THE FINAL MISSION

Spooky

BOB KING
St. Martin's Press ☙ New York

Library of Congress Cataloging-in-Publication Data

King, Bob.
    Spooky 8 : the final mission / Bob King.—1st ed.
      p. cm.
    ISBN 0-312-20579-1
    1. Intelligence service—United States Case studies.   I. Title.
  II. Title: Spooky eight.
  JK468.I6K49   1999
  327.1273'009'045—dc21   99–21988
                                                     CIP

First Edition: July 1999

10 9 8 7 6 5 4 3 2 1

This book is dedicated to the spirit and men of Spooky 8 and to all Special Operations personnel who served as this country's unspoken guardians.

Contents

Acknowledgments

To those warrior spirits, forced to live with the demons of their secret past, with no one to comfort them but themselves.

To those I have known who, over the years, have shown me the strength of my own spirit and the true meaning of honor.

To those who have guided and watched over me and have given me the courage to share their lives in this book.

To the thousands of young men and women who left their simple and uncomplicated lives to become entangled in this country's many hidden agendas.

To my friend Steve, who died in my arms one lonely Christmas day, and to the family of the MIA whose name is engraved on the bracelet given to me by Paco and team Spooky 4: SFC James D. Cohron, USA (SF), who became an MIA on 12 January 1968, a true American hero.

Introduction

In the beginning, this book was never intended to be read by anyone but a select few and, as those closest to me will attest, was an extremely difficult and emotional book for me to write. It was, however, written with the blessing and anonymous support of the survivors of Spooky 8 and a number of courageous members of government intelligence.

My reluctance to write this story gave way to the need to finally face the demons that haunted my team and myself. It was written as a means of therapy and giving closure to a secret life that was extremely difficult for those not involved to believe. It was my way of saying good-bye to those who have died and showing my respect and admiration to those who lived.

I know I have pushed the limits of what I could say and the threat of severe, possibly terminal reprisal will always be a lurking reality. Every effort has been made to re-create these events as accurately and safely as possible, taking into consideration the people, locations, subject matter, and span of time. To protect myself, the members of Spooky 8, and the other individuals for whom this book was written, certain names, dates, places, and events have been intentionally altered.

Understandably, I did not use my real name, nor did I use the name of David Chance when I was involved in covert operations. Chance was a nickname given to me by my men that I decided to use to represent my character in the book. Only those who were involved in these events will know the real names used by the people in this story.

This is my interpretation of events that took place between 1973 and 1992 and led to the betrayal, deadly ambush, and subsequent survival of a civilian paramilitary team operating in the jungles of South America in 1992. Because this team, as well as others, was employed by U.S. intelligence, I expect a

Introduction

considerable effort will be made to discredit my past, challenge my veracity, or even attack my mental state to make sure few will take this story and what it represents seriously.

This story is about a secret side of our government whose existence is unknown to most. It is not about the U.S. military, nor is it a story about the CIA, NSA, or any other specific government agency. It is a story about a dark side of U.S. intelligence—a side of government that is not elected by the people of this country but controls our lives and very possibly holds the destiny of the world in its hands.

Easy Breather

1992, above the Colombian Jungle, South America

The lush green canopy of dense jungle stretches out below a sky beginning to boil with color as the sun gives birth to a new day. A heavy layer of gray fog blankets the surrounding mountaintops like a thick crown of wet concrete. Soon the sun will begin to bleed its heat into the valley below. The humidity will grow as suffocating as a hot, wet blanket wrapped around your head. Yet now it seems so peaceful beneath us, so serene, and beautiful.

The peace turns to thunder as the rotor blades of our UH-1 helicopter knifes through the mist at 120 miles per hour. The seven men and I sit in camouflaged BDUs (Battle Dress Uniforms), trying to ignore the deafening whine of the Huey's turbine engines. Lucky, the oldest team member and our language expert, sits next to me, his head resting on the butt of his HK (Heckler and Koch) MP5SD suppressed submachine gun. Mike, Dave, Santana, and T J sit across from me, trying to get as comfortable as possible on the helicopter's webbed seats. Except for T J, they carry Colt M-4 (CAR-16) rifles. T J, our sniper, caresses his Robar 300 Winchester Magnum sniper rifle. Razz, the craziest one of us all, sits on the other side of me with an M203 (M-16 with a 40mm grenade launcher attached to it). Opey, the youngest member of the team and team medic, sits next to Razz. Everyone except Lucky and I is in his thirties. At forty and the team leader, I'm the other senior member of the team. I hold my MP5SD as if it is a beautiful woman. Strapped between Lucky and me lie two heavily padded aluminum cases containing sophisticated electronic surveillance equipment that we are assigned to set up.

These are the men of a team known as Special Projects team W45B7S8 but to people in this line of work as Spooky 8. Spooky 8 is one of the few remaining TRTs (Tactical Reconnaissance Teams) made up of former military and other ex–government employees. Spooky teams have been tasked with the mission of securing intelligence to be used in the ongoing "drug war" between the United States and the many drug cartels of Central and South America. Spooky teams have been working in this part of the world for several years on a clandestine operation known as Dark Eagle.

Been there, done that, I thought as I looked out over the jungle below.

"Hey, Chance!" yelled Mike. "You think we'll ever get real jobs?"

"Real job? I doubt it. Tried it once, didn't like it. Don't you worry, Mikey. Someday I'm sure you'll figure out what you want to do when you grow up."

As I looked out over the jungle, I realized I'd been doing this kind of thing for more than twenty years. Before this, I had served in the army. I had also worked as a cop during my early years with Spooky 8. I honestly didn't know what else I could do.

The flight to our AO (Area of Operation) felt cold and foreboding. The door on the Huey had been locked open, leaving us naked to the wind as we made our way through the damp early morning air. Off in the distance I could see the lights of small, nameless villages. They glowed like dancing ghosts through the mist of another world.

As we got closer to our LZ (Landing Zone), the pilot came over the intercom and told us to get ready: "LZ in sight. You'll be on the ground in five minutes."

As I sat there in the door of the Huey, I couldn't help thinking of a little saying that I've tried to live by all of my adult life: "Never go where your mind hasn't gone before." In my work, I've tried to cover every conceivable "what if" scenario in my head, but this one wasn't coming together.

I keyed up my team radio to alert the men, removed my intercom headset, and unbuckled my lap belt. I could see we were traveling at treetop level now. As the Huey slowed to a hover inches above the jungle, the events leading up to this moment came crashing into my mind.

The notification of the mission had come as most do, by a voice over the phone. Though I had left the military in 1975, I had continued to be active in the "Special Operations" arena as a civilian adviser and a member of a TRT. Most of the time I was working for a suborganization of one of our many government's intelligence agencies.

As a contracted civilian, I thought I had it made. I could accept or decline any mission or assignment offered me. Most assignments were intelligence-gathering missions that sometimes got a little hairy. The hairy part, frankly, was why I kept doing them. I was hooked on the rush. The money wasn't all that great, but it wasn't bad, either. I had been single for the last several years, so I could come and go as I pleased. Nobody bitched or asked a lot of questions, and I liked it that way. I had also been doing civilian executive protection details and other contract work for people out of Washington, D.C., so friends never wondered when I was out of touch for a while.

When a mission was "laid on," the sequence of events leading up to the job followed a routine. After being given the basic details about the assignment, I notified the rest of my team and explained the mission. They then had the opportunity to accept or decline.

The members of Spooky 8 had worked together for several years. If any member didn't feel right about the mission and declined to go, the rest of the team would also decline. Once in a while a member had commitments he couldn't break and just couldn't go. In that case, we would either get a replacement or go with one fewer member. When it came to "gut feeling," we were like the Three, or I should say Eight, Musketeers. It had to be unanimous.

All of us had prior training and experience, either military, federal, or from some other unusual "past life," that served as a valuable asset to the team.

The other team members' past lives didn't matter to me. What mattered was we were a damn good team and we depended upon one another. Everyone was jump-qualified and scuba-trained and had years of weapons and hand-to-hand combat experience. We had even developed improvisation to an art form that even McGyver would have been proud of.

My strong point was leadership. I had learned to earn respect without demanding it by always counting on the team's contribution to make my decisions. It was seldom that I made the final decision without their input. I was also good with tactics and explosives, and I had picked up a knack with electronics. But the trait most valued by Spooky 8 was my luck. I had a way of successfully taking chances and making some wild plan work. I guess that's why everyone called me by my last name, Chance, not David—I wasn't afraid to take a chance to accomplish the mission. My team had confidence that I would get them home, and I always did.

The next step of the mission was the choice of a location for preparation and rehearsal, usually decided by the authority that assigned the mission.

Sometimes we'd prepare in the United States, but often, especially if the mission was in Central or South America, we'd go to Panama, Honduras, Costa Rica, or Belize, where we could have a chance to become acclimated to the terrain, climate, culture, and food while we prepared.

Once the team was gathered at the briefing site, we were given the objective of the mission, or "mission statement." It was then up to the team to decide if the mission was within our means to accomplish. Once we determined the mission was within our abilities, the team would take the mission statement to the next phase, called isolation.

Once the team entered isolation, all contact with the outside world ended until the mission was completed. If someone was injured or dropped out, he would still be held in isolation until the mission was over.

The first order of business in isolation is the "in-processing." The in-processing phase usually takes only a few hours. This is when we make sure all wills, powers of attorney, and other concerns were correct and current. Physicals were brought up-to-date. All shots and dental needs were taken care of, and for any "meds" needed for the mission we went to the team medic.

Meds usually referred to any shots we needed for the country we would be operating in and sometimes "legal" speed, usually injected, for more "critical" missions. When these amphetamines were used, they allowed us to work at 150 percent for three or four days without sleep, but as with all drugs, they had a downside. At the end of the mission, your body shut down so hard, you might sleep for a couple of days.

We also used the isolation phase to prepare for a "worst-case" scenario. Worst-case for us meant somebody was severely wounded and about to be captured. Our standing agreement was that none of us would be taken prisoner. If one of us was wounded and couldn't be rescued, he was to die before he could be taken captive. We each carried a small injectable Syrette for just that purpose.

If one of us was captured and survived, the plan was to rescue him at any cost. This was kept strictly between the team members, however, as any rescue mission would be "unauthorized" through normal channels. I always figured if it ever came down to that, we would all just stay there and fight it out to the last man before we gave up and left someone. I don't think I would have the balls to "do" myself if the choice was left up to me.

After all of the paperwork had been taken care of, the team would then settle in for as long as it took to come up with a plan of action, or TACOP (Tactical Operation Order). Generally, we would have a large amount of intelligence supplied by several government agencies at our disposal. There aren't too many areas of the world where the United States hasn't been to "train" or "advise" and where we didn't have current intelligence. The United States has been in Central and South America "training and advising" for over forty years, so we already know a lot. With the satellite and spy plane overflight intelligence, combined with the hundreds of unattended solar-powered satellite transmitting sensing equipment, we're pretty well wired when it comes to our southern neighbors.

Once we had started our intelligence briefings, we would formulate our plan based on our mission statement, our assets, our liabilities, and our resources. Every man had a specific job to do to accomplish the mission. Once he knew his role, he learned to do the job of every other man.

Usually, any piece of information we needed could be obtained. We had briefings with doctors, lawyers, meteorologists, and the clergy. I even had, on a couple of occasions, people known as "remote viewers" consult with the team.

Remote viewers are psychic types who were used in secret government projects like Project Stargate, among others. They are supposedly able to use their mind to identify secret locations, find hidden people, even read classified documents held in other countries, and go back in time. The first time I ran across one of these remote viewers was while I was attending a briefing back in D.C. He told me he had been remote-viewing for the CIA for several years and teaching military officers the skill. At first I didn't believe he was able to do the things he said he could, so I gave him a location and asked him to go there in his mind. When he was able to describe the place in detail, I knew there was a lot more to this remote-viewing than I could ever explain.

When the briefing and planning stage ended, our plan, officially called a TACOP, was prepared for the next stage of the process, called the briefback. The briefback is where you sell your plan to the people who tasked you with the mission. A spokesman, usually Lucky or me, talked through the entire mission from rehearsal to extraction and answered the endless questions they would ask: "How many taxis are in the town?" "How long is the dirt airstrip you plan to use, and how do you know it will accommodate your aircraft?" "What will you do if a tractor or truck is parked in the middle of the airstrip?" "What is the third alternate radio frequency, and what type of burst transmission key will be used on your SATCOM?" "What is the location of your alternate mission staging site?" "At what point do you scrub the mission?"

The briefback usually lasted for several hours, until everyone was satisfied the mission would or wouldn't work.

If the TACOP passed, we got a "go." If it didn't, we went back and started the process all over again.

Once the TACOP had been approved and each man knew his and everybody else's job, all the equipment for the mission was acquired and checked. Anything that needed batteries received new ones. Communication equipment was checked and rechecked.

Normally we used secured burst transmission–capable radios. These radios used a special "frequency-hopping" chip in them that changed frequencies several times a second, making it almost impossible for someone to intercept and listen in. These radios could "burst-transmit" around thirty thousand bytes of information a second. We could talk from almost anywhere on earth to our control point in the United States as if we were right next door.

The radios could also communicate directly with the portable radios used by the team. These portable radios, usually Motorola Sabers, were also scrambled and configured with headsets. The headsets used bone induction earphones that left both ears uncovered. The "earpiece" would rest on the bone in front of the ear. The sound vibrated through the bone just as clearly as if the earpiece were on your ear.

Sometimes we would use a STU III, MX 3030 COMSAT mobile communications system. These are secure-voice portable satellite telephone systems that used "INMARSAT-M" technology for global telephone communications.

This type of communication was especially effective because it transmitted in the 1631.5 to 1660.5 MHz range and received in the 1530.0 to 1559.0 MHz range, so it is hard to intercept with conventional means.

Most of the highly sensitive equipment had a small built-in explosive charge for self-destruction purposes. If things got bad and we had to leave something behind, we just set it, and it blew itself up. This was handy because it could also be used as a booby trap. If someone was to find and use a piece of sensitive equipment, it was programmed to become a real expensive antipersonnel bomb. I made sure that if everything had gone to shit, we could drop every piece of nonessential gear we had and run like hell.

All weapons, night vision, remote-sensing equipment, and GPSs (Global Positioning Systems), *everything,* was checked, calibrated, and checked again. All equipment, including weapons, silencers, and uniforms, was "sanitized"—no serial numbers, no lettering, and no tags. Everything was committed to memory, leaving no markings on maps. Grid coordinates and "way-points" were preset on our issued GPSs.

For our own peace of mind, most of us brought some of our own equipment, like a GPS, small radio, or another handgun. We never overly displayed or acknowledged these, but we all knew we had them.

We tried to carry no information about anything in written form. All radio frequencies, codes, and passwords were memorized. Nothing was left to chance. There was to be no evidence left behind to indicate who we were, what government we worked for, or how many of us there had been.

Once the mission was a go, a launch window was established, equipment was checked again, and the rehearsals began. The complexity of the mission dictated the time spent on rehearsals. If the mission was similar to ones we had done before, we kept rehearsals to a minimum. Often missions were so routine that the entire process of planning, briefback, and launch took just a couple of days.

That's how things usually went. But the only normal part of *this* mission was the way it started, with the phone call.

The Ray•Ban Man

"Chance, this is Bates; you up to makin' a few extra bucks?" Ed Bates' call came on a Saturday afternoon.

"Sure. Let me get to the other line, and you can tell me about it."

"The other line" referred to a portable phone scrambler we used to communicate about sensitive things.

"That's not necessary, Chance. This one's an easy breather. All you'll need is your old group: you, Lucky, Opey, T J, Mike, Dave, Santana, and Razz. We need you guys to deliver and set up a couple of packages down south. It's a real easy breather, not much to it. I'll get in touch with Santana and Dave for you, and then I'll set up your transportation to Bogotá. You'll be meeting a Jack Springer at El Dorado. He'll take care of things from there. I'll call you in a few days with flight information."

"OK, I'll get everyone together. Scale's the same?" I asked.

"Ten for five. That sound OK with you?"

"Yeah. That's way better than normal; what's the deal?"

"I guess they figured you guys deserve a bonus or something."

"OK, I'll talk with you in a few days," I said, and hung up the phone.

I thought it a very odd that an easy breather would pay ten for five. "Ten for five" meant $10,000 for five days' work. Normally we earned $500 to $750 a day for an easy breather, not $2,000. "Easy breather" meant that it was a low-threat intelligence-gathering mission where no contact was expected.

I called the other members of the team, and like me, they were hurting for money and glad to take the mission.

On Tuesday, Bates called with flight information for the team and me. As usual, each team member would pick up his tickets at the airport he normally flew out of. I called the men, faxed them their flight info, and said I'd see them in a couple of days.

Our schedule had us leaving on Friday morning from Miami for El Dorado International Airport in Bogotá, Colombia. On Thursday night we all met in the Miami airport at our usual eating place, a restaurant that served typically bad airport food. It was great to see Santana and Dave again, and we hugged each other as if we were long-lost brothers. I hadn't seen them in almost a year, so it was like a family reunion.

"What in the hell is going on? We never fly straight to Bogotá," said Lucky as we met.

"Are we going as tourists this time?" joked Mike.

"Yeah, a group of Baptist ministers," Dave said with a smile.

"Bates told me this is an easy breather. Something we've done before."

Lucky and I were both uneasy about the easy breather label, but the rest of the team was focused on making a little money. Santana and Razz were, as usual, the least concerned, competing to see who could eat the hottest chili. The rest of us ate lightly and flipped a coin to see who would have to sit next to Santana and Razz and suffer the massive amount of gas they would be passing.

We talked briefly about our travel plans and decided they (government intelligence) didn't think we needed a long drawn-out briefing and rehearsal, so they were sending us right to our deployment point. The rest of the team figured we would just get our briefing and our gear and head out. Not me. That's not the way we'd done things before, and I wasn't too keen about changing now.

"This is bullshit, Lucky."

"Maybe they're just trying to save a little money or something. You know how those cheese-dick hill dogs [politicians] like to hoard money," said Lucky.

"I'll bet there's going to be new faces on this one," I replied as I stared at a glass of water.

"Damn, Chance, you must be getting old. You're starting to get too cautious," said Opey. "Santana, Dave, and Mike are in the same boat as me: broke."

"Fuck it," Razz put in. "What difference does it make? We haven't fucked up anybody in Bogotá for a while. Besides, who would recognize us anyway? We're not really here. Shit, we don't even exist."

Our American Airlines flight finally called for boarding, and we headed to the gate. This was one of the few times we flew commercial. We normally took a Great Air, Orange Air, or some other bogus airline south. These kinds of companies were rumored to be covert government airlines, like Air America was during the Vietnam days.

Lucky and I sat next to each other on the flight to Bogotá. It was a quiet trip, neither one of us saying much. We were having too much fun listening to Santana and Dave sitting behind us, talking about their problems. Dave had been in a relationship with a Mexican woman and was asking Santana what he should do. I guess Santana felt about women a lot like I had lately.

"Don't trust a fuckin' woman, especially a Mexican. She'll mess you all up," said Santana.

"Yeah, but she is so damn good in the sack," Dave retorted.

"That's what they do. They screw your brains out, and then they really stick it to you."

I had to laugh at Santana's attitude toward women. As I tried to relax, I thought how good it was to be back with my "family," who were, again, trusting Lucky and me to get them home alive.

While the team came together sporadically over the years, they had all became my closest friends. Lucky, however, was my oldest and most trusted friend of the group. We had met in the army in 1973, when we found ourselves involved in a couple of "untraceable" covert operations working for the CIA out of Thailand. Lucky took me under his wing, and before long we became best friends. Not only is he fluent in several languages and a photography expert, but Lucky also has an uncanny way of fitting in everywhere he goes. I knew he'd always be there to cover my ass. After the army, Lucky and I found ourselves again working together as civilians on operations doing pretty much the same thing we had done in the army. In late 1978, Mike and Dave came on the scene, and they, too, became close friends of ours.

Mike looks like he's around seventeen years old, and he hates the fact that he gets carded every time he tries to buy a drink. I'm young-looking, but Mike looks like a much younger brother. The women liked his jet-black hair and dark eyes, and he never has any trouble getting laid. His baby face makes it easy for him to get real close to people, then kill them. Mike is a true assassin. His father died a long time ago, and his mother died just a couple years ago. He has nobody but the team, and to him, we are his family. When he's home in Georgia, he's a civilian skydiving instructor with over four thousand jumps. I never could figure out how he made any money skydiving, but I probably didn't need to know what else he did.

Dave looks like a frat boy. Like the rest of us, he is somewhat quiet and laid back. He has a couple black belts in the martial arts and is as tough as nails. To him, a ten-mile run is just a warm-up. Even though he looked like he should be playing tennis with Buffy, he could take on a half-dozen guys and not even break a sweat.

Razz, sitting in the back of the plane, is a real loner. No wife, no family, just the team. Razz had worked with us a few times before permanently joining the team in 1984. He was an alternate team member while a member was away getting some specialized training. Once, while we were on a mission supporting another team, we were surprised by some bad guys. Razz saved our ass and became a full member of the team because of it. This was less than a year after the team was "officially" designated Spooky 8. He definitely is the craziest one of all. I saw him drink a mug of puke once on a bet in a bar. Blessed with an incredible ability to retain information, he knows something about everything. An added plus for Spooky 8 is that Razz is meaner than a junkyard dog and not afraid of anything.

On the other hand, Santana is always looking for the right woman to share his life with. Unfortunately, he was now getting over his third divorce. At least I've only been divorced twice. Santana must have a high testosterone count, because he was always looking to get laid. He had that Latin lover attitude, and he can always con a woman into believing she is the only one in his life. Santana and Razz were best friends. Santana came on the team shortly after Razz did in '84. Santana's real talent is his knowledge of electronics and his skill with sharp knives. He is so quick, he could cut you deep and you'd drop dead before you even know you had been stuck. Santana works as a computer tech in Albuquerque, New Mexico, when he's not with the team. Rumor has it he can hack his way into just about any computer system and has once or twice, but that's only rumor.

T J looks like a big country boy just off the farm. He always calls everybody sir and ma'am, and his slow southern drawl seemed to drive women crazy. A real gentleman until you put a rifle in his hands, then he becomes a stone killer. When he's not with the team, he works with his father selling farm equipment in Texas.

Spooky

T J joined the team in late '85 after showing me up at a civilian long-range rifle match. He was only twenty-four, with very little military experience to speak of, but he was a real natural when it came to shooting. After the match, I made it a point to get to know him better and found out he had been charged with manslaughter after a shooting accident in Texas. He was in the army then but was discharged because of the indictment. He was looking for work, so I hooked him up with a front company to give him some overseas experience and to find out what he was made of. He performed as expected, and within six months he was on the team.

T J told me that the man he killed was the same guy that beat up his mother. This guy had beaten her up one too many times, so she finally got the nerve to break up with him. A few months after his mother had broken up with this guy, T J was hunting with a friend. T J took a shot at a deer but missed. His shot accidentally hit another hunter almost eleven hundred yards away. Of course it was a total surprise to T J when he heard his bullet had killed another hunter over a half-mile away that happened to be his mom's ex-boyfriend. It was also a surprise that T J's bullet had hit this guy square in the chest just moments after he stepped from behind cover. T J never said anything more about it, and I never asked.

Opey, our medic, got his name because he looks like Sheriff Andy Taylor's kid on the old television show about Mayberry. Tall, lanky, with sandy red hair, Opey was always like a mother to us. He made sure we were in the best shape we could be. He joined the team in 1987 after our regular medic was suddenly transferred to another team. Opey was the best field medic I had ever seen, but we really didn't know much about his past. When he was home in Vermont, he said, he worked for a veterinarian.

Except for Lucky, we all look like a bunch of young kids. We all have personalities that complement each other and an infinite amount of trust. Our talents and abilities are amazing and ones I wouldn't trade for anything in the world.

We reached Bogotá at 1245 hours. Jack Springer waited for us outside the terminal, just like Bates had said. With his Ray•Ban sunglasses and khaki photographer's vest, he had CIA written all over him, and he stood out in the crowd like a whore at a church quilting bee. He recognized me, introduced himself, and told us to get into a waiting windowless passenger van. In big blue letters written on the side of the van was the sign FLORERIA DE BOGOTÁ. A divider between the driver's seat and the passenger compartment kept us from seeing where we were going. I wasn't overly concerned about this, as it was somewhat standard procedure. Cities like Bogotá have an abundance of people with cameras and camcorders taking pictures of people coming and going from airports, especially a vanful of Americanos.

We traveled for about an hour and a half in the stifling van, finally pulling into the driveway of an isolated villa. I heard iron gates open as we drove in. It was 1430 hours and extremely hot. We stepped from the dark van into the blinding sun on a large circular drive. We had to stop for a moment and let our eyes adjust to the light. When they did, I noticed that ten-foot stone walls surrounded the complex.

On most missions, our final destination before going to the AO was an airstrip or military-looking installation or maybe just a clearing with a few portable shelters in the middle of a forest. But on this mission we were to be briefed in a well-fortified compound. We passed several armed men, some of them obviously American, who were watching the villa carefully, and were led into the big house and ushered into a large living room. It clearly wasn't a house that somebody lived in. The living room contained a large once-elegant table and a bunch of folding chairs. The other rooms appeared to be empty. The large windows were covered with faded and stained sheets that looked like they had been there for a long time.

At the table were two more civilians who introduced themselves as Mr. Valley and Mr. Baines.

"Welcome, gentlemen; please make yourselves comfortable," said Valley. "Take a seat and we'll begin."

We each found a seat around the long table, which looked as if it once had belonged in a grand dining room with expensive paintings, crystal chandeliers, and a maid serving dinner. Now it had nothing on it but a briefcase, a bottle of water, and a stack of Styrofoam cups.

"First things first," said Baines. He opened his briefcase and took out eight white envelopes. He handed us each one with his first name written on it.

"We've decided to pay you up front. When you're done, you guys can take a little vacation or something. Some of you haven't seen each other for some time. It might be a good time to catch up."

I suspected my team members were all thinking the same thing I was: Why were they paying us now?

"You can count it if you want. It's all there," said Valley.

It was apparent that Springer and his crew were new to this and were not very comfortable. All three kept glancing at each other as if they were looking for direction. I wasn't about to let this go by.

"We've been paid in advance before, but always when we accepted the assignment, not as the briefing was about to start. We hadn't even received our mission statements yet. So why the cash?"

The knot in the pit of my stomach grew when Springer ignored my question. I could almost smell the nervousness of Springer and his two partners. The red flags were starting to go up like when an IRS agent knocks on your door and says he's there to help.

"We wanted to get right to business. We are in a bit of a time crunch," Springer finally said.

Here we were, wherever that was, in an empty house somewhere around Bogotá, with three guys we didn't know shit about, being paid in cash we couldn't do anything with until we were through. All of us knew something wasn't right, but we just sat there, not saying a word, thinking about the money.

"We didn't think you needed to know any more about this mission until now," said Springer. "It's one like you all have done before, a walk in the park.

"What we need you to do is take two electronic monitoring packages to a small airstrip about one hundred fifty miles from here, set them up, and make sure they're working properly. Then monitor things for a couple of days and leave. That's it. The airstrip is believed to be a major stopover point for drug shipments being flown into the States. Satellite reconnaissance has shown it to be active, but we can't seem to catch them on an overflight. We think they may know our overflight schedule, so we need some real-time surveillance."

"Excuse me," I interrupted. "You are paying us this much money to set up an LP/OP [Listening Post Observation Post] and then leave? That's it? I guess I don't completely understand. You could use any team to do this. Why did you specifically pick us?"

"It's really very simple—your track record," he said. "You guys have completed every mission you've had. You get in, do your thing, and get out. You don't have much trouble, and if you do, you always manage to handle it. Many of the teams are scheduled to be debriefed, then reassigned. You are one of the few teams that have the experience we can count on."

"The goddamn DEA wants in on everything, and, well, we just don't trust them. Don't get me wrong," Valley broke in. "What you're doing will benefit the DEA, but it will help other groups as well."

"There might be a leak somewhere," Springer resumed, "so we've decided to do this without anyone knowing. That's part of the reason why we didn't tell you any more about it. This equipment will monitor more than just what goes on at the airport. I'm sorry I can't tell you anything more about the equipment than that."

"So why so much money?" I asked.

"Some of you have been doing this for a long time," Baines said. "We know you guys have had it a little rough lately, and this is our way of showing our gratitude. This is highly secret; no one but us will know what you're doing. We figure you'll want to help us the next time if we take care of you now, right?" Baines looked at each of us.

"Are there any other questions before we continue?" Springer asked. "This is a real easy breather, you know, just a walk in the park, but a quiet one. You can still back out if you don't think you can handle it."

I knew if I told Springer that I wasn't comfortable with this, the rest of the team would just say, "That's it. We're out of here." But having an envelope with your name on it containing $10,000 in U.S. currency is a real strong settler of nerves.

"OK, let's get on with it," I said. I turned to the team, and they all nodded yes. It wasn't the first time things didn't feel right.

Over the years the game had changed. If someone new was calling the shots, we would have to learn how he wanted the game played. It was unusual, however, not to see any familiar faces. There were always one or two contacts we had worked with before.

Back in the old days when Ford ('74–'77), Carter ('77–'81), and Reagan ('81–'89) were supposed to be running things, their administrations kept a few of the "old-timers" around until everybody was up to speed with the new players. That seemed to change when Bush ('89–'93) took office. From then on, I never quite knew who was really in charge. Neither did anybody else.

The briefing only lasted a few hours. We were given the location of the AO, the mission objective, and the equipment we were going to be using. As the team inventoried and checked everything, I was given the surveillance equipment and briefed on how to set up and calibrate it. They were pretty high-tech toys, unlike any I had ever seen. Designed to monitor both ground anomalies and atmospheric disturbances, they could tell what types of vehicles, aircraft, and probably troops were within a two-mile radius. They were completely self-contained, and solar-powered, with battery backup.

While I was checking out the equipment, I was able to open one of the access panels and discovered these things did a lot more than just monitor movement. The two units would communicate with each other by a fiber-optic cable. The larger unit contained different transmitters and repeaters (microwave, HF, VHF, and UHF). I could recognize what looked like five different encrypted transmitting systems.

The smaller unit looked to be the sensing part of the system. I saw IR (Infrared), thermal, microwave, atmospheric, and seismic systems. As I examined both units, I discovered a self-destruct feature that I had expected, but not to the overkill level hidden within. Built into both packages was what looked to be about ten pounds of C-4 plastic explosives. These guys didn't want anybody to find any part of this. With this much C-4, these things become a fragmentation bomb that would kill everything within thirty meters.

Springer told me once the entire unit was set up and running we were not to disturb any part of it without setting a disarm code, or the thing would detonate and kill everyone within ten meters.

Yeah, no shit, ten meters! I thought.

A few ounces of C-4 were more than enough to completely destroy this thing. It was obvious that this surveillance equipment was going to do a lot more than what I was being told. There was even one component inside the larger unit that had a radiation warning sticker on it. These were some very serious electronics.

The rest of the equipment issue was pretty much what I had expected: sterile uniforms, Litton AN/PVS-7A night vision goggles, a twelve-man medical kit, HK MP5SD submachine guns, M-4 (CAR-16) rifles, one M203, and one Robar scoped rifle. We all also had HK .45-caliber handguns with threaded barrels. These handguns were SOCOM (Special Operations Command) issue, and I thought it was funny they would give them to us. They were big and bulky, and I didn't care for them much. I preferred the Sig Sauer P228 we normally carried. I was given a GPS, and each of us was issued secure communication gear.

The gear was pretty standard issue for this type of operation, but it was unusual to have it already waiting for us. Of course we had brought a few of our own "mission-essential" pieces of equipment, but I didn't think that was any of Springer's business.

We spent the rest of the day going over the mission and equipment. The following day we held a little rehearsal, setting up the high-tech surveillance gear and getting it calibrated. I never completely powered up the surveillance unit because of the self-destruct system. There wasn't any point in taking unnecessary chances. We checked our communications, weapons, ammo, GPSs, and other equipment, just like we would do on any mission.

After the rehearsal, Springer handed me a set of satellite photos and Lucky and I went over them carefully.

"OK, Lucky, you're our intelligence guru; make sure these satellite photos tell us everything we need to know."

"Well I don't see any dancing girls, but they look pretty clean otherwise."

"We don't have a large window of opportunity here. Let's get this show on the road." Springer was obviously antsy to get us out of there.

"Relax!" I said sharply. "This is our road show, and we'll leave when we're ready."

Springer seemed impatient with our preparation routine. He kept saying how unnecessary it all was. He wanted us to leave the day after the briefing, but I said there was no way. I told him that I knew he was new to this, but certain things had to be done first and if he didn't like it, he could get somebody else. When it escalated to the point where I had to get a little in his face, he backed off and let us finish.

When I was satisfied that everything was as it should be, we left at midnight and assembled in what looked to be a private hangar at El Dorado Airport. We were then taken aboard a De Havilland DHC-6 Twin Otter for a one-hour-and-twenty-minute flight to a small airstrip near San Jose del Guaviare. The Twin Otter had all of the seats removed and was obviously used for hauling heavy loads to unimproved airstrips. The Otter made the flight with all of its running lights turned off and never rose more than two hundred feet above the treetops.

The pilot didn't want to end up as a unknown on some airport or military radar.

Once we reached the remote airstrip, we did another inventory of our equipment and stowed it in the UH-1 helicopter we were going to use for our insertion. Valley and Baines didn't accompany us on the flight, and it was Springer's show from here on out. He sat up with the pilot and hardly said a word even after we landed and stowed our gear on the helicopter.

"What's the matter, Springer? Don't like helicopters?" I asked.

"No, Sergeant, I don't. The damn things have a tendency to fall out of the sky around here."

All of my senses snapped to red alert.

Sergeant? Nobody had called me that in years. And the only people who did were on my team. The military part of my life had been over a long time, and this guy had absolutely no reason to call me Sergeant. I watched him closely to see if he realized the slip. He didn't flinch, so I decided he wasn't even aware of what he had said. For some reason, or rather ten thousand of them, I let it go.

We had a little time before lifting off for our AO, so we finished stowing our gear in the helo, checked it all one last time, got comfortable, and tried to get some rest.

There was some activity on the airstrip, even at two in the morning, but no one approached us. I didn't think much of it, and I'm sure they thought the same thing. Most places where special missions are run have an unspoken rule: You don't fuck with us, we won't fuck with you.

Much too soon, 0345 came. The pilot of the Huey came out and started to make his preflight check. So did we. We finished putting camouflage paint on our face and hands, loaded our weapons, and powered up our communications equipment. We strapped in, made sure our equipment was secure, did a commo check, and waited to go. Springer approached the pilot with some last-minute instruction. The pilot seemed a little angry with Springer, but I couldn't hear any of the conversation. It ended with the pilot saluting Springer. Then Springer came around to me, shook my hand, and wished us luck.

As we were lifting off, he said, "See you guys in a few days," waved, and gave us the thumbs-up.

As the helicopter lifted from the pad, the pilot flipped down his ANVIS night vision flying goggles. I turned to see Springer standing there, staring up at us, in a cloud of dust illuminated by the Huey's running lights. Just as the pilot turned off the running lights and Springer disappeared from view, I thought I saw him snap a sharp military salute at me. Without a thought, I saluted back.

As the blacked-out Huey ascended into the darkness, I became numb to the cold wind and unaware of the eerie darkness that surrounded us. Trying to get the last little bit of rest before the mission, I thought about Springer and what his real story was. Before long, I found myself drifting back to another time and place: the seventies, when I really was a sergeant in the army and when I met another "Ray•Ban" man, a guy named Patterson. It was my first experience with black operations, when Lucky and I became delivery boys for the U.S. government on a secret operation called Dragon Flower.

Dragon Flower

1973, Somewhere over the Jungles of Cambodia

The sun has just set and night is coming on fast. Looking down upon the lush carpet of jungle canopy, you might think that all was at peace with the world. There is no anger, no hurting. People are not struggling for survival among the tangled, twisted maze of undergrowth below. It's as if the world were void of people and nature left to decide its own fate.

Without warning, the silence is shattered by the roar of twin turbines of a modified OV-10 Bronco fixed-wing airplane flying at treetop level, heading for the crest of a distant mountain. Having come from a small secret airstrip just inside the border of South Vietnam, the Bronco screams toward its secret destination dangerously close to the jungle canopy below. The plane has no markings and is painted OD (Olive Drab), with no lights visible. The pilot, "Buzz" Franklin, sits in the front seat of the tandem Bronco concentrating on the quickly disappearing skyline, his eyes straining to catch the last glimmer of sunlight before the jungle is engulfed in total darkness.

Buzz, a man in his forties, didn't talk much. He got his point across by his flying. Sometimes he would watch us as we walked to the flight line and just shake his head. The only thing he would say when he took us on our picnics, as he called them, was, "You guys must have cast-iron balls, or sawdust for brains." Funny; I always thought the same thing about him—the cast-iron balls, that is.

His backseat (copilot) has already put on his newly developed night vision goggles designed for night flying. Buzz waits until the last minute to use his—they're big and heavy and don't work all that well. Buzz has been flying these jungles for over six years as a pilot with Air America. He knows these jungles like the freckles on his Thai girl-friend's ass. All Buzz needs to do is get to the rapidly approaching mountain crest, drop his load, and return home. That is, if somebody doesn't shoot him down first.

Inside the belly of the Bronco sit four young, frightened soldiers dressed in tiger-striped fatigues and boonie hats, carrying sterile XM-177E2 (CAR-16) rifles. Each man has a special low-altitude parachute strapped to his back with no reserve. At this altitude, a reserve wouldn't do much good. There is something noticeably different about these men. They have no ID, dog tags, or markings or rank on their uniforms. Their weapons have no serial numbers or other marks, nothing to link them to anyone or anything.

Between them sit two large heavily padded cases attached to small cargo chutes. Over the roar of the engines and the screaming wind, Hollywood, one of the young men, yells, "Hey, Top, this carnival ride about over? My ass is about to go on leave."

"Hang on, sweet cheeks!" I yelled back. "You'll be earning your pay soon enough."

Our nerves were on edge. This wasn't like any other mission we'd been on in the past. We really didn't know what to expect.

The back of the Bronco was open, and, of course, I was sitting by that hole. Just a small hydraulic door kept us inside. The Bronco was small, cramped, and uncomfortable, every inch taken up by my men and equipment. I was going to be the first out, as if that mattered. Soon things would happen so fast that, well, it just didn't matter where you sat. When it was time to go, Buzz would pull the Bronco into a steep climb and drop the back door, and we all would be out before we had time to think about it. I sat there staring out over the dark jungle below, thinking how peaceful it looked and how we were going to be fucking all that up in a few short minutes.

Our mission was to meet a Cambodian colonel who had been working with a local CIA spook and deliver the two cases we had with us. At first you might ask: Why in the hell are Americans meeting with Cambodians? Aren't they the enemy? Yeah, that's what I thought, too, and in the normal sense, that would be the case. But as usual, I hadn't worked in the normal sense since I signed my army contract away at Fort Benning when I got there for jump school.

I was told my team had been trained specifically for POW search and recovery anywhere in Southeast Asia. That meant we would do whatever it took to return our POWs to the United States. We did our own intelligence gathering and analyzing on missions. We called this STRAT RECON (STRATegic RECONnaissance). We worked in small groups, usually four, six, or sometimes up to twelve men. We routinely relied upon the assistance of indigenous personnel (the local villagers that we would help). We were, for the most part, completely self-supporting. We didn't rely on the regular troops because where we went and what we did was classified. For all intents and purposes, the official rules of engagement were the opposite of the objective of our missions.

Spooky

We were trained to take the POWs by force, usually lethal. In the event our intelligence was accurate, my team was supposed to go to where the POWs were being held and take them, very quickly, very precisely. We weren't there to take prisoners unless it was for intelligence reasons. Sometimes it was necessary to negotiate a trade, but that wasn't our job. Trades were arranged by government officials or the CIA. Our job was to find POWs and take them. Up until now, I hadn't been involved in the trading game, and I didn't like the idea of buying and selling POWs. Locating MIAs and taking them back was real personal for us. I guess I liked the idea of leaving a little something behind for the enemy to remember us by. Unfortunately, we had never found any American POWs.

I was told the packages we were carrying this time contained money. It was payment for two American POWs this Cambodian colonel was supposed to have. After he received the money, he was going to make arrangements to deliver the POWs to a representative of the U.S. government in secret. I knew these types of arrangements had been going on for many years, but this was the first time I was directly involved.

Yeah, this really sucked, I thought. This was the CIA's job. They're the ones who arranged this kind of bullshit, not soldiers. This was the first time we were involved with the delivery of payment. We wanted to deliver something all right, but it wasn't money. We didn't like the idea of going home empty-handed.

Lucky, my number two man on this mission, made a final check of our packages while the rest of us checked out each other. Hollywood, the newest member of the team, looked up at me, and I could see the anxiety starting to show on his face. I knew what he was thinking, what all of us were thinking.

The last mission was a bad one, two people killed and five wounded. We lost our team leader and assistant team leader. It was one of those times when we found ourselves in the wrong place at the wrong time. I gave a thumbs-up to Hollywood, and he smiled and went back to checking his equipment. I looked at this bunch of guys and wondered how many other guys my age were doing this same thing.

We weren't like other units. Most soldiers were sent to Vietnam for a tour of duty, usually twelve months. Not us; we had it made. We came "in country" for a specific mission that might last anywhere from a few days to a month or so. When we were through, we went back to the world to train hard, party hardy, and get ready for our next mission. We might go to Thailand to train, then deploy to our AO. Usually we started at a secret airbase or possibly an FOB (Forward Operating Base) somewhere in Thailand or South Vietnam, then went on to wherever our mission took us.

My team was active toward the end of the Vietnam War, and yes, it was a war, not a conflict. By the time I visited Vietnam, things had changed drastically. Once, I accidentally went into what I thought was a command bunker. Inside were a dozen young men who were obviously frightened out of their minds. *God, what's happened to these men?* I thought. I asked one of them where his CO was, and I thought he was going to cry. They just sat there, staring at me. I was angered at first. They were passing a joint around and even offered it to me. I couldn't understand how these men could survive in this condition. *No wonder you guys die,* I thought. I had heard about the drug problem over there, but I was never around it. I didn't understand. My team had to stay as sharp as possible just to survive, but not these men. All they could do was make it from day to day, week to week. All they wanted was to do their time and get back to the world. I felt sorry for them. I knew I was lucky to have a team that cared for me. I was lucky I didn't have to stay in this shit hole for a year at a time. Yeah, we had it made.

I could hear the throttle increase as the Bronco started to make its climb up the slope of the target mountain and knew it was close to show time. The backseat driver of the Bronco clicked the mike on his headset to get my attention. I had slipped one of the earphones of the headset off my ear so I could hear my men. I put it back on so I could hear the backseat driver.

"Get ready, Sergeant. You boys will be out in two minutes," he said.

I acknowledged him and yelled at my men, "OK, boys, hook up and check 'em. We'll be out of this bird like bad berries through a goose in one minute."

Each man clipped in his static line to a steel cable that ran down the center of the roof. Lucky clipped in one of the package chutes. I clipped in the other. As each man checked his gear, he looked at me and gave a thumbs-up. I knew we were as ready as we could be and it was up to luck and God now. Each man knew he had only one shot at this, so everything had to be perfect. If his chute didn't open, he became part of the food chain.

It's amazing how many things go through your mind in the final minutes before you jump out of a perfectly good airplane. Most people believe you'd be thinking, *What in the hell am I doing here? Will I be alive when my body hits the ground? What's waiting for me out there in the darkness? Will my buddies make it? What will I do if I'm the only one who makes it and I'm left alone in the jungle?* The strange thing is that's not what I was thinking about. I've already thought about those things on that long and lonely ride that brought me to this place. I looked at these three guys, and I couldn't help wondering what brought us to this point in our young lives. What events and what choices brought us together? Just out of high school with our entire lives ahead of us. . . .

High school—God, what a great time that was. I spent more time skipping school and playing in the mountains of Washington State than anything else. Life was never more challenging than finding the next tank of gas for my Jeep. The summers were warm, the girls pretty, and life was centered on my new Panasonic stereo system I had been saving for all year.

I came from a long line of cops. My dad had started the local police reserve unit. My oldest brother, Randy, after doing a hitch in the navy became a cop in our hometown police department. My middle brother, Dick, after doing his time in the navy joined the sheriff's department. It seemed like I was surrounded by the law. Even my uncle was the chief of police in a resort town twenty-five miles north.

I guess that's why I wasn't part of the social crowd in school—they didn't like the idea of a cop's kid knowing where all the good parties were—but that was OK with me. Most of my friends were a lot like me. It was better for us to be outside enjoying nature and searching for the elusive Bigfoot than getting drunk out of the trunk of some football jock's car.

I didn't have a lot of friends, but the few I did have were true friends. There was one in particular, Jerry, and yeah, he was a cop, too, for the city. I really admired him. He was a former Special Force soldier who became my mentor. I got to know him because we were both scuba divers on the local dive rescue team.

One day I was riding with Jerry on duty and, as usual, we were talking about the army and Special Forces. Up until this point, I was a guy who planned to go into the Marine Corps. Jerry would make fun of the marines and tell me that if I were a real man, I would go into the army and become a Green Beret. One day Jerry was really raggin' on me when he looked me straight in the eyes and said, "You're not tough enough to be Special Forces." Well, the gauntlet of challenge had been thrown, and by God, I was going to take it!

I looked back at him, and without so much as a blink I said, "Take me to the army recruiter, and I'll enlist right now."

"Bullshit," he told me.

"No, I'm serious; take me there now," I said.

So he did! I enlisted right then and there.

The army recruiter was really glad to see me walk through his door. It was 1971 and for me the draft was not much of a threat, since my draft number was around 350. They liked guys who wanted to enlist, especially into a combat MOS (Military Occupational Specialty). I told him what I wanted to do. He said I couldn't enlist into the Special

Forces, but I could enlist into the eighty-second Airborne. "They're at Fort Bragg; that's where the Special Forces are," he said with a big grin. Damn, I took that hook, line, and sinker. The recruiter also said I could get a buddy to enlist with me and we would have a contract with the army guaranteeing our specialty choice and allowing us to stay together. That sounded perfect to me, so that was that. After Jerry took me home, I had to think about what I had done. But shit, I couldn't turn back now.

I came from an all-navy family. Boy, were people going to be pissed. I had a good friend named Tom that was my diving partner. After telling him how great the army was going to be, I finally talked him into going down and enlisting as well. I guess I wasn't as brave as I thought. It was nice to have someone I knew going with me. Tom had never given much thought to the military, but he was a lot like me. "What the hell, let's go for it," he said. So, there we were, in the army on the delayed entry program while still in high school.

Everybody I knew except for my lifelong sweetheart, Susan, thought I was crazy. Susan was my soul mate. We had been the best of friends since we were kids. When I was real young I liked to go over to my friend Jeff's house because it happened to be right behind Susan's house. Jeff and I would hide behind the fence and watch Susan play with her Blue Bird friends in her backyard. Susan was one of those rare people I could talk to about anything. I guess I was in love with her even then and probably always would be. Everyone but her would say, "Go to college, get an education, and make something of your-self," or, "Go into the navy and have a real military career." Susan knew my dreams, and all she wanted was for me to follow them. When I left for the army, we said our good-byes and she went off to college. She remained the one place I could always retreat to in my mind when I was afraid and needed to find peace.

As for me, I always knew what I wanted to do. The military was the life for me. It was as if I had some kind of destiny to be part of the military, almost like it was part of a past life or something. When the Vietnam War started, I hoped it wouldn't end before I had a chance to enlist and volunteer to be part of it.

I would get really upset when I saw some "hippie" burning the American flag on TV. I guess I was a real flag-waving patriot even when I was young. I had no desire to go to college and get a formal education. I had always known I was going to enlist in the military right after high school, and as fate would have it, this was my chance, so I took it.

I went home and told my folks what I had done, and of course my mother didn't believe me. "No way, you can just bag it," she said. She had always wanted me to get into football and go to college on a scholarship or something. She was kind of a hard woman and had a tendency to try to run our lives as she thought they should be.

When I told her I had enlisted in the army, she just laughed and said there was no way I was going into the military, especially the army, since after all, we were a navy family. I just shook my head and said, "You'll see."

I guess my family didn't really believe me until my orders came in the mail one day. My mom was in shock. She didn't know if she should cry or slap me. I guessed my dad was proud of what I was doing, and that's what really mattered. He didn't say much, just smiled.

As for the rest of my family, my uncle, who was retired navy, didn't talk to me, my two brothers thought I was nuts, and my sister, Donna, who was younger, was more worried about boys than what her older brother was doing.

Yeah, I know how I got here. By choice. . . .

That familiar smell of JP-4 jet fuel being sucked into those turbines suddenly filled my nostrils. Buzz was pouring the coals to the Bronco as we screamed toward the summit of our target mountain. It was time!

Total focus was on my men and the mission. Was my equipment checked? Was their equipment checked? Was my static line properly secured? Were theirs? You knew these men knew what they were doing, but you were responsible for them. I guess it's like being a mother and worrying about your kids, except my kids kill people for a living. Now is the time when it all comes together: the training, the preparation, and the soul of your warrior spirit. You go over and over everything in your mind, and for the most part, you're totally focused on the *mission*.

Yet there is one thing that seems to always fester in the back of my mind. You know if anything happens to you, you're totally alone. Technically, you don't even exist. If you're killed, you *will* be left in the jungle forever. If your extraction is missed, you might get out, but on your own. If the mission gets screwed up, there is *no* support, no help. Knowing this from the beginning brings you and your team much closer than any other humans can be. You live because of your team. They live because of you.

No one but the people who are directly connected with this mission will ever really know what happened to you if something goes wrong. It's like a cancer that's in check. You know it's there, but you know you're good and your men are the best, so you accept it. You have confidence in your ability, your training, your team, and your warrior spirit. Because of that, the cancer won't get you. The cancer of non-existence is in check, and it will stay that way as long as you stick together. Because of who and what you are, your confidence is high; but like the thought of cancer, the fear is there, gnawing at you, ever present.

As the Bronco passed over the mountain crest, Buzz lowered the nose into a shallow dive, gaining airspeed. I knew that in a few seconds we would be out of the cramped, but safe, confines of the Bronco and on our own. The jungle dropped sharply on this side of the mountain. Suddenly Buzz pulled the Bronco into a steep climb that almost took my breath away.

I watched the pair of lights, one red, one green, above the hole at the back of the Bronco. It always reminded me of a giant open mouth waiting to swallow me into never-ending blackness. Within seconds the light switched from red to green, the door snapped open, and it was time to go.

In seconds, we were out. The cool night air slapped me as I hit the slipstream. The sudden jerk of my chute opening was a chilling jolt back to reality. I could see the Bronco above us standing on its tail, then rolling over, heading in the direction we had just come. I felt I could read Buzz's mind as we drifted so briefly to the canopy below: *Good luck, you crazy bastards. You're going to need it.*

The peaceful ride to the anger below was a short one. We all hit the ground about the same time. It was almost funny listening to us crashing through the tops of the trees. Everyone was OK, and we had all of our equipment. Now the games began.

First order of business was to secure the parachutes. Of course the damn things were caught in the trees. This LZ was picked supposedly because there wasn't much dense jungle. So much for good intelligence.

It took about twenty minutes to clear the chutes from the trees and bury them. Normally the next thing I would do was radio our SITREP (SITuation REPort) back to our CCP (Command and Control Point), but this mission was different. We were not supposed to use our radio. We were to maintain radio silence until just before our extraction.

This was something we hadn't done before. It made me nervous, not letting someone know we were on the ground and proceeding with the mission. It made me feel very alone.

The mission sounded simple, an easy breather. Just walk through the jungle to this road, wait for this guy in a truck, give him a couple of packages, and leave, right? WRONG! Besides the fact that the two large containers weighed about a hundred pounds apiece and there was only four of us, the rendezvous point was three clicks (kilometers) from our LZ through enemy-held jungle at night. *No sweat, piece of cake,* I thought. *Yeah, right.* We took a compass heading and started toward our objective, slowly, cautiously.

Getting in a hurry is one of the biggest mistakes you can make on an operation, so you learn certain habits to keep you from getting killed. Without so much as a second thought, we would walk a short distance, often using ranger beads, stop, and check things out.

Ranger pace beads are a set of beads on a leather strap. One side of the set has nine beads. Every time your left foot hits the ground you count it as one. When you have counted sixty-five paces, you slide one of the nine beads down. Each bead would represent 100 meters. At 1,000 meters, or all nine beads plus sixty-five, one of the four beads is pulled down and you start over again with the nine beads. You could measure up to 5,000 meters with a set of ranger pace beads.

Depending on the terrain and the likelihood of Indians (enemy), we would stop, listen, look, for what good it would do, then continue. I often trusted my senses of hearing and smell over my eyesight at night. Our eyes could trick us, but our other senses usually wouldn't. Sometimes we would hang a three-foot piece of string from the front of our weapon. If the string caught on something we couldn't see, it would start to bend back toward us. This usually meant the string had caught on a trip wire.

Our orders for this mission were not to make contact with anyone, friend or foe. This was not a strike mission. We knew there were SF (Special Forces) advisers in the area, and we had heard rumors that a SEAL team was also working nearby. We could not make any contact with them, even if they were in trouble. We weren't given their radio frequencies or radio codes to make contact with them even if we needed to. If we were to come upon any other round eyes, we were to avoid contact at all cost.

The SF advisers and SEALs didn't know we were there, and it was to stay that way. It was common not to make contact with another team, so I figured if we saw the SF guys, they would think we were the SEALs and leave us alone. With only three clicks to make by 0700 the next morning, I knew we had plenty of time, so there wasn't any reason to get in a hurry.

Walking at night in the jungle can be a real bitch. You can't imagine how dark it gets. Sometimes we would have to stop and wait for the moon to come out from behind a cloud just to see the ground. We had some night vision optics with us, but when I tried to walk with them I would get dizzy and almost sick. In addition, we were trying to carry two packages that were getting heavier with every step we took.

We knew the spot where we were supposed to meet the Cambodian because of a small Buddhist temple that was next to the road. A few weeks earlier, we had been to that same spot trying to gather intelligence on the very same Cambodian asshole we were now en route to meet.

It was real ironic to me that we were going to meet the very enemy we had intended to kill a few weeks earlier. As a young soldier, you're not supposed to think about things like that. It wasn't your job to think about anything other than the mission.

About 0200 hours we heard a terrible firefight off in the distance. Immediately we stopped, stashed our packages, and set up a quick defensive position. Was that those SF advisers getting their asses kicked? Or the SEALs wishing they were back in the water? *Those poor bastards,* I thought.

Every fiber in me screamed to forget those damn boxes and find out what in the hell was going on. You don't have to be in very many gun battles to recognize an AK-47 firing against an M-16. If those were Americans in trouble, we needed to help. That's our fuckin' job. We sat there in the dark helplessly waiting. I really wasn't sure what we were waiting for. It seemed like the battle lasted ten minutes or so. It would get quiet for a few seconds; then I could hear an M-16 opening up or a grenade going off. *Thump,* then the *ka-whoom* of an M-79 grenade launcher could be heard. *Yeah, those are Americans, and they're not that far away,* I said to myself. I had to force my mind to stay focused on the mission, *the mission of no fucking contact.*

After a time, the raging battle was silent. We sat for a while, thinking of what the outcome might have been. Could we have just heard the taking of more U.S. prisoners? Could we have helped? Would we have made any difference? I knew we did the right thing, but the "what ifs" started, and that's all I could think about for a while. We waited a short time, making sure there weren't any Indians coming our way, got our boxes, and continued on toward our objective.

At night your mind tends to play nasty little games with you. You start thinking about all of the things out there in the jungle. You know there are a lot of things both two-legged, four-plus-legged, and no-legged that can maim or kill you. You know they're there, close, real close, looking for you, waiting for you, hungry for you.

Are you going to be killed by some lucky VC, step on a land mine that blows your legs off, snag a trip wire, or become part of the food chain by some stinking act of nature? The thought of dying becomes a very personal and consuming thing. You think about it, but you control it and move on. *The mission.*

The trip to our objective was as fast and as cautious as I could make it. Except for the distant firefight and trying to keep our imaginations in check, we had no problems.

Steve, whom we called Chief because he was part Indian, was someone to whom I was closer than anyone. "Chance, what do you think is really in these boxes? You know it's not money," he said.

"Stow it, Chief. This ain't the time to start questioning what we're doing. Besides, what difference does it make if it gets our men back?"

I knew where Chief was coming from. There were only four of us to protect all that paper money. My gut feeling was to open boxes up and find out what was really inside. If I'd known then what I found out later, I would have destroyed the cases and delivered something else to our contact in Cambodia.

"You know this is bullshit," Chief said. "We're not spooks. We're soldiers, not goddamn delivery boys."

"I know," I replied. "That guy Patterson, he's a CIA spook. I heard him say to Captain Harris if this worked, we'd be doing a lot more good than we've been doing in the past."

"What does that mean, 'if this worked'?" asked Chief.

"I don't know," I replied. "Hang with me on this. I'll find out what's going on when we get back."

"No sweat," said Chief with reservation.

The rest of the journey was smooth but never routine. You learn to become a chameleon in the jungle. If they can't see you, they may not shoot you. Your training becomes second nature. Camouflage, cover, and concealment become a way of life, literally.

Three hours early for our rendezvous, we stopped some distance from the road and made sure we weren't walking into any trouble. We took a position about twenty meters off the road and settled in. It was still dark when we set up, and everything looked good.

The sun came up like it always did: hot. We watched as civilians walked by with everything they owned on a cart or in a bundle on their back. Most were women and children, with an occasional old man or cripple. People with nothing except each other and all in a hurry going nowhere.

I couldn't help wondering about the hell these people must be going through. I knew they were refugees looking for a place to be left alone. The kids had no expression, no smiles. They just trudged by, staring without feeling.

One of the things I really liked about this job was that every now and then we were able to set up an aid station to help these people. We would give medical aid to civilians, mostly women and kids. It would break my heart when some little kid came in with his foot blown off by a mine. Then, after you fixed him up, he would hug your neck with incredible strength, the strength of a child crying, *Please help me; let me live.* All they wanted was a place where they could be safe. Where they could wake up each day without the fear of dying.

The plan was for me to make contact while the others provided cover. This was the first time I had ever done anything like this, and I was scared shitless. I preferred hiding in the jungle unseen by man or animal to standing up next to a platoon of enemy soldiers waiting for me with AK-47s.

It was hot and humid, real fuckin' humid. The sweat ran down my face. My camo paint tasted like shit, my eyes burned, and I had to scratch my ass but couldn't. If I moved, I might have been seen. I had to piss for two hours, but it was not the time. I could feel what I thought was sweat running down my spine into the crack of my ass, and I prayed that it was sweat and not one of those six-inch centipedes I could see running underfoot.

Goddamn it, I said to myself. *I thought this was a good spot this morning in the dark, but it really sucks. The only reason nobody can see us is because we aren't moving. God, if we were only twenty feet farther back.*

Right at 0700, two military trucks pulled up next to the shrine and stopped. It was weird how all the traffic had suddenly stopped just minutes before they showed up. The dust hadn't cleared when out stepped a short, hard-looking man dressed in Cambodian jungle fatigues. There was no doubt he was in charge. A dozen or so soldiers piled out of the other truck and lined up. When the hard-looking man barked orders, the soldiers with him looked like they were shitting little pith helmets trying to obey. I would have laughed if I weren't so damn scared.

They stopped across from the shrine on the opposite side of the road from where we were. At least something went right. The soldiers' backs were to us, so I took that opportunity to move my men. They made their way to a better spot about twenty feet behind me. I stayed where I was so when I went to make contact I wouldn't give the others' position away.

I sat there thinking I must be nuts. I'm going to just stand up and walk over to a bunch of Cambodian soldiers with guns.

I must have watched them almost an hour. It was becoming obvious that the colonel was getting impatient, and so was I.

OK, Chance, show time, I said to myself. I stood up slowly and started walking toward the colonel. *God,* I was so afraid, I didn't know if I was going to shit or throw up.

You dumb shit, what the fuck are you doing? I kept asking myself. *You're just walking right into their waiting arms. I hope this works. I hope one of these fine pieces-of-shit gooks isn't having a bad hair day and decides to blow my cast-iron balls away.*

No one noticed me at first. I walked slowly and deliberately. Suddenly one of the soldiers saw me and looked like he about shit. So did I. I had a death grip on my M-16, but I froze and didn't move a muscle. I did have one comforting thought, however. If anything happened and I was killed, these poor fucks were really going to get some shit. The night before, we had daisy-chained three Claymore antipersonnel mines about ten feet in front of them.

I waited to make sure I wasn't going to get shot. Then I walked right up to the colonel. That's when things got even stranger.

"Good morning, Sergeant Chance," the colonel said, in almost perfect English.

I stopped dead in my tracks. How did he know my name?

"I've been waiting for you. You have something for me?" he asked.

"Colonel, I will need to have your password first, sir," I replied, trying to keep my voice from showing my fear.

This was one of the strangest conversations I had ever had. I should be shoving my weapon up his ass and taking him prisoner. Instead, I'm having this conversation with him like I did it every day. Damn, is this fucked up or what?

"Dragon Flower," he replied.

"Very good, sir. If you would keep your men right where they are, I'll get your packages."

From what Cambodian I knew, I could tell the colonel snapped out some orders for his men to stay exactly as they were and not look behind them. It was like they weren't supposed to know about this little transaction. I went back to where the boxes were stashed and carried them one by one to the colonel.

"Can I have one of my men give you a hand?" he asked politely.

"No, sir, I can handle it."

"You are very cautious, Sergeant. Relax; no harm will come to you. You have my word."

I didn't reply; I just looked at him. He knew what I was thinking. His face was cold and hard. I stared at him, wondering how many Americans he had killed. I saw that part of his left ear was missing and thought, *Someone almost got you, you piece of shit.* I turned away and went back after the last package.

After the colonel had put the packages into his truck, he walked over to me and led me away from his men. "Tell your people it was nice doing business with them, and I hope to be doing a lot more."

He stuck out his hand for me to shake, but I couldn't shake it. I wanted to cut it off and shove it down his throat. "I will relay your message, Colonel," was all I said. I turned and walked away, thinking he would put a bullet in the back of my head. He climbed into the truck containing the packages as the rest of the soldiers got into the other vehicle. As quickly as they had arrived, they were gone. As they drove away, I thought I was going to puke....

Delivery

The Huey banked sharply off to the east. The sudden turn brought me crashing back to the present reality. I watched as the lights of San Jose del Guaviare faded off into the distance. The air became suddenly colder, so I rolled down the sleeves of my BDU top and buttoned up, then turned and looked at the rest of the team. They were all looking at me as if they knew something. It was almost frightening, looking into their eyes. I could tell by the looks on their faces that they also sensed this wasn't going to be an easy breather. It was as if we some-how knew that all of us weren't going to be coming home.

The helicopter hadn't completely stopped its forward movement when we exited, four out each side. Santana took one of the packages, and I took the other. Immediately upon hitting the ground, we fanned out about ten yards from the helo, stopped, and took up a position until the helicopter was out of sight. Within a minute, the helicopter was out of hearing range, disappearing over the crest of a near by hill.

The surrounding jungle seemed shockingly quiet. We froze, not moving a muscle, waiting to see if anything was going to approach from the dark tree line that encircled us. Soon the horde of night creatures began their chorus. Thousands of frogs began their ritualistic mating call. The noise was startling at first, but I quickly recognized them as part of the jungle sounds I was used to. I felt comfort in the night sounds. I keyed up my Motorola and checked everyone out.

"Sound off," I said quietly over my headset.

"Two's OK," said Lucky.

"Three's OK," said Santana.

"Four's OK," said Razz.

There was a long pause.

"Five, you OK?" I asked.

"Yeah, I'm OK. I fell and knocked the wind out of me, but I'm fine," said Dave.

"Six's OK," said Opey.

"Seven is just fine," said Mike.

"Eight as happy as a pig in shit," said T J.

"Can it, T J. Wait until we move out before the jokes," I said.

The fog was starting to move down from the tops of the mountains, and it was getting extremely dark. We all formed up at the edge of the clearing and checked our gear. I double-checked the frequency on the SG-715-DE HF-SSB radio that Santana was carrying, then radioed our control point, Springer, to let him know we were proceeding to our objective.

"Park Ranger, this is Easy Breather, over."

"Easy Breather, this is Park Ranger; I read you Lima Charley, over," replied Springer.

"Park Ranger, the package is in the mail, over."

"Easy Breather, copy, over and out."

Springer, Valley, and Baines used the phrases "easy breather" and "walk in the park" so much, I decided to use them as our call signs. I was "Easy Breather" and Springer "Park Ranger." What the hell, I figured, they're encrypted radios.

I checked our position on my own GPS, against the one I'd been issued. Lucky double-checked it with a compass and map. We got a heading to the AO and set off. Once we were on the ground, I figured we were playing by my rules, not Springer's. Before we left, I had plotted our routes, including a few alternates, into my GPS. I then programmed everything into the issued GPS and gave it to Lucky.

We had decided as we started to travel that if we ran into any trouble we would separate the team. Lucky would take Santana, Razz, and T J. I would take Dave, Mike, and Opey. If we had to separate, we would meet at the next way-point we had stored in our GPSs. We started off toward our AO in two teams, with Lucky's team about a hundred yards behind mine.

I had learned a long time ago that it was a good idea not to have all your assets in one place, especially when you're traveling in Indian country. It was very important to have backup that could come to your aid if needed.

When I felt secure in the fact that we weren't going to be compromised by any unexpected guests, we linked up and traveled together, staying about five yards apart. It didn't take long before we got into our travel routine. We had done this so many times in the past, we all knew where we needed to be and what to do. As usual, I rotated point with everybody except Opey (our medic) and Santana (our radioman), whom we kept in the middle of the team.

The jungle sounds were comforting. We knew if things got quiet, we weren't alone. Moving was relatively easy, as the jungle had numerous trails and paths. The foliage grew only moderately thick, and the humidity had not gotten too high, yet. As we traveled, the forest occasionally opened up into areas of fewer trees, reminding me of some of the mountains back home in Washington State. The big difference was that the mountains back home didn't have the smell of rotting vegetation and the musty odor of mold.

The morning light revealed everything covered with dew. Because everything was wet, it was easy for us to tell if anyone was using the trails. It was also easy for someone else to see where we had been walking. I frequently stopped and checked our rear security to make sure we weren't being followed.

An hour and a half later we reached the perimeter of the airstrip. We found and secured the area where we were supposed to plant the LP/OP. The equipment we were carrying was going to act as a remote LP/OP that would continue to operate until it was removed, somebody found and destroyed it, or it was remote-destroyed by whoever in the government was running this show. Equipment of this type could be remotely turned on and off via satellite. Cutting the power was an extremely important element, as it would prevent the enemy from triangulating on the signal and discovering its location.

When we secured the LP/OP's location, I realized it wasn't the best site for the equipment and decided to place it on an adjoining hill about 150 yards LOS (Line Of Site) across from the original spot. I sent Lucky and Razz to the new area to make sure it was secure.

It took them about thirty minutes to make their way to the new site. In the meantime, the rest of us established a defensive perimeter and waited. Once Lucky and Razz had secured the site, Lucky radioed me that everything was OK and we moved all of our equipment to the new location.

Mike had brought an NVEC TRC/3A wireless seismic intrusion detection system that he set up as part of our perimeter defense. The system consisted of a base station receiver with headphone and four sensor/transmitter "geophones." With this system, we could place a remote sensing transmitter up to a half-mile from the base station receiver. Each sensor/transmitter could detect someone walking 250 feet from the sensor or vehicles moving up to 1,200 feet away. This system could operate for about one hundred hours before needing new batteries. If anybody was to enter the area protected by the sensors, a tone, a light, or both would alert the base station. Each sensor transmitted a different tone, so you could tell what direction the intrusion was coming from. This was part of the equipment that Springer didn't know we had. But I wouldn't think of taking my men anywhere without it.

Once we had our perimeter security in place, Santana and I proceeded to set up the electronic LP/OP. The location I had selected was closer to the west end of the airstrip than the middle. The site had a complete view of the strip and a good view of the flight corridor that any approaching or departing aircraft would use. I secured the sensing unit about six feet from the base of a large tree and put out its two seismic detectors.

The sensing unit secured to the ground with anchors and remained hidden under a ceramic shell that looked like a rock. Valley had told me that the cover would promote the growth of moss and vegetation on it. Somebody had really put a lot of thought into this toy.

The seismic detectors connected to the main sensing unit with cables that were made to look like vines that had grown into the undergrowth. The covering of the cables had an irregular texture and was camouflaged in color. The cables almost disappeared when we laid them out on the ground.

Santana had the job of climbing the tree and placing the transmitting unit toward the top. This needed to be as high above the other unit as possible for better transmission and survivability. The top of the transmitter had a solar panel a foot square. The solar panel sat about six feet above the transmitter. Once the units were in place, a sixty-foot fiber-optic cable was connected and secured between them. The cable was covered in the same material as the other cables and placed in an irregular pattern up the tree. I connected a small interface terminal to the sensing unit and powered up the system.

The next step was the calibration. I positioned a small directional microwave antenna on top of the ground unit so it "looked" at the transmitting unit in the tree. When the antenna was in place, Santana adjusted the same type of antenna on the bottom of the transmitter in the tree so it pointed down at the ground unit. I watched the control terminal until three small aiming LEDs turned green. Now we could begin the next phase of testing.

Santana covered the transmitter in the tree with its own organic-looking cover and climbed down. I removed the antenna from the top of the ground unit and attached it to the inside of the unit's cover. I was not told why the two units had to be aligned, but I figured it was a redundant system in case something happened to the fiber-optic cable. My guess was the transmitter in the tree was able to function independently. So if the ground unit was discovered, it would self-destruct, leaving the tree unit to continue on.

I placed the system in the "standby/test" mode so a series of tests could be performed over the next twenty-four hours.

It would be all to easy to get too focused on the testing and forget we were in Indian country, so I took my time and made sure we maintained proper area security. One of us always monitored our own perimeter-sensing unit while those who weren't involved in testing kept watch. At one point, a small plane made a low pass over the airstrip but didn't land. As we heard it coming, we covered up what might have been exposed and waited for it to pass. Since we were all camouflaged and our gear was under cover, it probably wouldn't have seen us even if it had landed on us.

T J had moved to another hilltop where he could watch our position. He was our sniper, complete with Ghillie suit (made from strips of burlap and camo netting to blend in with his surroundings). His suit helped him hide almost anywhere, becoming invisible to the untrained eye. His Robar sniper rifle was a .300 Magnum, giving him maximum long-range cover fire.

Our mission was to maintain the area for forty-eight hours. After doing a series of tests on the unit, we were to sit and wait for any activity to make sure the LP/OP was working properly. The first battery of tests involved the unit's ability to detect flying objects. I sent two men to either end of the airfield to shoot small golfball-sized metallic-looking balls toward the center of the airfield.

I had packed a "wrist rocket" slingshot, which would do the job of launching the balls. I had actually brought the slingshots to fire "flash balls" in case of an emergency. About the size of large marbles, they served as a diversion, hitting with a brilliant flash and smoke, hopefully providing us enough of a distraction should we need to escape. Over the years, I'd learned to shoot them about one hundred yards with surprising accuracy.

I sent Razz and Dave to the west end of the airstrip and Lucky and Mike to the east end. As each of the metallic balls flew down the airfield, the control terminal, which looked like a small computer key-pad with an LCD screen, registered detection, listing altitude in feet, speed in feet per second, direction, and duration of the detection. This was some very sensitive shit, I thought.

We did this for two complete cycles three hours apart, then proceeded with the next phase of testing. Lucky and Razz each had a small seismic "thumper." A thumper was a small, round rod about two inches in diameter and about twenty-four inches long and pointed at one end. They would push the probe deep into the ground and detonate a small charge in the end of it. As they detonated the thumpers, I couldn't hear or see anything, but the two seismic probes connected to the sensing unit sure could.

The testing took most of the day. It would have only taken a few hours, but when you're in Indian country you have to do everything very slowly and cautiously. Santana and I did most of the actual calibrating while the rest of the team helped and watched.

T J served as our remote security until the end of the day. Sunset came before we finished all of the testing, and Lucky had been out scouting our AO. He was about to return when he noticed something down a narrow path that led from the east end of the airstrip.

"One, this is Two; I've spotted something down here. It might be some kind of building. Do you want me to check it out?"

"Two, can you tell what it is?"

"Negative, One; I can just barely see it through the trees. It looks like it might be an old shed or something."

"Do you see any activity from where you are?"

"Negative. I can't tell for sure, but it doesn't look like anybody has been there for a while."

"OK, Two, get back here, and we'll check it out on our way out," I said.

When Lucky returned, he said he couldn't tell exactly what he saw. He glassed it with his binoculars, and it looked like an old storage shed. The building stood on a dirt path about a quarter of a mile off the end of the airstrip.

"I didn't see anything on the satellite photos. Did you?" I asked Lucky.

"No. I looked at them very carefully, and there were no structures anywhere on the photos."

"The more I look at this place, though, the more it doesn't look anything like the photos," I said.

"No shit," Lucky interjected. "I started thinking that as soon as we got here."

"Great. That's all we needed, bad intelligence. I wonder what other bad information we got," I said. "We can't worry about that now. Let's get this shit set up and get the hell out of here."

I figured there were so many of these small airstrips out here that it would be real easy to have the wrong set of photos.

By the time we finished testing and the team regrouped, the sun had set. We had set up our ROM (Remain Over Night) position about fifty yards from our remote LP/OP equipment and got out our MREs (Meals Ready to Eat) for chow. It's easy to get dehydrated, even in the jungle, so Opey made sure we all were drinking plenty of water. All of us had two canteens of water on our sides and a two-quart bladder in our packs.

One of the little tricks we learned was to always drink from your canteen in your pack first. That way, if you had to drop your pack in a hurry, you still had water with you. We each had extra survival straws so we could drink the local water. There was a small creek not too far from our ROM, and Opey made sure we had plenty of clean water.

It was a beautiful evening as I sat overlooking the airstrip eating my MRE. I started to feel the $10,000 in my pocket. This was starting to look like one of those assignments that most people only dream about.

Dead Neighbors

At 1900 hours, I radioed Springer to give him our SITREP.

"Park Ranger, this is Easy Breather. Do you copy? Over."

"Easy Breather, this is Park Ranger, I read you, over."

"The mail has been delivered, over."

"Affirmative, over and out."

We secured our site and settled in for the night, rotating a two-man watch every two hours, with one man monitoring the TRC/3A base station while the other maintained a position where he could keep watch with his night vision goggles. T J had rejoined the team after giving our perimeter a once-over. Once we all got settled, we had to find a soft spot as bug-free and dry as possible and try to get some sleep. Preferring to sleep as high above the ground as possible, I managed to sling my hammock about ten feet up between two trees.

At 2330 hours, Santana woke me with a radio call from Springer.

"Easy Breather, this is Park Ranger. Do you copy? Over."

"Yeah, Park Ranger, this is Easy Breather. Go ahead, over."

"A postcard shows you may have some new neighbors that have moved in on our block to the east. Can you check them out? Over."

A "postcard" referred to a new satellite photo taken of an area. "Neighbors that have moved in" referred to buildings, structures, or vehicles in the photos. I had been told that the photos we saw before the mission were less than twenty-four hours old. They showed no buildings. I knew then that Springer hadn't shown us the right photos in the briefing. A sick feeling was starting to grow in the pit of my stomach.

"Affirmative, Park Ranger," I said. "We'll check it out before we leave day after tomorrow, over."

"Easy Breather, contact me after you've checked it out, over and out."

"Easy Breather out."

I got Lucky up and we went off down the hill from our ROM so we could talk about this in private. I told Lucky about the radio conversation I just had with Springer and about the "neighbors." I said I had told Springer we would check out the neighbors in a couple of days, on our way out. Lucky felt the same way I did—uneasy. We decided we would check out the building at daybreak, then get the hell out of the area. Though the mission called for us to stay here for a couple of days, we felt compromised now and decided to terminate the mission early. Spooky 8 was more important than a bunch of hardware. This wasn't an easy breather any longer.

At 0430 hours, I woke the team and we prepared to check out the northeast end of the airstrip. We decided that Mike, Santana, and I would approach the building from the airstrip on the east side of the path coming from the strip to the building. Opey would stay behind us and give cover fire. Razz and Dave would take up a position on the east side of the building, and Lucky would cover the northwest corner. T J would find a position to the west of the path where he could see the south and west sides of the building. T J would head out first in his Ghillie suit and be our advance scout. We all had night vision goggles, so I decided that starting in the dark would be the best way to go. If any bad guys were around, the time to catch them was when they were most vulnerable, tired, and sleepy.

It took T J about an hour to make his way to the agreed cover position from where we were on the southwest side of the airstrip. He went around the west end of the strip, then east to the path, which turned out to be a road that led from the east end of the strip north to the building. When T J was about halfway there, Lucky, Razz, and Dave followed T J's route partway, then headed through the jungle to the north side of the building. Opey, Mike, Santana, and I started around the east end of the airstrip and made our way to the east side of the road, south of the building. T J was the first to get into position and get a good view of the building Lucky had seen earlier.

"One, this is Eight," radioed T J.

"Go ahead, Eight," I replied.

"There are three buildings here. They're in a clearing about a quarter-mile north, up the road from the airstrip, over."

"Eight, do you see any movement or vehicles?"

"Negative. It looks to be an old house with a storage shed about twenty yards to the east and a small outbuilding to the right of the house on the west side. Two, what color was the building you saw yesterday?" T J asked Lucky.

"Faded blue."

"I can't tell through the goggles, but that must be the storage shed to the east. It's a different color from the main building. The main building is probably white, and is straight west from the blue shed about twenty yards. The grass has been trampled down around the buildings, and it looks like it's used regularly. I don't see any power lines or radio antennas on any of the buildings. There is what looks like an outdoor shitter right next to the house to the east, over."

"Roger, Eight. All right, boys, you know the routine. Once everybody is in position, let me know. We'll move once everybody is set," I said.

We were using secure radios, so I wasn't too worried that anybody was listening. If they were, we were screwed anyway, and we would just have to deal with it. I had programmed the radios myself before we left, and nobody had the frequency we were using, especially not Springer.

We had all reached our positions at about 0515 hours. At one point, I thought I smelled a cigarette, but the smell didn't last. There are many smells in the jungle. Plants can give off odors that can fool you. Some even smell like rotting flesh.

One by one, the men radioed that they were in position.

"This is Two. I'm on the west side, and it looks like there is a well-used path leading from the jungle to the house," Lucky reported.

"Does anyone see anything?" I asked.

"Negative," said Razz.

"Nothing here," added Dave.

"Is everybody ready?" I then asked.

They all gave an affirmative, so I waited for a few minutes until the sun was up enough to give us light, then motioned Santana and Mike to move out. I took the lead, Santana behind me, then Mike. Opey stayed back to provide cover. We moved along the tree line on the east side of the road that led from the airstrip to the buildings. As we crept toward the house, we kept about five yards between us. As we got closer, I found evidence that somebody had been here within the past couple of days, a cigarette butt that hadn't yet started to fade in the sun with its tobacco still intact. It was store-bought, not hand-rolled. Most locals didn't have money to buy cigarettes, so I was pretty sure whoever had been here didn't live here.

"Tighten up, guys. Somebody's been here recently, and we may not be alone," I radioed.

The tenseness of the situation was unbearable. I was so on edge, my sweat hurt. Every sight, every smell, every thing I sensed processed at a tremendous rate. No computer on earth could match what our brains were doing with the information we gathered.

We proceeded up the road to within twenty yards of the storage shed. Then suddenly and without warning, the peaceful quiet erupted into a mass of gunfire. From what I could tell, a man had been concealed about thirty feet from where Lucky had taken up a position. I couldn't tell exactly where the man was or who he was shooting at, but I could hear his AK-47 belching out rounds. As I heard Lucky's MP5 open up and silence the shooter, two more men came out of hiding behind Razz and Dave and opened up on them.

A massive ambush had started. I saw a man, about ten yards away, stand up between Dave and me. Then I heard the .300 Magnum of T J's rifle bark out its awesome killing power. T J's shot struck the man in the chest with the force of a truck.

Just as I started to run to the west side of the road, I felt several muzzle blasts, then heard a loud slap. I knew Santana, who was right behind me, had taken a hit. I felt blood and pieces of Santana's skull splatter my back and turned to see Santana fall to the ground, face first. A large piece of his head had been blown away, and there was an empty hole where his brain used to be. As I was turning back to my left and starting to run, I felt another burst muzzle of blasts then a sharp burning pain as a bullet penetrated my right thigh. The muzzle blast was close, real close.

The bullet hit me like a hammer, catching me off balance and spinning me around, slamming me to the ground. I landed on my left side, looking at the shooter. A man with an MP5 machine gun stood about fifteen feet away, trying to put a new magazine in his weapon. As I hit the ground, I was lying on my MP5, so I drew my handgun and fired one round, striking the man in the face, just below his right eye. The .45-caliber slug hit him with tremendous force. Pieces of skull, brains, and blood dripped from the tree behind him as he dropped to the ground.

I looked back and saw that Mike was OK and was returning fire. I could hear other M-16 rifles, but I couldn't tell whose they were.

Mike and I were in the open, and I knew we had to find cover or die. It took a moment to get up, but the pain in my leg was something I couldn't do anything about now and I had to keep moving. I felt the shock wave and heat as a bullet cracked by me, only inches from my face. Mike and I made eye contact, and I pointed to the tree line to the east.

As we ran for the trees, we almost tripped over two guys who were lying behind a fallen tree. Mike and I opened up on them before they even knew we were there, killing both of them instantly. We jumped over the log and took cover, using the tree and their bullet-riddled bodies as shields. I had emptied my weapon at them, so I grabbed one of their AK-47s and began to fire. After I had fired the AK out of rounds, I reloaded my weapon and continued.

I could hear commands in Spanish being yelled from the house. The Spanish was good, but it didn't sound fluent. It sounded to me like an American speaking Spanish—someone I really wanted to meet. When Mike and I could see no more standing threats, we made our way around the east side of the clearing, then north toward the house.

Mike took up a position and provided cover fire as I moved toward the house. I heard that same American voice, so I stopped and waited a few yards from the house. A man with dark blond hair and light skin, definitely American, ran from the house toward me yelling commands in Spanish.

He got about ten feet away before he saw me. He stopped in his tracks, and our eyes met for an instant, his in fear and mine in rage. I watched the expression on his face change when he realized he was about to die.

In calm, almost perfect English he yelled, "Fuck you, you son of a bitch!"

"No, fuck you," I said as I aimed my MP5. He started to dive for cover, but it was too late. I fired a burst into his chest, and he fell to the ground.

As he lay dying at my feet, he looked up at me and said, "They'll find you." He struggled to raise his weapon and finish the job, but I kicked it from his hand. I stared at him with intense anger.

"Who sent you?" I yelled.

"Fuck you," he tried to say.

"Last chance, you piece of shit," I replied calmly. He only stared at me, then grinned. I finished him off with a few more rounds, reloaded quickly, then headed for a large tree where I had spotted one of the men who was firing on Razz and Dave. By the time he saw me, I was so close he didn't have time to react. I emptied a full magazine into him as I ran by. I was so close it almost cut him in half. I found cover, reloaded, and looked to find my next victim.

Rage and hatred were driving me. I wanted to kill every stinking son of a bitch here, then hunt down their entire family and kill them, including their dogs and cats and anything else living that belonged to them.

The bullet in my leg had buried itself in the muscle but wasn't bleeding heavily yet. If I hadn't been so pumped, I probably wouldn't have been able to handle the pain without a little help from Opey. It ached, but so little I had almost forgotten about it.

As I moved to give Dave and Razz some support, I could see at least five more men had emerged from the house. I heard two more rounds from T J's position and was sure he was taking them out. I made my way around to where Razz and Dave were. I found Razz dead, shot several times. Dave was a few yards away and had been wounded in the hand and shoulder but was still fighting. I was down to my last magazine, so I had to stop and get the extra magazines from my pack before I could continue.

The firefight only lasted six or seven minutes, but it seemed like much longer. Opey had moved across the road to the west and was working his way north to help Lucky. I could hear M-16s, MP5s, and AKs being fired. It was a totally intense, totally insane few minutes.

As quickly as it had begun, it was over. The smell of gunpowder hung thick in the air, as did the smell of death. It happened so fast, all we had time to do was react. I hadn't had time to think of our wounded until now. Once the shooting had stopped, I started to check everyone's condition. I knew that Santana and Razz were dead. Dave was wounded but OK. Mike was covering me, so that left Lucky, Opey, and T J.

"Lucky, you OK?" I asked.

"Fuck no, I got a goddamn bullet in my ass, but I'll live," he said.

"Opey, how about you?" I then asked.

"Yeah. I'll check on Lucky," he said.

"T J, how does everything look?" I asked.

No answer.

"T J, come in. Does anybody see T J?" I asked.

I could hear the panic in my voice. The severity of the situation was starting to sink in. I knew we had been set up, and my fucking leg was hurting like a mother.

"T J, goddamn it, come in!" I yelled.

Opey came on the radio. "T J's gone."

I stopped for a moment, trying to get my shit together. The wound in my leg was hurting, and I was starting to feel the after affects of my adrenaline rush. I limped to where T J was and found Opey checking him out. T J had been shot sometime during the firefight, although I couldn't see how he could have been shot by anyone near the house. Someone had to have worked around behind him, but that seemed almost impossible. T J had been wearing a Ghillie suit and was almost invisible. He had lain a good 150 yards from the fighting, totally concealed. The only person that could have possibly found him was someone who had the same type of training as another sniper or us, not this bunch of asshole mercenaries. It had to be somebody who knew how to find and kill a trained sniper.

I told Opey to get back to Santana and get his radio. I had to stay with T J for a moment and try to figure out what might have happened. I scanned the area, trying to tell where the shot might have come from. The only people that might have been able to get to T J would have had to come from the house or be waiting in the trees where we couldn't see him. Maybe Lucky, Dave, or Mike might have seen someone. They were in the right position to see.

T J was lying on his stomach in a prone position. There was blood on his rifle, which was lying in front of him. I took a closer look and found that T J had been shot in the back of the head with a small-caliber bullet. The exit wound was small, like what a handgun would make, not large like a rifle's.

This suddenly scared the shit out of me. Somebody snuck up behind him and killed him. Somebody was out here in the trees waiting for him. Somebody knew we had a sniper and knew how we were going to use him. It looked as if he had been stalked by a fucking sniper. A pro that could get close enough to use a handgun.

I went over to where Opey was checking the spot where Santana had fallen.

"We can forget the radio. It's shot full of fucking holes," Opey said.

I rolled Santana over to see that he had taken a round through the right side of the head, I'm sure from the same man who shot me, and died instantly. I rolled Santana back over and discovered the radio had two bullet holes in it. It appeared they had come from behind, like the bullet that killed T J. These were rifle rounds, though, not from a handgun. Someone didn't want us to radio anybody, and they damn sure didn't want us to leave, either. I felt Opey and I might still be in this asshole's killing zone, so we hurried back to the house to check on Lucky and Dave.

The smell of Santana's body stuck to my clothes like the blood that was running down my leg. My adrenaline was starting to wear off, and my leg was starting to throb intensely with pain. It was as if someone had taken a white-hot poker and pushed it deep into my thigh. *I don't have time for this shit right now,* I kept saying to myself, but my "mind over matter" skills had been pushed to their limits, and the pain wasn't going away. I knew the battle was over, and now I needed Opey to give me a shot to ease the pain.

Of my team, Santana, Razz, and T J were dead. Lucky, Dave, and I had been wounded but not seriously. Mike and Opey were OK. The bad guys weren't so lucky. I counted thirteen dead. I didn't think anybody got away, but there was no way to be sure. I knew that somebody would be checking on this place real soon and we had to work fast. There would be a satellite overflight soon, and the heat given off by bodies decomposing in the sun would light up their thermal imaging like a bonfire. If they wanted a body count, they were going to get one.

We finished clearing the house and found that the men had been living there for several days, obviously waiting for us. No wonder Springer had rushed us. The house had been booby-trapped in case their plan hadn't worked, a real professional job. The hides, small holes in the ground that conceal a sniper's position, were well built and had been designed for extended use. They were obviously not dug yesterday. The dirt had been taken into the jungle and dumped. Each position had a hard-wired field phone in it, which connected to the main house. It looked as if this place was used for drug deals that needed a little extra security. On the outside, it didn't look like much, but it was well used. Somebody had gone to great lengths to hide the real purpose of this place from surveillance overflights.

By now, my leg wound's pain was unbearable. I could barely walk. The hole in my leg went deep into the meat, but, luckily, my leg wasn't broken. Lucky had taken a round through the cheek of his ass, but it wasn't serious. Dave had been shot in the shoulder and hand. Both wounds didn't break any bones and had gone clean through.

Opey had to dig the bullet out of my leg before we could continue on. Infection would have killed me, so he did what he could, and then he sewed me up. Opey was an excellent medic whom I had complete faith in. He tended our wounds, then hit us with morphine for pain. He was able to patch us up so we could get the hell out. None of our wounds was serious enough to keep us from moving out quickly. Fear and rage are amazing motivators. I wasn't sure what we were going to do, but I was sure we were going to fight like hell to make it out.

We had to leave a body count, so my plan was to dress the bad guys in our clothes, give them our equipment, then burn everything so they couldn't be easily identified. I was hoping that the equipment left would stall whoever set us up. All I needed was twelve hours to give us a chance that they would never find us. We found five bodies that were about our size and changed clothes with them. I then had my men pair up one bad guy each with Razz's, Santana's, and T J's bodies to make it look like they had died together.

The rest of us took our dead counterparts and positioned them so they looked like our dead bodies. We then made sure that all of our issued equipment was left, plus the $10,000 we each had. After things were put in place, we prepared to burn everything. I was going to burn the bodies of the bad guys, leaving T J, Santana, and Razz for them to identify. We took the rest of the bodies into the jungle and hid them. The jungle has a way of recycling that is hard to beat.

I hoped that it would take a few days for anyone to figure out what really happened. Most of the dead didn't look like regular soldiers, so I figured they were probably mercenaries who knew we each were carrying $10,000. If they were mercenaries, any survivors would want to get the money and leave the area as soon as possible. Most of the time, mercenaries are hired by a third party. They would go in and do a job and often never know who they did the job for. They were happy as long as they got paid. If a bunch of mercenaries were hired to ambush and kill a bunch of people, especially Americans, I wouldn't think they would stick around too long. They would probably destroy any evidence of their action and meet up at some later date. At least, that's what I was counting on. If they did come back, they would find a few of the unidentifiable bodies carrying $10,000 in U.S. currency and be able to report that they had gotten the right guys.

Before we started to burn things, Mike and I went back to the LP/OP site and destroyed the equipment we had set up. The LP/OP had not been completely powered up, so I had to set it to blow itself. I was hoping it didn't have some kind of fail-safe that would be able to transmit what was happening before I was able to destroy it.

Next we set fire to the buildings, then to most of the bodies. Leaving my teammates was one of the hardest things I have ever had to do. When they died, a part of me died with them.

We made sure we didn't take any of the equipment that Springer had issued to us. I didn't know if there was a locator beacon built into our radios or if our night vision equipment was made to detonate by remote control. I had used some of the toys employed by our government before and knew that anything was possible.

We took what supplies we needed from the bad guys. We kept our personal equipment we had brought: my GPS, a couple of Motorola Expo radios that were modified to work in the aircraft band, a .22-caliber suppressed pistol, and the wireless perimeter ground sensor. All the clothes, other weapons, food, and water we took from the bad guys.

When things were burning, we headed northeast into the densest jungle we could find. We had to move as quickly as humanly possible and put distance between the airstrip and us. The smoke from the fires and the explosion from the electronics might bring someone faster than I wanted. South would have been a much easier direction to take because we would be heading away from the mountains and could use the waterways for travel. That was precisely why we headed northeast, to the shittiest part of the jungle.

I had an idea where we should go. I had set up a safe house some years ago in a town called Sogamosa. The village lay about one hundred miles straight north of the airstrip, and I already had its location plotted in my GPS.

We humped the bush for more than six hours nonstop. By this time, we were running on nothing but pure adrenaline. None of us had time to think about what had happened. We finally stopped around 1900 hours and set up our ROM. Mike put out the wireless ground sensors, and we settled in to rest, eat, and check our wounds. Before it got too dark, Opey went out and did a perimeter check about a hundred yards out from our position. He had one of the Expo radios with him in case he had any problems, but everything was quiet.

Even though every sound got our full attention, the familiar jungle noises were comforting. As long as things were noisy, we knew we were probably alone. The sounds of the hundreds of unseen creatures seemed to magnify as the events of the day started running through my head. The smell of blood filled my lungs. The pain of my wound now consumed me like a raging fire.

I was too tired to eat or drink. Opey came over and made me take some water, then gave me another shot of morphine for the pain. Within seconds, the fire in my leg diminished to a dull ache, as if someone had hit me with a baseball bat. This was much better than the fire. I could handle this. I found a place where I could watch my surroundings, grabbed a couple pieces of bread we had taken from the house, and tried to eat. *God, what I would give for a cold Corona right now,* I thought.

I tried to close my eyes, but all I could see was the hole where Santana's brains used to be. My rage remained intense, and so did my fear. Deep down, I knew I was going to make it. I knew we all were going to make it. All I could think of was revenge. I wanted to cry, I wanted to scream, and, most of all, I wanted to kill someone. *The payback will come later,* I thought, *and it will be sweet.*

But then the reality of what had happened hit me like a grenade thrown in my cornflakes. We had been left in the jungle to die, no trace, no questions. We were somebody's trash, ready to be taken to the dump. I remembered my good friend Paco, a Spooky team leader who, like me, had been sent on a routine mission and, like us, met with a well "dug-in" enemy. My memory clicked into the phone call from Paco, and thoughts of the mission that had followed replaced the pain in my mind.

Paco

"Four-Way, wake the fuck up. It's party time in the Southland."

I knew when I was called Four-Way and by the phrase "party time in the Southland" it was my old friend Paco. Four-Way was a nickname given to me by a civilian whom we had rescued the year before. This civilian had watched me dispose of four of his captures, each differently. He was so shaken by the events that from then on he started calling me Four-Way. Paco knew to use the name Four-Way to signal things were not well and he needed my to help.

"Hey, Beaner, what's up?"

"Fuck, man, I'm in some really deep shit here. I have to talk quick. The battery in this sat phone is almost gone. You remember what we talked about last?"

A couple of weeks earlier we had met over a Corona to talk about a mission Paco and Spooky 4 were scheduled to go on. Paco told me it was supposed to be an easy breather mission in Nicaragua. But had some real bad vibes about it—too many new faces and a lack of proper intelligence. He and I planned an unauthorized rescue mission if anything happened.

Political times had changed in the past couple years, and people in our business seemed to just disappear. We had heard rumors about people being left to die but tried to blow them off as just rumors. We didn't trust anybody we didn't know.

"Yeah, I remember."

"Four days, man, that's all I can hold out, four days, got it?" Paco said almost in a panic.

"Don't you worry, just like we planned. You hang in there, damn you. Don't you do something stupid and mess this up. You understand me?"

I could hear Paco breathing hard. "Yeah, I hear ya. Only four, goddamn it, only four. They fucked me real bad, Chance."

He was about to lose it. I knew that he didn't have much time, and I was going to do everything I could to get him out.

"OK, Paco, I'm en route now. You be there no matter what! You be there, Paco! I'll see you in two days, three at the most. On the lake. Everything is going to be OK. You know you can count on me. You hang in there."

Then his satellite phone faded and went dead.

Paco's call meant he had no options left. I was his last chance of getting out. He and his team had been operating in an area between the cities of Juigalpa and Acoyapa, about ten miles north of Lago de Nicaragua, a lake in southern Nicaragua. If things went bad, he was to make his way to Lago de Nicaragua and wait.

When Paco hung up, I called Lucky, Santana, Razz, Opey, Dave, Mike, and T J and brought them all together for an emergency meeting. At the time, we were all living within 150 miles of each other, so we were able to meet that night. Dave and Mike immediately headed to Puntarenas, in Costa Rica, to arrange for transportation to the Yucatán Peninsula in Mexico. I knew an exporter there who regularly flew to the Yucatán on "business" and who earlier that year had a little problem with a DEA Blackhawk. I had overheard the aircraft radio traffic about him while I was in another Blackhawk and was able to pull the dogs off his tail. He owed me, big-time.

The rest of us left for La Cruz, Costa Rica, the following day. We rented a couple of trucks and made our way to a fishing village on the Tempisque River about three miles north of La Cruz, where we found a man with several fishing boats who rented us one with a captain. He also supplied us with a small rubber Zodiac boat and some weapons he thought we might need: four M-16s, ammo, and an American M-60 machine gun with two cans of linked ammunition.

The thirty-foot boat we rented looked like it had been used for this type of adventure before. It had a gun mount for the M-60 on the front of it and a large supply of camouflage netting stored on deck.

T J and Santana stayed back at the village to make sure our boat owner friend didn't decide to change his mind and let somebody know what we were doing.

After fueling the boat and securing enough supplies for a few days, Lucky, Razz, Opey, the boat captain, and I headed upriver for Nicaragua. The river crossed the Nicaraguan border and fed into Lago de Nicaragua. As the border was not being monitored too heavily, we had no problem crossing. We found a small inlet at the mouth of the lake and pulled in and dropped Lucky and Razz off on the shore for security. We covered our boat with camouflage netting and waited until dark before continuing on. About an hour after dark, we stowed the netting and made our way across the lake to where Paco and his team were supposed to be waiting.

Paco had an IR "Fire Fly" he was supposed to turn on at night that I could see with my night vision pocket scope I had brought. The Fire Fly is a battery-powered flasher about the size of a large pack of gum.

It had three infrared light-emitting diodes on top that blinked about eighty times a second. You couldn't see it with the naked eye, but on the lake you could see it for a mile or so with night vision equipment.

It took about two hours of searching the shoreline before I saw the Fire Fly. I launched the small Zodiac, climbed in, and headed for shore while Opey and the rest went back out to the middle of the lake to wait for my radio signal. I got to shore, pulled the Zodiac up on the beach, and hid it about a hundred yards south of where I saw Paco's Fire Fly. We had arranged for him to wait to the south of his Fire Fly signal.

Paco had one of the Expo radios like ours that was used for just such emergencies. He knew not to turn on the radio until the day of the scheduled pickup and to only turn it on at night. This way, the battery would last two or three days.

It only took about thirty minutes before I heard Paco on the radio.

"Four-Way, this is Paco; I copy. We are about half a mile south of the Fire Fly; copy."

"I must be right on you. Come down to the water, and I'll find you."

I saw Paco and three of his men coming from a small shack about fifty yards from me, about half a mile south from where I first saw the Fire Fly. They were hungry and tired, and three of Paco's men were hurt but able to move. Paco said they had come across a Nicaraguan patrol the day before and had to take them out. He figured somebody should be looking for them by now and we needed to get out fast.

We hadn't quite reached the hidden Zodiac when a small boat appeared from the north, heading for us down the shoreline. We froze as it stopped just a few yards from where I had hidden the Zodiac.

We watched as men got into a small boat and came ashore. I figured it was a Nicaraguan patrol boat because I could see by the moonlight the men wearing some type of military uniforms. The crew of three had come ashore to take a leak or something and were standing around talking next to where the Zodiac was hidden. The Zodiac was still covered with brush, and it didn't look like it had been discovered, yet.

We took cover in the tree line and waited for the patrol to leave. They had been standing around for about ten minutes when one of the men went over to the brush hiding the Zodiac and tore off the cover. He started yelling and the rest of his men came over to look at what he had found.

"OK, Paco, you ready for this?" I asked.

Paco knew what I meant. We had to kill the patrol before they could alert someone to our presence.

"Fuck yes, I'm ready. Let's do it."

Paco and I drew our knives and made for the men. As we reached them, one of the soldiers turned, only to meet my knife being buried deep in the top of his chest. Paco grabbed one of the men by the hair from behind and pulled his head back, exposing his throat. Paco pulled his knife hard across the man's throat, almost cutting the head completely off.

As I pulled my knife from the Nicaraguan soldier's chest, I could hear a wheezing sound coming from him as his last breath escaped through the hole in his lungs. As my knife pulled clear of his chest, the soldier collapsed at my feet, dead. I turned to see the last soldier pull his side arm and start to point it at Paco. I managed to grab the soldier's weapon, shoving it to the ground, then drive my knife deep into the side of his neck.

As the blood from his neck pumped out and flowed down my arm, he stared at me in total terror. He knew he was going to die and couldn't do anything about it. He grabbed my hand in an attempt to remove the knife, but he could only hold on for a few seconds before he started to fall. He tried to gasp for air but couldn't. With his strength gone, he fell to the ground, rolling onto his back. His eyes were wide open, staring at me in complete fear. I felt pity for the man. He had done nothing wrong, except been in the wrong place at the wrong time. I knelt and closed his eyes, trying to leave him with a little dignity.

No sounds came from their boat, so I figured no one waited on board. We dragged the three bodies and their small boat into the trees and covered them with brush. Paco and his men uncovered the Zodiac, and we slid it back into the water.

We slowly made our way out to the anchored patrol boat to make sure there wasn't anyone else on board. As we approached the boat, I slipped over the side of the Zodiac and made my way to the opposite side of the patrol boat.

We had gotten lucky. It wasn't a real patrol boat. The three soldiers had been doing some fishing, and it didn't look like anybody knew where they were. They were just out having a good time. Inside the boat were their rifles and a cooler full of beer. They didn't even have a radio. The boat was an old wooden one about sixteen feet long with an outboard motor. I pulled the drain plugs at the rear of the boat and was able to knock a couple of holes in the bottom to sink it. I didn't know how deep the water was, but it didn't really matter as long as the boat sank before sunrise. By then we would be long gone, and nobody would be the wiser. We put the cooler of beer in the Zodiac along with anything else that might float and steered for the middle of the lake.

We had no trouble locating Opey and the others. Loading Paco and his men into the boat, we tied the Zodiac to the stern. Opey gave medical attention to Paco's men as we headed for the Tempisque River.

The night had turned perfectly clear and calm. Paco sat in the back of the boat not saying anything, just staring out at the water. I got a couple bottles of beer out of the cooler we had taken from the soldiers' boat and handed one to my old friend.

"We're going to be OK. Everything is being set, just like we planned," I said.

Paco took the beer, snapped the cap off using the boat railing, and drank it down without taking a breath. I opened mine and sat next to him.

"We had really bad intelligence," Paco told me. "This is bullshit, Chance; they were waiting for us, dug-in good. We didn't even see them until they opened up on us. The assholes running this show don't have a fuckin' clue what's going on. We've had it. This was the last time. They're going to get us killed."

"Fuck 'em" I said. "You made it this far, and you're damn sure going to make it the rest of the way."

I reached over to pat Paco on the shoulder, but he had fallen asleep. I looked over at Opey, who gave me the thumbs-up, letting me know that the rest of Paco's men were OK.

The sun was just starting to rise when we picked Lucky and Razz up and headed downriver toward T J and Santana and the fishing village north of La Cruz. The trip across the Nicaraguan border was as easy as the first time. T J and Santana met us at the docks, where we loaded up the trucks to make for Puntarenas, about ninety miles southeast on the Gulf of Nicoya.

By noon that day, we were in Puntarenas. Mike and Dave had found Mr. Cunningham, my export friend, and were waiting for us at the airport to fly to Veracruz, Mexico. The twelve of us boarded an old DC-3 that belonged to Cunningham's export company.

I had all of Spooky 4's passports with me. This was part of our emergency plan. Paco had given them to me before they left. All of the passports had aliases but were registered in the United States. When we cleared customs, they would check out as valid passports.

The flight to Veracruz took about five hours. We landed, checked in through Mexican customs, and got a hotel for the night. The next morning we left Veracruz, taking a cruise ship up the coast 500 miles to Brownsville, Texas. From Brownsville, Paco and his men disappeared.

A couple of weeks after I left Paco in Texas, he showed up at my door. He said he could only stay a minute but wanted to give me something—an MIA/POW bracelet. It was always our team's promise to each other not to let anyone become a name on a bracelet. An engraved inscription on the inside of the bracelet read: "CHANCE (4-WAY), THANKS FOR GETTING US HOME, TEAM SPOOKY 4."

Paco said he wished he could be there if I ever needed him but knew he never could. He never found out if his team had been sent to the jungle to die or it was just a bad mission. He was out of it now and wasn't going to see if somebody might try to finish the job. He was leaving, and I would never see him again.

Ghosts in the Jungle

The stench of jungle decay and the fear of being taken by an unseen enemy jolted me back to reality. I guess Paco wasn't going to be alone with his nightmare, I thought. I looked at the bracelet given to me by Paco as tears welled up in my eyes. The pain in my leg had reached an unbearable level again, and I looked around to Opey for help.

The sound of intense buzzing distracted me. I looked at my thigh to check the bandage and saw that my entire leg was a swarm of mosquitoes and flies. My blood-soaked pant leg had drawn thousands of bugs like flies to shit. I beat at the black-and-gray undulating mass that was once my leg like a crazy man. I fell to the ground screaming. Opey and Mike came running over to me, trying to keep me quiet.

"Chance, calm down. Take it easy! You're OK!" yelled Opey.

They were able to calm me down enough for me to realize the pain and exhaustion had made me delirious. This was the first time I had ever lost touch with reality. Losing control is something I didn't allow myself, and it added fuel to the intense rage that was already burning inside me.

Opey changed my dressing, then sprinkled sulfur powder over the outside of my leg to help keep the bugs away. Another morphine shot eased the pain, so we started to plan our escape out of our intended grave.

God, I wish I had Paco out there to come after us, I thought. This mission had been put together so quickly that we weren't able to plan for a rescue like we did for Paco. It left me with one contingency plan. One I made a couple of years earlier on another mission. One made for this exact situation. One I thought I would never be using, especially to escape from my own government. It was hard to keep focused on our escape. Than overwhelming panic felt like it was going to explode from my chest. I had to focus on surviving, focus on getting the team out, focus on revenge.

My plan was to make our way to the town of Sogamosa. I hadn't been in contact with the man that had been taking care of the safe house in more than a year, but I was betting he was still there and everything would be as I had left it.

We needed to rest, then start for Sogamosa at dawn. Sleep never really came, however. Everyone was totally exhausted, but fear and adrenaline kept our senses on high alert.

The morning was chilly and our wounds made it difficult to get going. I was so stiff I could hardly walk. My pain had leveled out to a dull throb that only hurt when I breathed or moved. Opey wanted to give me another morphine shot, but I told him I didn't want it. I needed to be as alert as possible now. Lucky was having a hard time with the hole in his butt, but he didn't complain, keeping pace with the rest of us. Mike, who was uninjured, took point and set the pace for the rest of us to follow.

The jungle was particularly dense now. The trees, vines, and thick underbrush made travel very slow and difficult. It was a clear day, and the humidity climbed rapidly as the sun poured out its relentless heat. Within minutes, we were covered in sweat. We were also covered with hundreds of tiny cuts and bug bites that burned as the salty sweat ran down our bodies. We didn't have the water we needed to continue at this pace for very long. If we didn't slow down or find clean water, we might not make it.

The first day was agonizingly slow. We were used to traveling five miles a day, but that day we made only two. On our second day, we headed for the mountains, which I knew would be our most difficult challenge. We had to get over the mountain range before we could reach our objective, Sogamosa.

About four hours into the day, I thought I heard water. I stopped the team and had Mike go check out the sound coming from a slope a short distance away. Mike walked off cautiously and disappeared into the bush. We waited quietly for several minutes, listening to what sounded like water rushing over flat ground.

Suddenly we saw Mike running back to us. "We've got to get the hell out of here, now."

"What is it? What did you see?" I asked.

"Fuck, man, ants, millions of them. They're coming this way. They're eating everything in their path. God, you can't believe it. The ground is alive with them. They must be twenty yards across, as far as I could see. Nothing but millions of ants."

We knew that this was no place to hang around. I had heard of the ant migrations but had never seen one. I wanted to go and take a look but knew that in my condition that could be fatal.

Suddenly I felt a slight breeze coming from the direction of the ants. The breeze brought with it the most disgusting odor. It was a smell unlike any I had ever smelled, the odor of a forest being destroyed by creatures only a half an inch long. The realization of the power that Mother Nature possessed motivated us to move out and move out *now.* I decided that we needed to continue in our present direction, getting across the ants' path as quickly as possible.

As we hiked, my mind flashed back on how I thought my leg had looked, covered with mosquitoes and flies. Could that have been a warning of what would happen? Of the team, only I had heard the ants. What would have happened if I had chosen that place to rest? What would have happened if we had fallen asleep? I knew that the warrior spirits of my dead teammates were with us. I knew they were watching us, and I counted on them to help us make it out.

By day three, we found the strength needed to overcome any obstacle that might get in our way. When we rested at night we didn't waste time trying to understand why this was happening to us. We needed to stay focused on getting out, but every step was a step into the unknown. Every noise could be the enemy waiting just out of sight to finish the job. We were able to survive on small animals, along with the food and water we had brought with us. We knew if you took time to look around, the jungle could provide everything you needed for survival: food, water, shelter, and medicine.

Around 1000 hours the third day, we heard a helicopter off in the distance. It wasn't a Huey, but it was a large helicopter that sounded like it had landed and shut down. Within an hour, we came upon a clearing, and there it was, our ride out—an old Sikorsky 58 helicopter was sitting there as if it were a gift from the gods. The side of the Sikorsky bore the name "OXY Lumbering" in large red letters. I thought it was odd that this logging helicopter was out here. There wasn't any logging going on within a hundred miles. I figured these guys were here on private business and could probably be persuaded to give us a ride out.

We hid our rifles and put our handguns under our shirts, and Mike, Opey, and I headed for the chopper while Lucky and Dave covered us. Two guys were sitting in the door talking, acting as if they were waiting for someone. They didn't see us at first, but when they did they acted like they knew us. As we came nearer, they realized we weren't the ones they were waiting for and became very quiet and suspicious.

"Hola, senor. Habla ingles?" I asked.

"Yes, I speak English," said one of the men.

I introduced myself as a member of an environmental conservation team that had been in a helicopter accident and explained that we needed to get to Tunja right away.

At first, the spokesman, who turned out to be the pilot, said he couldn't help us because he was working and needed to wait for his boss. I knew that this fat piece of shit was just another fucking doper who was probably waiting for another shipment of drugs.

I then explained to him that we weren't really environmentalists but businessmen and that we had been in a little trouble with the local authorities. I told him they were not too far behind us and were really pissed. They would probably think he and his helicopter were the ones we had intended to meet and wouldn't take the time to listen to his story. I told him we needed to get to Tunja, which was about forty miles west of Sogamosa. We would meet friends there who would pay him handsomely for the use of his helicopter.

The pilot agreed that it might be better for everyone if he gave us the hour-and-a-half ride to Tunja. We climbed aboard the old Korean-vintage Sikorsky while the pilot and his buddy climbed up to the cockpit and warmed up the old 58. We found seats among several bundles of what looked like drugs, and within minutes we were heading toward Tunja. I kept a close eye on my GPS to make sure the pilot stayed on course.

About fifteen minutes from Tunja, I took Lucky's radio and switched it to the one aircraft frequency we used for special occasions. I told Lucky to listen to his radio and go along with anything he heard. He looked at me with a grin and said, "OK." The Sikorsky's cockpit was about four feet higher and forward of the cargo area. I knew it was difficult for the pilot to see us and he wouldn't know what Lucky and I were planning. I went up to the cockpit and asked Carlos, the pilot, if I could use his radio. I told him I was going to call my friends in Tunja and have them waiting for us with a little bonus for him and his friend. He nodded yes. I asked him the location where he intended to land, tuned his radio to the frequency of Lucky's Expo radio, and began to call.

"Crystal Palace, This is Lone Eagle; you got a copy?"

For the sake of realism, Lucky did not respond immediately.

"Crystal Palace, we are headed your way. Had to hitch a ride; do you copy?" I tried again.

This time Lucky responded. "Lone Eagle, this is Crystal Palace. I have a copy; repeat your message, over."

I asked Carlos how far away we were from landing. He said we were about ten minutes out.

"Crystal Palace, we are about ten minutes away from your location. We will be landing one mile south at the old OXY lumber company helipad. We need to pay for a chopper rental and a lot of help. Do you understand?" I asked.

"Roger, Lone Eagle," he said. "All I have is five grand. That sound OK?"

I could see the grins on both Carlos's and his friend's face. I asked them if that would be enough for them. They both nodded, each with a shit-eating grin.

"That sounds real good, Crystal Palace. We'll see you on the ground."

I turned to Carlos, patted him on the shoulder, and gave him the thumbs-up. These two dumb shits didn't have a clue about what was going on. All they knew was that they were going to make $2,500 apiece for taking a three-hour detour.

Within minutes, the Sikorsky was setting up to land in the clearing. I could see the outskirts of Tunja to the north about a mile, just like Carlos had said. We landed in the middle of the clearing, and the team got out to make sure it was secure. I stayed with Carlos and his friend, telling them I would wait until my friends arrived to make sure they got what they deserved. In a few minutes, Mike returned and told me everything was secure. Nobody was around.

Carlos and his friend had been sitting in the cockpit waiting for me to explain what was going on. When Mike returned, he brought Opey's medical bag, hoping our two fliers would think it was their payment. I climbed up the side of the Sikorsky with the medical bag and a big grin on my face. Carlos and his partner were sitting there like kids waiting for a Christmas present. I reached inside the bag and took out my suppressed .22 Colt Woodsman pistol. Carlos and his friend looked in total disbelief. They both continued to grin, thinking it was some kind of American joke. "Sorry, you pieces of shit; wrong place, wrong time," I said.

Then, without hesitation, I shot them each once in the side of the head. Only a small trickle of blood marked the place of each fatal wound. It was deadly quiet in the cockpit of the helicopter. The slight smell of sulfur from the .22 rounds was in the air. I stood there staring at the two dead Colombians without any feeling of regret. It was sobering to think I was becoming so callous that the taking of a human life didn't mean anything. I was filled with so much rage, life meant little to me at this point, especially that of a drug runner.

As I climbed down from the helicopter, the part of me that was afraid I had lost all feelings began to talk to me. Two more people in the wrong place at the wrong time—God, will this ever end? Will we ever be safe again? Will we ever be able to stop running and hiding? I could put the gun to my own head, but that would have been the coward's way out and they would have won.

Mike and Opey took the two bodies from the helicopter and hid them in the jungle. We tore up the inside of the Sikorsky as much as we could to make it look like a dope deal had gone bad, then left for Tunja.

It was around one o'clock in the afternoon, and the thought of getting out of the bush had given us strength but also made us more vulnerable. We made our way to the south side of Tunja, where we found clothes hanging out to dry in the sun. I was the biggest of the team and had a hard time finding anything that would fit. Finally, I found a clean pair of pants and shirt, then proceeded to look for something to take us to Sogamosa.

Vehicles had been Razz's field of expertise, but Mike said Razz had shown him a few tricks, so he would try to find some wheels.

We waited just outside of town, watching the people go by on the road. Every time a vehicle slowed, our hearts stopped, as we expected our presence had been discovered and it was going to be a fight to the death. Finally, Mike returned with an old beat-up International Travelall. It ran, but not much more. All of the glass had been broken out, and the seats were gone except for the driver's. Mike said he had bought it for 100 U.S dollars. The owner didn't ask any questions, Mike said, so he took it. It didn't matter where or how he got it as long as it got us to Sogamosa.

Mike said he had driven around town for a while before returning to make sure he wasn't being followed. He pulled off the road, close to where we were waiting, and acted like he had had a breakdown. We waited for a few minutes to make sure he didn't have any company, then climbed in, and we were off.

The road to Sogamosa was a narrow, winding dirt road full of holes you could lose a cow in. It seemed like nobody had a clue who we were. I was as if we no longer existed. I was starting to believe my plan had worked. We were, as far as anybody knew, dead. We were now just ghosts in the jungle.

Sogamosa

As we entered the outskirts of Sogamosa, it looked like the outskirts of any large town in this part of the world, mostly slum. People here try to survive by any means they can. Small shacks for houses, kids running around half-naked, dogs digging through the trash, and the smells of raw sewage and rotting garbage surround you. The perfect place to get lost in.

A few years earlier, after finishing a mission in Colombia, my contact told me he was from Sogamosa. He invited me to come and spend a few days there before heading back to the States. The second night there, he and I were at a small cantina, enjoying some of the local color, when a disturbance started just as we were leaving. Two of the local militia thugs were giving the waitress a hard time as she was trying to close and leave. At first, I ignored it, but soon it became clear that these men were doing much more than just demanding another drink and a free feel for the road. They dragged the young girl into an alley and were attempting to rape her. I've always had a problem with people who were predators, so I wasn't about to let that happen. I told my partner to watch the alley and make sure nobody else interfered while I went to give her a little help. The two militiamen attempted to turn their aggression toward me but soon realized that was a bad career move on their part. I left them unconscious in the alley and took the girl home to her family. Her father, Juan, was very grateful, thanking me over and over and begging me to stay. I sent my partner on his way and spent the rest of the evening with Juan and his family. We quickly became good friends.

Over the years, I would help Juan and his family by sending them money or doing other small favors. In return, Juan kept a few supplies for me in case of an emergency. He also had a place where I could go and hide out, a site where no one would stumble onto me.

We hadn't showered in several days and were starting to get pretty ripe. I had Mike ditch the truck after he dropped us off a few blocks from Juan's house. Lucky and I had been to Sogamosa a couple times in the past, but Lucky didn't know where Juan lived. I didn't want Juan to be scared off by too much company too fast, so I sent Lucky, who spoke Spanish fluently and looked like he belonged here, to hang around the local watering holes to see if he could pick up any gossip.

As I walked the two blocks to Juan's house, I couldn't help noticing how things looked like they had gotten worse, not better. The street people were very cautious of me, so I tried not to make any eye contact. As I reached Juan's house, I checked around to see if anybody was paying attention to me; then I knocked and waited to see who answered the door.

As I waited, my heart started to pound in panic. What if Juan no longer lived here? What if they knew about Juan and were waiting for me? I waited and knocked again. No answer. I figured Juan hadn't gotten home from work yet but should be home soon. I decided to go back to the team and wait to hear from Lucky before I tried again.

Lucky returned around seven that evening and told us that everything in that part of town was quiet. There wasn't any word of someone looking for Americans or of a truckful of strangers coming from Tunja. The town was quiet that evening, so we decided to head for Juan's house about eight. I had the team spread out down the street while I went to the door and knocked. I could hear Juan inside talking on the telephone. He hung up the phone and was cursing when he opened the door. He stared at me for a moment, and then he threw his arms around me and gave me a big hug.

God, it was good to see him. I noticed that time had not been kind to him, however. His face had aged a lot since the last time I saw him. The deep wrinkles looked like a Martian landscape on his parched leather skin. His eyes seemed hollow, lacking the life I had remembered. He sensed I wasn't alone by the way I acted, so he told me to get my friends and come in. I motioned to the rest of the team, and we all went inside.

Juan's house hadn't changed much in the past few years. We started talking about old times and how glad we were to see each other. I asked him about his family, and Juan got real quiet. He told me that the local drug gang had killed his wife last year and that his daughter had disappeared shortly afterward. I could see that Juan was a hard man now. Everything that meant anything to him was gone. I began to understand the sadness in his eyes and the pain in his heart.

He told me he had started an underground movement to take care of people who were being terrorized by the drug lords and corrupt police. I told him about what had happened, and he said he would help us any way he could. Juan was the only person, aside from what was left of Spooky 8, I trusted in this part of the world.

We were able to bathe and get clean clothes. Then we sat, ate, drank, and talked about old times for several more hours before falling off to sleep. Juan told me that the safe house remained as I had left it and we could stay as long as we wanted. Juan knew the local players very well and had established a superb network to transport people all over South America.

I knew Juan was not working for anybody but himself. He didn't trust the U.S. or his own government, but he did have loyalty to those who had been screwed by them. I invited him to come back with us, but he refused. He said he had to find out what had happened to his daughter and make sure she was at peace. I didn't try to change his mind because I knew he was on a mission, just as I was on my own.

Around ten o'clock the next day, Juan and I headed to the cache site that he had been keeping for me over the years. I told Lucky to keep the team together and not let anyone leave Juan's house. I didn't want any attention brought to Juan by a few Anglos walking about.

Juan had moved the cache to a new and better location on some property that had been owned by his father. Juan told the locals his father had died of a very contagious disease and it was unsafe to go into the house. It had been a grand home in its day, surrounded by a high rock fence and lots of trees. Now it was just a run-down shell of a house that smelled like dog shit and was full of birds. There was a secret cellar under the kitchen floor that Juan used to hide his precious belongings. Pictures of his family and other valuables were kept in boxes on the dirt floor. Hidden behind some bricks in the wall was a canvas bag containing all the things I had left for Juan to keep.

There was $5,000 in U.S. dollars and a half-dozen blank passports. I also had stashed an old portable shortwave radio and a hand-held scanner. I had even scrounged an air force survival radio with ELT (emergency locator transmitter), a couple of handguns, and a book of safe houses and contacts to get out of South America. It included a list of different contacts with cruise ships, tour groups, and airlines that might be used in an emergency.

Before we left, Juan showed me pictures of his beautiful wife and daughter. They looked full of life and love for each other. Tears welled up in Juan's eyes as emotion overcame him. He told me he was glad

I came to him for help—he needed to be with someone who could remember his wife and his daughter.

We spent the next two days trying to make contact with a few of the names I had in my book, but they all came up dead ends. The book was a couple of years old, but I had thought somebody would still be around. The more I tried, the more paranoid I got. I finally decided to stop using the old system and come up with a new one on my own.

I knew if we were able to get to a large tourist city like Caracas, Venezuela, it would be a simple matter to disappear into the crowds like tourists. Then we could individually make our way back to the States. We used the scanner and shortwave radio to monitor the local police and military as well as private business frequencies. We also scanned a few of our own government frequencies, trying to catch any hint of the events at the airstrip a few days ago. Juan had friends in Bogotá, Girardot, and Medellín, and he had them snoop around for information about any bodies that might have been found in the jungle. Bodies found in the jungle were a fairly common thing down here, but American bodies weren't. That usually got somebody talking. Somehow we had continued to stay lucky. There were no rumors of anything that had to do with us. It was like we had never been there.

I figured to get to Caracas we would drive to Bucaramanga, about 150 miles from Sogamosa, then another 100 miles across the Venezuelan border to San Cristóbal. From San Cristóbal we would catch a commercial flight to Caracas, then home. We had enough passports and traveling money for everyone. Juan knew a man who could get us the photos, stamps, and signatures that we needed for our passports.

We met Juan's friend in a safe place away from Juan's house. He was able to fix up our passports with the proper information and signatures. I was concerned about this man, but Juan assured me he was OK. Juan's friend had lost his son the same way Juan had lost his wife and, like Juan, was on a mission.

Spooky

We left Sogamosa the next morning by bus. Juan and I hugged, knowing that this was probably the last time we would ever see each other. Juan had saved our lives, and I knew I could never repay him. I almost envied Juan and his life. Things were much simpler. It was just a matter of day-to-day survival. He knew whom he could trust and whom he couldn't. Friends were friends to the end.

The trip to Bucaramanga took almost seven hours in the old bus. We stopped at every shit hole town along the narrow two-lane road. The bus was hot, humid, and dirty, but it didn't matter. I kind of liked the chicken feathers and dog hair that swirled in the stagnant air. I knew it would be easy to disappear here, to become one of the many nameless faces that struggled for existence in the dirty streets. I sat next to Lucky on the ride to Bucaramanga. Our wounds had stopped bleeding, and the pain was bearable. Opey sat with Dave, making sure he was all right. His wounds had been causing him pain and were starting to get infected.

About three in the afternoon, we pulled into Bucaramanga. A run-down bus station teeming with people greeted us with noise and more dirt. We had a meal and caught another bus to San Cristóbal. This bus was more of a tour bus, with seats that even had padding on them. Our first obstacle was the border of Venezuela. We stopped at a small border station, and two soldiers boarded.

My passport was American, as was Lucky's. Mike had a Canadian passport, and Opey and Dave both had British. I knew this wouldn't be a problem if everybody acted like a tourist. Dave wasn't feeling too good and was afraid he might get noticed. He told one of the soldiers that the local food didn't agree with him but he wanted one of the soldiers to pose with Opey for a picture anyway. The soldier was glad to be part of a European photo album and stood next to Opey looking as tough as he could. The soldier finished checking our papers, and we were on our way. Because we looked somewhat the same, I told the soldiers we were traveling for pleasure but looking to possibly start a tour service in this part of South America. I knew that tourism was something these people didn't have much of and they were always looking for more ways to make money.

The sun was getting low in the sky as we entered San Cristóbal. The bus station was quiet and suspiciously void of activity. I told everybody not to gather in a group when we got off the bus but instead stand alone and look for a taxi to the airport. I told them we would meet out front of the airport in one hour, then continue on to Caracas.

Mike, Dave, and Opey looked beat. They all wanted to get cleaned up a little before the flight. Lucky wanted to go and grab a bite to eat before we got to the airport. As he started to walk away, he signaled me to meet him. The rest of the team had already started to go their separate ways and didn't see Lucky and me together.

He told me we needed to talk and he didn't want any of the other men around. I flagged down a taxi. We got in, and Lucky asked the driver to take us to a restaurant near the airport. The driver took us to a small place a few blocks away. I told him that all I had was U.S. currency. He smiled and said, "OK, that will be fifty dollars." I wanted to take the bills and cram them down his throat, but I just smiled and handed him the money. Lucky and I went in, found a table near the door, and sat down. Lucky ordered a couple beers, then began to tell me some of the feelings he'd been having.

"I've been thinking about this since we left Juan's. I've got a real bad feeling we have a fuckin' mole on the team," Lucky said.

"What the hell are you talking about, a mole?" I asked.

"I think there is somebody on the team that was supposed to walk away from the airstrip. Somebody who was to make sure we didn't."

"Why would you say that? Everybody had to fight like hell to stay alive. Did you see something I didn't?" I asked him.

"I can't stop thinking about T J and Santana. Who shot T J from behind? How could two shots hit Santana's radio?"

I sat looking at my beer trying to find the courage to face what I knew was true. I was glad that Lucky was feeling the same way I was. It was much easier to face now that I wasn't alone in the thinking.

"Yeah, I know," I told Lucky. "I didn't want to say anything until we got back to the States. When I said I thought we had a sniper problem, I wasn't really thinking sniper. Maybe you're right, Lucky. One of us was there to make sure we didn't get out. I just don't want to believe it."

"Holy shit, Chance," Lucky replied. "You knew this mission was going to go bad, didn't you?"

"I knew something was going to happen, but I never expected this. I figured we'd get screwed out of our money or get stuck doing some shit job."

"Who do you think it is? God, we've been together so long. Why in the hell would someone do that to us? Who could do it?"

"I'm not sure; hell, I'm not even sure there is a mole," I said. "Look; when we get to Caracas, make sure everybody gets on a plane to the States. Make sure everyone knows we'll meet up with them the next day. Once everybody is gone, you stay back with me. If we get separated, meet me at the Puerto Viejo, Oceana Hotel. It's about two miles from the airport. I'll be there under the name James Beckett."

It was time for us to meet everyone at the airport, so we paid our bill and grabbed another taxi. There was only one plane leaving in several hours for Caracas, and we all were on it. I had Lucky sit with Dave to make sure he was OK. Opey sat with Mike, and I sat with a smelly fat woman who hadn't brushed her teeth since the sixties. It was about 450 miles by air to Caracas, about one and a half hours.

At the Caracas airport, I checked to make sure my men had enough money to get home. We had spent most of our traveling money buying bus and plane tickets, eating, and paying Juan's friend for the work he had done on our passports. We had enough money to get Mike and Dave tickets, but I had to try to locate an old friend to help with more money for the rest of us.

"Mike, you and Dave hang with Opey at the airport. Lucky and I will be getting some more cash for the rest of us. If something happens, get back to the States any way you can," I said. "Dave, make sure everybody stays together. Nobody uses the phone. The NSA is monitoring all calls into the U.S., and I don't want some NSA puke to get lucky and screw this up. We're too close to home."

"No problem, boss," Mike said. "We'll be here when you and Lucky get back."

Lucky flagged a taxi, and we headed off to find a woman I knew that lived near the waterfront. I had met Debra in 1989 back in Virginia while on business. We had become very good friends and stayed in touch. Last year, she had sent a postcard to one of my post office boxes letting me know that she had moved to Caracas to take a position as a hotel manager. She told me if I ever got to Caracas to look her up.

Debra was pretty well off financially. Her family owned the hotel she was managing along with some twenty others. If I couldn't reach Debra, I was going to head for the bad side of town, find a doper on the street, and rob him if I had to. Nothing was going to stop us from getting home. I had the taxi driver take us to the waterfront, where I found a pay phone and called her.

Debra was at work and thrilled to hear from me. I asked her if I could meet her at her job and talk and told her I needed her help and not to tell anyone I was coming. She said, "Of course," so I told her I would see her in ten minutes. The hotel she was managing was the Puerto Viejo, Marina Hotel, the one I had told Lucky to meet me at. The hotel was only five minutes from where I had called, so we decided to walk. Debra was standing out front of the hotel waiting for me. When she saw Lucky and me walking up the drive, she ran out to meet us and gave me a big hug and kiss. She was as pretty as I remembered, prettier. She couldn't believe I was there and wanted to hear all about what I'd been doing. I introduced Lucky to her as she showed us into her office and closed the door.

"Debra, this isn't a social call. I need your help," I said.

"That's what I figured," she replied. "I knew it was too good to be true, you coming all the way down here just to see me. What do you need, Chance? You know I'll help you any way I can."

"I've got some friends that had a little trouble last week. We need some money to get back to the States. Can you help me out?"

"You know I will. How much do you need? Will three or four thousand be enough?" she asked as she took her purse from her desk.

"A couple thousand will do it. I don't know when I'll be able to pay you back. In fact, I don't know if I'll ever be able to come down this way again."

"Hey, I might need your help someday," was all she said as she pulled $3,000 out of her purse.

"You always carry that kind of money in your purse?"

"No, I'm a little short today," she said with a smile. "You're lucky. I was planning to go to Miami next week, but the trip got canceled. I had some U.S. cash with me to take on my trip."

I knew she wasn't telling me the truth. Her trip was probably canceled the moment I asked her for money. She looked at me with her big green eyes and smiled, letting me know she understood and it didn't matter if I wasn't able to pay her back.

"One more favor, can you book me a room for the night under another name?"

"Sure, what name do you want? James?"

When I first met her in '89, I had used the name James. It was one of those situations where I wasn't supposed to tell anyone who I really was, but she was the hotel manager and I had to tell her something. She didn't learn my real name for almost a year, and she had been a little pissed when she found out.

Debra booked me a room under the name James Beckett. I told her I needed to get back to the airport and take care of some friends, but Lucky and I would be back later that evening. She said she would check on me later to make sure everything was OK, gave me a hug, and told me to be careful. I think she sensed that I had been pushed to my limit. My leg wound had settled into a pounding throb, and I'm sure I looked like I had just crawled out of a gutter. Lucky and I headed back to the airport to buy tickets for the rest of the team.

Mike, Dave, and Opey were where we had left them. I gave Opey and Lucky enough money to buy their tickets back to Miami. We separated, got in line, and waited our turn at the counter. Opey got on a flight with Mike that left almost immediately. Dave's plane left in a couple of hours. Lucky's and my flight was scheduled to leave the next day at noon. I told everyone to wait in Miami at the Pirates Cove Inn, a cheap motel we all knew about, until Lucky and I got there. Opey had been acting real concerned ever since we got to Caracas. He looked like he was close to cracking, so I pulled him aside to calm him down.

"Chance, I think I need to get Dave some medical attention. He's not doing all that well, and I'm not sure Miami is the best place for him. I need to get him to someplace quiet."

"OK, you're probably right. Mike, do you remember the safe house in Manitou?"

Lucky perked up at the mention of Manitou, so I asked him if he had any objections.

After a pause, he nodded and said, "Sure, she'll be glad to see me. I probably owe her money anyway."

The safe house belonged to one of Lucky's old girlfriends. She lived just a few miles outside Colorado Springs in a town called Manitou Springs. Opey had never been there and I was sure had never heard us talk about it. Only Lucky, Mike, and I knew of its existence and how to get there.

"Yeah, I remember," Mike replied.

"Mike, you stick with Dave and Opey," I said. "Lucky and I will meet you there in two days. Make sure you contact no one. Got it?"

They all nodded yes.

"Don't panic. A few of us have special insurance in case something like this happens. We need to get together in the States and figure out what we're going to do with it. Everything is going to be all right if we can just stick together." I looked each of them in the eye.

After you've done a few missions, you learn to plan ahead. Lucky, Mike, and I had talked years ago about establishing an information network to be used in case one of us disappeared under unusual circumstances. We all had been in the game long enough to know you have to have a little "private insurance" put away for a rainy day, information you could use in case someone decided to make life hard for you. Ever since Paco, I had made it a point to put aside little bits of information: names, dates, places, and events that could be used to trade for my safety. It was becoming clear that someone, somewhere, felt Spooky 8's existence was a liability that could damage his career or political ambitions. And he must have figured that the only way to keep that from happening was to get rid of the threat, namely us.

If somebody on the team was a mole, as Lucky and I thought possible, I wanted to string him along. He would need to find out what kind of insurance we had before he was allowed to finish his mission or give us up to another group of assassins to hunt us down in the States.

Now, rat-holing information was a very dangerous game, but a common one. When you hide top-secret information, you violate almost every national security regulation there is. You essentially ignore all the little government documents you signed over the years guaranteeing your silence. The ones that say you could spend the rest of your life in prison for doing what we had been doing for years. We wouldn't be sent away for the dirty work, but for telling the fact that we'd done it.

Obtaining, copying, and hiding sensitive information was something people often disappeared over, permanently. I knew if somebody thought we had information that could hurt him even after we were dead, he would want to know what that information was. I was counting on this buying us a little time back in the States. Time so if we had a spy, we could find him and deal with him.

Mike and Opey left on the same flight, but Dave still had two hours to go before his departure. He, Lucky, and I waited in an airport restaurant for his plane to board. Instead of talking about the mission and taking a chance of being overheard, we talked about home. It's funny how special the little things become when you face losing them. Lucky told us how he missed classical music. That was a surprise to me. He didn't strike me as one who appreciated classical music. I had always taken him for a sixties rock 'n' roller. Dave said he missed his dad, whom he considered his best friend. They did a lot of things together: fishing, going to football games, and hanging out. I had to agree with him. I missed my dad, too. I had been gone for twenty years when I moved back home, and I wanted to be the son I hadn't been. I told them I didn't think my dad was going to be around much longer and I wanted to try to make up for all the shit my parents had to put up with from me over the years.

When Dave's flight boarded, Lucky and I watched as he disappeared into the crowd of people. As Lucky and I watched the plane lift off, I felt terribly alone. I knew that one of my men could be poised to try to finish a job that was started on a remote airstrip just over a week ago.

Lucky and I didn't speak on the way back to the hotel. My mind was tired of trying to sort it all out. I went to the front desk for the room key that Debra had left for me. She had booked us a VIP suite on the top floor with all of the goodies. We had no luggage for the bellman, and I felt a little funny going up to the suite with just Lucky. But at that point, I would have gone up with anyone just to get a little rest. We had a view of the ocean and the clean beaches. All I needed was a hot tub, a couple of naked women, some cold Corona, and I would be a happy camper.

Debra had left a message saying she would check on us that evening, so Lucky and I decided to clean up, get a little rest, then go down to the restaurant for some food. Lucky went in to take a shower, so I lay down on the bed to think. What had we done to become such a liability? Who did we piss off enough to have us killed? What did we know that we weren't supposed to?

When Lucky finished showering, I told him to start thinking about why this had happened before we started to think of who. He took a bottle of wine from the small refrigerator while I went to shower. Lucky and I were alike in many ways. I guess that's why I liked to have him around. Of all the members of Spooky 8, he was the one person I completely trusted. The only one I knew wasn't a mole . . . I hoped. I finished my shower, found some clothes that Debra had left, and joined Lucky.

Lucky had finished off the bottle of wine and was starting on a second. I found a cold Corona in the refrigerator with a note from Debra tied to it. The note was written in red lipstick: "Enjoy." I read the note and smiled. It was nice to have somebody looking out for me.

"Were they after just one of us or the whole team?" I asked out loud. "You and I are the only ones who have been together since the military. Shit, Lucky, who knows how many people, let alone governments, we've pissed off? But I don't think it has anything to do with our regular army shit."

"We need to find a common denominator," said Lucky. "Something that ties it all together."

"You know," I replied, "there are some things you and I did that have always bugged me. Back in '73, those operations we did. That bullshit operation Dragon Flower was just the beginning. That fucking *Hag* and Hope and Glory are the ones that probably started the nails in our coffin. That whole thing was fucked up. I've always felt that someday those would come back to bite us in the ass. We should have stayed doing regular army crap, not that spook shit. . . ."

The Hag

Two Days Following Operation Dragon Flower

Captain Harris instructed me to return to my team and explain to them that I was going to remain for a couple of weeks and would link up with them back in the States. I was then to pick one of the most seasoned members of my team for a mission I didn't know anything about. Chief and Lucky were the two men I had in mind. But which one?

Chief was the closest friend I had, going way back, even before the army. Chief came from my hometown, where we had been friends until he moved away in the seventh grade. After I enlisted in the army, I had gone through basic training, changed my army enlistment contract, and was back starting jump school at Fort Benning. I saw this guy in training that looked like someone I knew. It was almost spooky. It took all of five minutes of talking to him to realize this was the same guy I knew from grade school. Chief had moved to Texas, where he grew up and, like me, enlisted in the army while still in high school. And also like me, he had been asked to change his contract with the army and enter a special training program. Our friendship was soon as strong as it ever was, and our adventures began.

Lucky, on the other hand, was prior service. He was older than I and had been in the army seven years before I met him. He had already done two tours in Vietnam with the 173d Airborne. He was our intelligence NCO and had become one of my closest and most trusted friends. Lucky was like a seasoned street cop. He knew the tricks of the trade.

The choice was a difficult one to make, but Lucky had the experience, if nothing else, to look after me. I talked with Chief in private about my decision. I told him that I needed him to look after the team while I was gone, making sure they all got back home and our routine continued.

Our team leader, Captain Harris, and our XO, Lieutenant Lansing, weren't like our other commanders. They didn't spend as much time with the team as I thought they should. We were pretty much left to do our own thing, and I became more or less the team leader by proxy. I wasn't the oldest, the smartest, the highest in rank, or the most experienced, but I was one who wasn't afraid to take a chance and speak my mind and push us to the limit. We had such a cohesive team that no one was really in charge. Everything was done together.

Chief completely understood my decision and said he would have made the same one if he were in my boots. I made sure everyone was set for the trip home. We said our good-byes, "see you in a couple weeks," and I saw them off. Lucky and I then returned to Captain Harris's office for the mission briefing.

As Lucky and I entered the briefing room, we were met by Mr. Patterson and Mr. Baker. Patterson told us that we were not going to have the briefing now but would meet that evening at 2000 hours in a hangar on the airfield. He added that someone would pick us up at our billets and drive us to the hangar. We were to be in civilian clothes for the rest of the mission, which started now.

We were instructed not to talk to anyone about our activities. If anyone asked, we were to tell him we were starting a little R and R, waiting for a military hop to Krung Thep (Bangkok). We were told to pack all of our military clothing and any personal belongings into duffel bags and mark them with the numbers W45B7 in yellow. I was to make sure the driver that picked us up loaded the bags as we left. We were to receive civilian clothes from a special supply point on the compound. Patterson said they would know what clothes to give us when we got there. We were dismissed to get our clothes and pack our military gear. As Lucky and I walked out of the briefing room, we were both in a state of confusion.

"What in the hell have you gotten us into?" asked Lucky.

"Beats the shit out of me. I guess we'll find out tonight."

We were given directions to a Quonset hut that was to supply us with our civilian clothes. We found the building and walked down the hall to a room that was marked: PUBLIC AFFAIRS. The door was locked, so I knocked. When the door opened, there stood the prettiest American woman I had ever seen, well, in Southeast Asia anyway.

This woman was bulletproof. *What a looker,* I thought.

"You must be Chance and Lucky," she said.

Lucky and I just stared at her. Wow, was this a surprise! Maybe this wasn't such a bad decision after all.

"Yes, ma'am," I answered.

"Please, call me Samantha," she said.

"Yes, ma'am, I mean Samantha." I found it a little hard to talk.

Now, as they say, Lucky and I were typical military and all male,

Spooky

"young, dumb, and full of cum." We both had one thing on our minds, and it wasn't getting into our new civilian clothes. Samantha, on the other hand, was all business.

"Relax, boys," she said. "You have a lot more dues to pay before you'll be members of my social club."

I didn't know what she meant exactly, but by the look on her face I took her word for it. She handed us a medium-size gym bag, told us to enjoy our new careers, then closed and locked the door.

We just stood there in the hallway like two young teenage schoolboys who just saw their older sister in her underwear for the first time. We looked at each other for a moment, then went back to our billets, not even thinking to look in our bags.

"So, Lucky, what do you think?"

"Beats the hell out of me. This isn't like the last time."

"Last time! Sounds like you've been here before. Have you?"

"I thought you knew what I was doing on my last tour."

"No, I didn't. All I knew was what you told me about your past. Is this like before?"

"No," he replied. "Before, we did our covert ops, but they were all military. We didn't wear civilian clothes and meet in hangars in the middle of the goddamn night."

"You OK with this? You sound a little bugged."

"Hell, yes, I'm OK with this. I was getting a little tired of the same old shit anyway," Lucky said with a grin.

We changed out of our fatigues into the clothes we had been given. "Now, these are my kind of clothes, jeans and a T-shirt. I wish they would have thrown in a pair of sneakers," I said.

There were two new duffel bags on our bunks when we got back to our room, the numbers "W45B7" and "Chance" on one and "W45B7" and "Simpson" on the other, painted in yellow.

"Damn, these guys don't waste any time, do they?" I said.

"These guys must have a damn crystal ball or something. If I didn't know better, I would think these guys knew what we were going to do all along."

We didn't say much to each other the rest of the day. I was nervous about what was going to happen, but I couldn't help being excited. I had given the playing spook thing a lot of thought since I started working around them. I liked the loose cannon attitudes and not having a lot of rules to run your operations by, especially since our last mission.

Hell, nobody knows what I'm doing anyway, so what difference does it make? I thought to myself. Lucky was real quiet. I could tell he was troubled and had something on his mind that wasn't settling well. He lay down on his bunk and dozed off to sleep.

About 1950, we heard a car pull up out front. My heart started pounding, as I wondered what was about to happen. There was a knock at the door, and Lucky got up and answered it. A man in his thirties, wearing civilian clothes, was standing at the door.

"Are you ready, gentlemen?" he asked.

"Yes, we are," I replied.

"Put these padlocks on your bags and put them in the trunk of the car," the man said.

We put the padlocks on our duffel bags and put them in the trunk of the waiting sedan like he asked. Lucky and I got into the backseat, and we headed off to our briefing.

"How's things going?" I asked our driver.

He said nothing, just kept driving. Lucky and I looked at each other and didn't say anything else. The driver took us to a hangar that was all by itself on the airstrip. The hangar door was partly open, and the lights were off. We drove in. I watched as the hangar doors closed behind us, then the lights came on. Inside stood Patterson and Baker.

"Welcome, gentlemen," said Patterson. "If you will follow me."

We followed Patterson to a room that was at the back of the hangar and went in. Baker closed and locked the door. Inside was a familiar face: Buzz Franklin. I started to say something, but Buzz motioned for me to be quiet. Standing next to him was a man I didn't know.

"I think you both know Mr. Franklin," said Patterson. "This is Jon; he will be Buzz's copilot on this mission. Please sit down."

We all sat down at a table in the center of the room. There were no charts, reports, maps, nothing. This didn't look like any briefing I'd ever been in. *What the hell is going on?* I wondered.

"Gentlemen, from this point on, you and this mission do not exist. The only people that will know about your mission will be you, Mr. Baker, myself, and the people you will be meeting during your trip, and they will only know what they're involved with. This mission is top-secret. From this point on, you will not be working with the United States Army, as you know it. If you want to back out, now is the time. Once you are briefed, you will not be able to change your minds."

"Do you understand?" asked Patterson

Lucky and I nodded yes.

"Do you have any questions?" asked Patterson

"Yes, sir," I said. "Where is Captain Harris?"

"Captain Harris is not a part of this mission. You have been temporarily assigned to me," said Baker. "Now if there are no other questions, do you wish to proceed?"

We both said, "Yes."

Then Patterson continued, "As you may already know, the United States' involvement in South Vietnam is coming to an end. Within a few short weeks there will be no combat troops in this country. We still have a lot of work to do, however. At twenty-two hundred hours this evening, you will be on a flight that will take you and a load of supplies to Thailand. From that point on, your operation will be staged out of Thailand.

"At this time, it is not important that you know where in Thailand you will be going. Buzz, you and Jon will be briefed at twenty-one thirty hours. You two will be piloting the C-119 to Thailand. Once you have arrived, you will be met, and the mission briefing will begin.

"Do you understand?"

All of us looked at each other, then nodded yes.

We had an hour to kill, so we decided to go the officers' mess and get some chow. On the way over there, I listened to Lucky, Buzz, and Jon talk about the other missions they had been on over the years. They all agreed that this one was different. I could tell that there was a lot of tension in the air while Patterson and Baker were talking to us. It was as if they, too, were doing something they weren't comfortable with.

We ate, had a couple of beers, and headed to Hangar Number 7 on the airstrip. Lucky and I went to the C-119 cargo plane parked on the tarmac and checked in with the loadmaster. Buzz and Jon went into an office to get their flight briefing.

The loadmaster and I went over the cargo manifest of equipment that was already loaded on the plane. The manifest said it was mostly food, shelter material, communication equipment, and small arms and ammunition. It was on three large pallets and took up most of the cargo area inside the plane, leaving just two seats up front for Lucky and me. It was a well-used, rather beat-up-looking C-119, so Lucky and I nicknamed her the *Hag*. Naming her after the operation (Hope and Glory) seemed appropriate to us, and besides, men always named airplanes after women. Around 1950 hours, Buzz and Jon boarded the plane. We buckled up while they did their preflight and prepared to take off.

"Chance, you guys strapped in?" Buzz asked.

"Yeah, Buzz, we're ready to go," I replied.

"Once we get airborne, you might want to find a comfortable place and try to get some sleep. We'll be in the air a few hours," said Buzz.

"You got it, Buzz. We'll be fine back here," I replied.

Lucky and I sat there in the dark, waiting for the plane to get airborne. The old *Hag* rolled down to the active runway, then paused for a moment. The two 3400-horse engines began to roar. Buzz released the brakes, and the plane lurched forward. We were on our way. Inside the plane, it was dark except for a couple of small lights in the cargo area and a shining red hold light at the back by the loading doors.

Lucky and I were sitting up front toward the nose in a couple of nylon web seats. The seats were next to small windows located under the cockpit. I sat there looking out over the lights of Nha Trang, knowing this would be the last time I would ever see them, probably the last time I would ever see Vietnam. Off in the distance I could see the glow of fires from an area of the city that had been under attack by the North Vietnamese.

In a few minutes we leveled out and were heading west toward our destination somewhere in Thailand. The night air was smooth and calm. There was a pile of camouflage netting on my side of the plane, so I found a soft spot, lay down, and tried to get comfortable, using the netting as a cushion. The sound of the engines soon became hypnotic. I lay there staring into the darkness almost as if I were in a trance. Lucky had found a place and was settled in to get some sleep, too.

Jon had come down from the cockpit and done a check of the cargo to make sure that everything was secured for the flight. He finished checking things, and I settled back to sleep. Looking toward the back of the plane, my eyes focused on the small red hold light shining above the cargo door. Before long, all sense of sound faded away, and all I could sense was the presence of the light as I drifted off to sleep.

BBBLLLAAAAMMMMMMM! A tremendous explosion ripped me from my sleep. I was picked up and hurled across the belly of the C-119 like a rag doll. *CRASH!* I slammed against the side of the plane next to Lucky. Lucky grabbed me and asked if I was all right.

"Holy shit! What the fuck happened?" I yelled.

"We've been hit! I think we took a SAM in the ass!" yelled Lucky.

I looked to the rear of the plane and saw the pallets were a blazing inferno. There was a huge gaping hole in the plane where the rear cargo door used to be. Jon came down from the cockpit looking for the loadmaster.

"Where is he? Where's Kelly, the loadmaster?" screamed Jon.

"He was sitting at the back of the plane!" yelled Lucky.

The back of the plane was gone, blown away by the explosion. The smoke and fire were becoming so intense, it was getting hard to breathe. Jon grabbed me and told me we had to jettison the cargo or we would crash. I grabbed Lucky, and we started to unhook the tie-downs that were securing the pallets to the floor of the plane. Jon was trying to clear some of the shredded metal that used to be the cargo door. There was a loud bang when the rest of the cargo door fell away. Jon returned, and we started pushing the pallets toward the back. I couldn't tell if we had lost any altitude or if the damn plane was even flying. All I knew was to get the burning cargo off the plane.

Lucky and I pushed with all our strength. The thick black smoke made it impossible to see. I knew if we didn't get rid of the cargo, we were going to die anyway, crash or not. We pushed as if our lives depended on it. They did. Finally the pallets started to move, ever so slowly. I yelled at Lucky to push harder, but the pallets suddenly stopped. I looked for Jon, but he was nowhere to be seen. He was at the front of the plane trying to get a fire extinguisher from under a seat.

"Jon!" I yelled. "Forget that. If we don't get this out, that won't matter. Help us push."

Jon got between Lucky and me and started to push. We strained every muscle in our bodies. Slowly the pallets started to move again. Suddenly the pallet closest to the back of the plane started to pop. *Oh, shit,* I thought. *That ammunition is starting to go.* Cases of ammunition were catching on fire. Almost as soon as the bullets started firing, the pallet fell from the plane. The other pallets started moving faster toward the open hole. Once we got the momentum going, Jon ran up front to help Buzz control the plane.

Within seconds, all three pallets were out. Lucky and I stood there, holding onto the sides of the plane, looking at the huge hole that used to be the cargo door, watching the burning pallets fall to earth. Suddenly there was a tremendous explosion as the first pallet hit the ground. A shower of white phosphorus streamer lit up the night sky like a Fourth of July celebration. I knew that cases of WP (White Phosphorus) had exploded. The other burning pallets could be seen hitting the ground with another tremendous explosion.

I looked over at Lucky. He just stood there, staring.

"Lucky, you OK?" I yelled over the roar of the open hole.

"I am if I'm not dead," he said.

I made my way across the plane, grabbed Lucky, and took him to the front. He was in shock. He just sat there, looking at the open back of the plane. "Fuck, man, this is why I hate flying. I fuckin' knew I would get killed in a goddamn plane."

"What do you mean? We're still alive. Shit, man, that was the most exciting thing we've done in a long time," I said with a grin.

"I knew you were nuts, but not this fuck'n' nuts," he told me.

I'm sure Lucky knew I was as terrified as he was. Things happened so fast, I didn't have time to be afraid. But now I was about to shit my pants. We sat there looking at each other; then we both broke out in uncontrollable laughter. We laughed so hard, tears started running down our faces. Buzz and Jon both looked down at us in total amazement. I'm sure they must have thought we had lost our minds. We hadn't lost it. We were just trying to get rid of all the adrenaline we had inside. Some people would get sick; some would cry. Guys like us, well, we usually broke down and had a good laugh—that is, if we weren't throwing up.

After I composed myself, I went up front to check with Buzz.

"Damn, Chance, I knew you had cast-iron balls, but this is ridiculous," he said.

"Hell, Buzz, we're not dead. I'm just real happy about that. Besides, that was pretty damn exciting."

"You're one sick motherfucker."

I asked Buzz what had happened. He said we had taken a SAM in the ass just as we passed over the border into Thailand. We had lost a few hundred feet, but the plane had held together, and we should make it to our destination. It was still dark, so I couldn't see the damage to the tail of the plane. From the looks of the insides, though, the plane had pretty well had it. The back half of the plane was shredded from the shrapnel of the explosion. The cases of bullets going off had added a few more holes. The fire had melted all the wiring in the back of the plane, and Buzz wasn't sure the landing gear was going to come down. Other than all of that, I thought we came out pretty damn good.

It wasn't long until the sun started to come up. When there was enough light, Lucky and I went back to the rear of the plane to see if we could tell how much damage had been done. *Oh, God,* I thought as I stared at the tail. Over half of the tail section was missing on one side of the plane. Gaping holes were visible on both tail booms and in the control surfaces. The back half of the cargo area was being held on by slim pieces of metal ribs. The cowling under the right engine had been blown away, exposing the landing gear. The right wheel had been shredded by the explosion. I could see oil streaming out of the right engine. The smell of fuel was becoming stronger as it got hotter.

I went up front and told Jon he'd better come to the back and look at the plane, then looked up at Buzz and asked him if he had any parachutes on board. I don't think he thought that was funny. Jon went to the back of the plane and just stood there, staring. We went to the right side and saw the condition of the landing gear. I asked him if this thing was going to get to the ground in one piece. He told me that of all the pilots to crash a plane, Buzz was the best. I didn't know if I should be reassured or start to pray.

Spooky

Jon went back up with Buzz to let him know the condition of the plane. I went up front and asked Buzz if there was anything Lucky and I could do. Buzz said we needed to get rid of everything that wasn't tied down. He wanted us to lighten the plane as much as possible. We were losing fuel, and we might have to shut down one engine to make it to the airbase. I told Lucky what we needed to do, and we started to get rid of what little was left inside the plane. Dying in a plane crash was something I had never really considered before. I was afraid, but at the same time I knew I had very little control over the final outcome, so I wasn't going to worry about it. If it was time for me to bite the big one, then there was nothing I could do about it. Yet inside I knew we were going to be OK. I knew my guardian angel was taking care of things.

Lucky and I tore out the seats, cargo racks, netting, fire extinguishers, and first-aid kits, anything that was not essential to fly the plane. As we threw things out the back of the plane, I noticed a large crack in the right tail boom that seemed to be getting larger. I ran to the front to tell Jon about it. He came to the back of the plane to take a look.

"Oh, shit," he said. "We're not going to stay in the air long at this rate."

Jon ran back to tell Buzz what he had seen. Lucky and I continued to find anything we could to throw out and make the plane lighter. Buzz slowly put the crippled plane into a shallow dive to get us as close to the ground as possible. He leveled off about one hundred feet above the treetops.

We'd been flying at that height for about an hour when suddenly the plane started to shake violently. I could see Buzz and Jon struggling to keep the plane in the air. The control wheel Buzz was holding was twisting and shaking so hard that I was sure Buzz was not going to be able to hold on. I looked out the back of the plane and saw what was causing the trouble. The right tail boom was about to fall off. Only a few small bands of metal were holding the boom on, and I could see that the control surfaces were no longer working. I ran to the front and climbed up to the cockpit to see if there was anything I could do. Buzz was fighting the controls with all his might. Sweat was pouring from his head as he tried to maintain control.

"You guys better grab your ass and hold on. This isn't going to be easy!" Buzz yelled. "We're not going to make it to our airstrip, but I think I can get us to an alternative strip just a few miles ahead. We have no landing gear, so I'm going to belly her in. Stay to the middle of the plane, just behind the cockpit. If the wings get torn away, you should be OK."

Now things were getting a little too exciting. I went back to Lucky and told him what Buzz had said.

"*Shit!* I knew it. I'm going to die in this fuckin' plane. Oh, well, it's been fun," Lucky said as he looked at me with a grin.

"We're not going to die. They don't make planes like this anymore. Hell, these things are like tanks. Just make sure you don't shit your pants when we hit the ground. I don't want to spend the next few days with you smelling like a drunk marine on shore leave," I said.

Lucky and I found a place as close to the middle and as far forward as we could. The cockpit was elevated above the cargo deck, so we held onto the supports of the flight deck. I could hear the right engine being shut down. The smell of fuel was real strong. I looked out the right side of the plane and saw JP-4 pouring from the wing. I was praying all the fuel would be gone before we hit the ground or we really would be in a world of shit.

I could see the tops of trees just a few feet below the plane. Lucky and I were sitting, bracing ourselves against the flight deck supports, waiting. I didn't really know what to expect, but I knew I probably wasn't going to like it. The smell of fuel seemed to start to dissipate when I heard the left engine start to throttle back. Only seconds separated us from the ground. Lucky and I looked at each other. Stupid grins came across our faces. I think we both knew we were going to be OK. I yelled at Lucky to get the hell out when the plane came to a stop.

Suddenly the plane smoothed out for just an instant before we hit the ground. I expected a tremendous jolt, but instead it was a smooth, almost normal touchdown. I knew we were on the ground because of the loud sound of the ground scraping away the bottom of the plane. Suddenly the plane started to bounce and pitch violently. I could see trees, brush, and dirt flying everywhere. The cabin filled with a choking dust.

There was a tremendous crash, then ripping sounds as the left wing was torn from the fuselage. Lucky was thrown to one side of the plane, then to the other. I gripped the I-beam supports so hard my hands started to bleed. I started to grab for Lucky but didn't for fear of being thrown from the plane. Lucky managed to grab onto the side of the plane until it finished its wild ride.

When the plane came to rest, I grabbed Lucky, who had been knocked unconscious, threw him over my shoulder, and ran out the back of the plane, expecting it to burst into flames any second. When we were a safe distance away, I laid Lucky down and started back to the plane for Buzz and Jon. I hadn't yet reached the plane when Buzz and Jon came running at me, almost knocking me down. We ran to where Lucky was now sitting and jumped behind some fallen trees for cover. But no explosion followed. The dust and flying debris that had filled the plane finally settled. The plane was not burning, not even smoking. Buzz said we had run out of gas before we hit and the wing with any gas in it was torn off. We all stood up, staring at what was left of the *Hag*.

"Damn, Buzz, think you can fix her?" I asked with a nervous laugh.

"Nope, I think she's dead," he replied.

Jon just stood there, staring. Blood was pouring from a cut above his eye and an obvious broken nose.

"So, Jon. Hell of a rush, wasn't it?" I said.

"Buzz was right; you guys do have cast-iron balls," he replied.

"I've got to give birth to another lieutenant," said Lucky.

"What?" asked Jon with a strange look on his face.

"He's got to take a dump, you know, drop a turd, take a shit," I translated, smiling at Jon.

"OK, boys, we're about a mile from our new home. Let's get what shit we can find and get moving. I don't want to run into any Thai border guards right at the moment," said Buzz.

We took a few minutes looking through the wreckage of the *Hag* but found nothing. Buzz grabbed a couple of canteens, and we started off to our new home, somewhere in the Thai jungle.

"See; I told you. You weren't going to die. You know I'm always lucky. Shit, that's why you guys like having me around. It couldn't be for my good looks and quick humor," I said to Lucky.

"I don't know how you do it. You always make it. You're right; you are lucky, you crazy fuck. You must make your guardian angel work a lot of overtime."

We headed off into the jungle. I didn't know what direction we were heading or how far we were going to go. But I knew Buzz knew where he was, and that was all that mattered. Every muscle in my body was starting to tighten up. I knew I was going to be a hurtin' puppy in the morning. Except for Jon's cut, broken nose and the goose egg on Lucky's head, we were all OK. I think Lucky might have needed to change his shorts, but that was OK too. At least he didn't smell like a drunk marine.

We had been walking fifteen minutes or so when we came across a dirt road. Buzz said this was the road to our compound and we would be there in just a few minutes. We started up the road in single file, Buzz first, followed by Jon, Lucky, then me. Even though we were in civilian clothes and in Thailand, I felt naked without a rifle in my hands. We were pretty much at the mercy of anybody who happened to be passing our way. Buzz waved at the locals and acted like he had been here before. I figured his Air American buddies were probably waiting for him with cold beer at the airfield.

We'd walked about ten minutes when we came upon an airfield out in the middle of nowhere. Parked on the dirt strip were two C-123

Providers, another C-119, a couple of smaller single-engine PC-6 Porters, and an old Cessna O-1 Bird Dog. The O-1 was painted Olive Drab. The C-123s, C-119s, and Porters were their usual silver aluminum. None of the planes had any numbers. In fact, two of the small planes had peace signs painted on them. All of the people milling about were dressed in civilian clothes, many wearing shorts. *Yeah, these are friends of Buzz,* I thought. Sure enough, when we got close to the planes, two guys came running up, each holding a cold beer.

Hope and Glory

The airstrip we finally ended up on was typical of those used in clandestine operations. Everybody wore civilian clothes and called each other by their first names or nicknames. One of the men ran out to us and handed Buzz a beer, asking if we were the new girls. They'd heard the crash of the *Hag* and were glad to see us alive.

"Damn, Buzz, looks like you survived another one. We heard you go down. One of our planes was near you and watched the whole thing," Scotty said.

"We were taking bets to see if you were going to make it to A4 (the name of the airstrip we had crashed on). Shit, I knew you would. You're the best I ever saw at crashing planes," Scotty said as he slapped Buzz on the back.

The other man with Scotty looked at Jon and stated, "Shit, Jon, your woman beat the crap out of you again? You look like hell."

Scotty led us back to the compound, talking to Buzz all the way. Scotty and his partner ignored us, acting like we didn't exist. Jon turned around and told us that's the way they always treated new guests. It was just a matter of trust and getting used to new faces, he said. When we got to the compound, Jon went off to get his face fixed and Buzz left with Scotty, leaving Lucky and me standing by ourselves.

"I need a beer," I said. "Let's go find the local watering hole."

We found the local bar, the Peckers Pub, went in, and ordered drink. At first, the bartender just looked at us. "Who the hell are you?" he asked, in a not so friendly way.

"Relax, Tom," said Buzz.

Buzz was already in the back of the place, slamming down some of the local brew. He was sitting around a table with a half-dozen men, talking about his brush with death, as he called it.

One of the men yelled at Lucky and me to come over and have a seat. "So, you're the guys with the cast-iron balls Buzz has been talking about," he said as he took another drink.

"Cast iron? More like rice balls and rocks for brains after flying with Buzz," I replied with a laugh. "Can we get some of that hooch, or is it just for special guests?"

Dean, the loudest of the bunch, yelled at Tom, the bartender, who brought us a round of drinks. The drinks looked like gasoline and smelled like formaldehyde. "Drink up," Tom said, then toasted all the crazy bastards that didn't exist anymore. I chugged a shot of the home brew and almost choked. It even tasted like gas, bad gas. I asked him what the drink was, but he said I probably didn't want to know. I figured he was right, so we had a few more and sat around telling lies about each other.

I guess we stayed there about two hours or so. After a while I didn't really care. I didn't realize how strong the drinks were until I got up to take a leak. I tried to walk about two steps, then fell flat on my face. Of course the whole place thought that was pretty funny. I looked like I was fifteen years old anyway, and making a fool of myself didn't help. One of the guys sitting at the table started to comment on how much I looked like a little kid. Lucky leaned across the table, grabbed the man by the throat, and got in his face: "Don't let his looks fool you. He's probably killed more people than you've fucked." The subject of my looks was never brought up again.

By that afternoon we were getting hungry, so Dean showed us where we could get something to eat and where we were going to be bunking. We took a warm shower, got a change of clothes, and had some chow. The food was great: steaks, baked potatoes, and salad. I thought I was back in the States. One thing about these "Sneaky Pete" guys—they ate well. We ate all we could, drank a few more beers, and hung out the rest of the evening. We all knew tomorrow was back to business, back to what was left of Hope and Glory.

That evening was pretty much like that afternoon. We did nothing but hang around, eat, and drink. About 2200 hours, I turned in, but Lucky wanted to have a few more drinks. He said he needed to get rid of a little more stress. I knew Lucky was going to try to get Buzz and Jon drunk so he could find out more about our mission. I told Lucky he probably was wasting his time. I was right.

0800 the next morning came way too soon. Buzz came to our hooch and woke us up. He was smart. He stood at the door and threw junk at us instead of coming over and shaking us awake. Too bad; I really wanted to knock him out, just for a couple more hours of sleep. It was time to get back to the business at hand. Buzz told me we had to get some food in us because we were going to be gone all day picking up supplies. We got up, cleaned up, and found some breakfast. About 0930, Lucky and I found Buzz out by one of the Porters looking at maps with one of his buddies.

Buzz told me to get in front and Lucky to climb in the back and sit on the floor. Buzz warmed up the plane, and we taxied out and took off. It wasn't until we were airborne that Buzz filled us in on where we were going and what we were going to do. He said we were picking up supplies for a "humanitarian mission" to the people of the area. I knew Buzz knew more than he was telling, and I figured this was as good a time as any to ask. We had been flying for about fifteen minutes before I started asking questions.

"OK, Buzz, I think it's time you tell us what is really going on. Those weren't regular supplies on the *Hag*. That shit exploded. It was full of ammo and white phosphorus. That wasn't what was on the manifest. Who was that shit for? What in the hell are we going to be transporting, and to who?"

The only thing I knew about Operation Hope and Glory was that Lucky and I were supposed to escort certain highly sensitive materials, not humanitarian supplies, then deliver them to a certain operative that I would recognize. They didn't tell me who this person was, but he knew me, and I would know him. I figured it was one of the guys I had worked with over the last year or maybe one of the spooks that I knew. It was just supposed to be a delivery, nothing more.

"All right, Chance, I guess it's time you know what's going on," said Buzz. "We've been supplying certain guerrilla forces in the region with arms. These secret armies are all that's left to fight against the communists. Our government is about to pull completely out of Southeast Asia, and we are trying to get them as many supplies as we can before then. The shipment we were carrying was the first large shipment being delivered to our contact in Laos. It wasn't our main shipment, more like a bonus. We are going to get part of the main shipment now. You and Lucky need to make sure it gets to the right guy. All I know is you have dealt with him before and you will know him when you see him."

What in the hell was he talking about, I was supposed to know him? *I hate this secret shit,* I thought. *Why in the hell couldn't they just tell me who he is? It's no big deal. We're just delivering supplies.*

We've been doing that for years. Why all the secrecy all of a sudden? Somebody was going to a lot of trouble to keep this quiet.

"Why all this secret bullshit?" I asked. "What's the big deal about delivering supplies? Haven't you guys been doing that for years?"

"Just following orders, Chance, that's all I know. I'm supposed to fly you guys to a couple of different airstrips, pick up some packages, and deliver them. You are supposed to know the rest," said Buzz.

I was confused and a little mad. I couldn't figure out why I wasn't told who I was supposed to contact. Lucky was listening to the conversation I had with Buzz, but he didn't have a clue, either. I sat there looking out over the jungle thinking I might have really screwed up by taking this mission. This sure wasn't like the army. At least there you knew something about your mission. I knew we were heading north from our home base, but I didn't know where we were supposed to pick up these supplies. About an hour into the flight, Buzz turned the plane almost due west. We'd been flying west for another hour when Buzz told me over the intercom we were going to land. I looked out the front of the plane, but I couldn't see an airstrip anywhere. All I could see was a small clearing on top of the mountain and a lot of dense jungle.

"So where exactly are we going to land?" I asked.

"Straight ahead," said Buzz.

All I saw was that little dot of a clearing. "Tell me you don't mean that?" I asked, pointing to it.

"Yep, that's it. Hang on; you're going to love this."

I turned around and looked at Lucky. His eyes were about the size of silver dollars. He was staring out the front of the plane, shaking his head.

"No way, man, there's no way you're going to get this plane in that little clearing. OK, Buzz, this ain't funny," said Lucky in a panic.

"What's the matter, Lucky? You don't like jumping out of airplanes?" I asked with a laugh.

"Fuck that, man. The last time we landed with Buzz, he almost killed us."

"Hey, Buzz," I said, "I don't think Lucky appreciates your flying."

"He will in about thirty seconds," replied Buzz.

Buzz had dropped to below the clearing. We were now looking up at the clearing at the top of the tree-covered mountain. Buzz had applied full flaps and full throttle to get the nose up and slow the plane down to almost a stall. The sound of the engine screaming and the stall-warning horn was enough to make any normal person want to jump without a parachute.

I had all the confidence in the world in Buzz, but I was holding onto the dash as hard as I could. The plane was barely flying, just mushing through the air. The clearing was not flat, not flat at all. The plane looked like it was going to settle into the trees at the bottom of the clearing when Buzz raised a little flap. Just as the plane started to climb, we hit the clearing and bounced about three feet in the air. We were on the ground at the top of the clearing before we knew what had happened.

"Let me out of here! Open the goddamn door!" yelled Lucky. "That's it, no more. I'm walkin'. I can't take this crazy flying shit. You just point me in the right direction, and I'll walk back."

Lucky threw the door open and jumped out of the plane. I was laughing so hard, I had to get out before I wet my pants. God, it was so funny. I had never seen Lucky this nervous, out of control. I didn't realize he didn't like this type of flying. I thought it was an incredible rush, and I would have thought Lucky liked it, too. Wrong!

Buzz shut down the plane and got out. Buried under some brush at the edge of the clearing was some camouflage netting. Buzz got the netting, and we helped him cover the plane. Buzz said this area wasn't real secure and every now and then a "fast mover" (military jet) came flying by looking for something to shoot. He was right. We hadn't been there long when we heard a jet off in the distance. It never got close enough for us to see what it was, but that was OK.

"Damn, Buzz, you fly like that all the time?" I asked.

"Yeah, that's what we do here a lot. You get used to it after a while. These planes are incredible. They'll take about any punishment you can dish out."

"So why are we here, and where is here? I don't see anybody around. Are we killing time or what?"

"Well, we're still in Thailand. We're going to meet some people here. They've got part of your shipment. They'll be here in an hour or so. I wanted to get here early to make sure everything was OK."

About four o'clock that afternoon, we heard a truck coming toward the clearing. Buzz uncovered the plane, started it up, and taxied to the top of the clearing and turned it around facing down the mountain. Lucky looked at the plane and just shook his head. I guess it was my turn to figure out what was going on. I watched a military truck come through the trees and stop at the edge of the clearing. A man got out and started walking over to the plane. I had Lucky take a position off in the trees with an M-16 to give us as much cover as possible. The man walked up to me and spoke.

"Hello, Chance, nice to see you again," he said. He stuck out his hand to shake. It was Patterson, the man we had met in Nha Trang.

"Patterson, isn't this a surprise," I replied, shaking his hand.

For some reason, seeing Patterson didn't actually surprise me at all. There was something about him and Baker I didn't trust, especially Patterson. He had an air about him. I knew he was well experienced by his cold, hard look. He struck me as someone who could stick a knife through your heart and like it. I didn't trust him when I first met him, and I didn't trust him now.

"I have the first shipment in the back of the truck. I'll take it to the plane. You can have Lucky come in from the trees. We're by ourselves. He won't need to keep watch," he assured me.

I waved to Lucky to come in as Patterson drove the truck up to the plane. Yeah, he'd done this before. He knew Lucky was out there. In the back of the truck were six duffel bags stuffed to the brim. Each bag weighed over a hundred pounds. The bags were locked with the same type of lock that Lucky and I had put on our duffel bags back in Nha Trang. We watched as Patterson loaded the six bags into the back of the plane. He looked at us as if to say, "Give me a hand." *Fuck him*, I thought. Buzz didn't get out of the plane. His orders were to stay in the plane in case we had to leave in a hurry. Only Lucky and I were to make contact on our deliveries. Patterson closed up the plane and walked over to me.

"Tell Buzz that the next delivery is on schedule. You will take this and the next shipment to Bravo-6. Make sure you tell Buzz Bravo-6, not Alpha-4," said Patterson.

"Bravo-6. Got it. Anything else?" I asked.

"Nope, that's it. I'll see you in a few days."

Patterson went back to his truck, got in, and drove away. I turned to Lucky, who had one of those looks like he was about to do something he really didn't want to do.

"Let's go, Lucky. Let's get the hell out of here," I said.

"I know I'm not going to like this," he replied.

We climbed in the plane and put on our headsets. Lucky climbed in the rear with his back against my seat, bracing his feet against our cargo. Buzz didn't wait for my door to close before he had given full throttle. The plane vibrated and strained against the thrust of the engine. Buzz then released the brake, and we launched forward. We were off the ground before we reached the middle of the clearing. The plane slowly crawled its way into the sky. Once we were above the trees, Buzz raised some flaps and lowered the nose, and we started to fly like a normal plane again. Lucky didn't say a word, just sat there. I could feel him pushing against the back of my seat.

"Holy shit, Buzz, that was great. You've got to teach me how to do that," I said excitedly.

"Not with me in the plane. I've seen you fly. You like to do crazy shit," Lucky commented. "I remember your first helicopter lesson."

"You lived, didn't you?"

"Yeah, but the pilot will never be the same."

"Don't believe him, Buzz; the pilot just wasn't used to somebody trying to park his helicopter inside a bunker," I told Buzz with a laugh. "Nobody was hurt, and we almost made it."

"We'll wait until we get rid of this load before I give you any lessons, OK?" said Buzz.

"Deal," I agreed with a big grin.

"Great. Now I get to have you try and kill me in a helicopter and a plane. I can hardly wait," Lucky said.

We flew for about an hour before Buzz told us where we were going. He said we were landing at an airstrip in Laos, about fifty miles over the border. He said there had been arrangements made to have the strip secure and we shouldn't have any trouble getting there. I didn't like the *shouldn't* in his comment, but I figured he knew what he was doing. I preferred being on the ground and taking my chances in the jungle to sitting up here in this plane.

I felt like a fly in a spider's web, waiting for the spider to come and eat me. The strip looked large enough to handle a C-130. There were no buildings on it, but I could see where there had been a tower and foundations of a couple of hangars. It was a dirt strip, but it was in good shape. We landed, and Buzz taxied the plane to the center of the strip, then pulled off to the side.

We got out of the plane, and Buzz told us to off-load our cargo. Then he went over to a clump of brush and opened up a door to an underground room. Inside the room were several bags of rice neatly stacked on wooden pallets. Lucky and I took the duffel bags and stacked them on the floor next to the rice. Buzz said they would be safe here and we needed to get going before it got dark, then closed the door and locked it. He put a small wire on the edge of the door as we were leaving. I went back to see what he was doing and saw that the whole place was booby-trapped. He said if anybody got into this place that wasn't supposed to, there would be nothing left but a large crater.

We got back into the plane and took off. Buzz told me that we weren't going back to our base but were going to another place for the night. I asked him if the strip we had left was Bravo-6. He said it was. He said the other strip, Alpha-4, was a few miles from there, but it probably wasn't secure, so that's why we had to use Bravo-6.

Buzz flew us back into Thailand and to a small farm he said was about forty miles from our base. This was his home, and he felt it would be safer if we stayed there tonight.

I'm sure he just wanted to get laid, but that was OK with Lucky and me. The beds were soft, the food was good, and Buzz's family was great. He had a Thai wife and three kids, a boy and two girls. It was like being in another world.

I thought about my own family and home, what my folks were doing, and what they thought I was doing. I thought about Susan, my childhood sweetheart, and how good she smelled. I could almost feel her arms around me. I could almost taste her kiss.

I look back now and wonder if I had known the truth about my mission, would I have been there, envying Buzz and his family and missing mine?

Buzz was a different person when he was around his family. I looked at his wife and wondered if she knew what he really did. She looked like she really loved him. More likely she just accepted it. All she probably cared about was that he came home to her and their children.

Early the next morning we got up, ate, said our good-byes, and were on our way south toward Cambodia. Buzz was very careful not to tell us the exact location of our destinations. I asked him if we were going to fly into Cambodia, but all he said was we were going to Alpha-2.

Buzz had fueled up at his place, so I knew we had an easy four hours of flying time to play with. We flew south, southeast for three hours before he said we were going to land. He kept low, below the mountaintops, flying in the valleys and through mountains passes just out of reach of small-arms fire. He obviously knew his flying. Lucky just wanted back on terra firma. I thought it was a gas, flying at treetop level.

Alpha-2 was a small strip, this time in a valley. It was long enough to handle a bigger airplane but looked as if it hadn't been used in years. Trees and brush had overgrown the airstrip, leaving just enough room for a small plane like ours. We circled the field and saw a couple of trucks parked at one end. Buzz got on the radio and was talking to someone, but I couldn't hear who it was.

We circled as soldiers off-loaded cargo from their trucks and left it piled at the end of the field. The trucks left, and we set up to land. Buzz told me that this was going to be fast. He was going to land, taxi to the supplies on the ground, and wait. Lucky and I were to get out and load the supplies as fast as we could. We landed, and Buzz taxied to the waiting cargo. He spun the plane around as Lucky and I jumped and ran to the supplies. Piled on the ground were six more duffel bags, just like the ones we had picked up from Patterson. They even had the same type of locks on them. Lucky and I threw the heavy bags in the back of the plane and climbed in, and Buzz took off. Sweat was pouring from Buzz as he climbed into the air.

"What's the matter, Buzz? You looked scared shitless," I said.

"Man, I don't like this place. There are no friendlies around here," he replied.

"So we were in Cambodia?" I asked.

"No, damn it. That was Alpha-2," was all he said.

Buzz didn't say anything as we flew back north. I could tell that he was really bothered about this. He looked scared. There was something more, but I couldn't put my finger on it. We flew for another thirty minutes, then landed at a small strip. Buzz told us to stay in the plane while a truck came out and fueled us. We weren't on the ground twenty minutes, and we were gone.

The flight to Bravo-6 took around three hours. We landed and off-loaded our baggage as before, storing it neatly in the underground room. I noticed there was an extra duffel bag.

"Buzz, somebody else know about this? There's an extra bag here," I asked.

"Yeah, that's what I need to tell you. You and Lucky are supposed to stay here tonight. There's food, a radio, and a couple sleeping bags in there. This is where I leave you until tomorrow evening," said Buzz.

"What the hell are you talking about?" I asked. "What the fuck is going on?"

"Your contact is going to fly in here tomorrow and pick this stuff up. This will be the guy you're supposed to know. When the three Hueys fly in here, only one man is supposed to get off and make contact with you. If you know him, open up the room and give him everything in it. If you don't, blow the damn thing up and get out," Buzz said.

I was in shock. Lucky and I stood there not saying a word. What kind of bullshit was this? We were supposed to hide in the jungle, baby-sitting who knows what, waiting for three helicopters belonging to someone I was supposed to recognize. But if I didn't know this asshole, I was supposed to blow this shit up and get out. Great! Get out from where? "Bullshit. I think you better tell me what the fuck is going on, or you and I are going to have a serious problem," I said, staring at Buzz.

Lucky knew me well enough to realize that I was dead serious. He had gotten the M-16 from the plane and was standing away from Buzz and me, ready to pull down on Buzz. I pulled the .45 from my holster and had it in my hand. Buzz just stared at me, not knowing what to do.

"It's time, Buzz. I've known you for some time, but that doesn't matter now. The only thing that concerns me is Lucky and me. I'll fly your fuckin' plane out of here myself if I have to," I said.

"God, Chance, that's all I know. I swear," Buzz replied. "I'm supposed to return tomorrow, late afternoon, and pick you up. The radio in the bag is tuned to my frequency in case you have to move. That's it; I swear to God."

I could see the fear in Buzz's eyes. He didn't know if I was going to believe him or put a bullet in him. Lucky was watching me closely as I stared at Buzz. He knew what I was thinking. I had to make a decision, and I had to make it now. I stood there for a few moments before I spoke.

"Sorry, Buzz, this took me by surprise. I wasn't going to kill you, just wing you."

The relief that came to Buzz's face was almost funny. He looked around, then ran to a tree and took a piss. Lucky winked at me and grinned as he took the extra duffel bag from the hole. Inside the duffel bag were two sleeping bags, an M-16 with a dozen loaded magazines, a portable radio, and some MREs, enough to make our overnight stay bearable. Buzz showed us a place, across from the cache site, where we could set up camp. There was a wire and explosive detonator there that was connected to the cache site. We were supposed to use it to blow the site if things went wrong. Buzz said the door was locked but not wired, so we could get in it tomorrow. Buzz told us he would see us tomorrow evening, gave me the key to the cache door, got in his plane, and was gone.

Lucky and I made up our ROM site the best we could and settled back to watch the sun go down. I didn't know exactly where we were, but I guessed we were in Laos. The scenery around us was beautiful, so lush and green. I could hear birds and monkeys off in the distance as we sat watching the sun slowly setting. We had two M-16s and a couple .45s to protect us. We didn't have a compass or map, so it wouldn't do us any good to try to leave.

It was very uncomfortable to have to rely on someone else to come and get us. Not having any sort of a plan really sucked. Lucky and I took turns watching our position and the cache site throughout the night. We didn't see or hear anybody all night long. No aircraft or vehicle came within hearing distance. About 0200, I had to climb in my sleeping bag to stay warm. I had another hour of my watch left, but I was starting to freeze.

At 0600 hours, Lucky woke me up. We cleaned up our camp and headed to the cache site to check it out. Everything was as we had left it. As I unlocked the door, I couldn't help thinking of those booby traps. *Shit, I hope there isn't something here I missed*, I thought as I slowly opened the door. Everything was in order, a total of twelve duffel bags and two pallets, each with twenty bags of rice. I wondered what was in the duffel bags. I tried to look through the top of one, but it was too tightly packed.

I could feel the bags were filled with something I thought might be smaller bags of money. The rice bags seemed to be heavier than they should have been. I poked around and discovered that the bags of rice had something else hidden in them. I had started to open one of the rice bags when I heard helicopters off in the distance. Lucky was topside and yelled that our guests were arriving. I climbed out of the room and closed and locked the door. I told Lucky to get across the airstrip and go to the detonator. He was going to cover me from there and, if anything happened, blow up the site.

Lucky had just made it across the airstrip when three Hueys appeared above the trees, heading straight at me. I was standing in the tree line, and I was sure they couldn't see me. The helicopters circled once, then landed in the middle of the airstrip. I waited for a few minutes, expecting someone to exit one of the helicopters, but nothing happened.

Shit, I've been here before, I thought. Then I saw the side door of the closest Huey slide open and out stepped a man in a military uniform. I was too far away to recognize him, and I started to get a little panicked. I felt totally naked. All I had was a side arm. My M-16 was lying down behind some cover I was planning to get to if things went to shit. The man stood by the Huey as if waiting for someone, me. *Here I go again,* I said to myself as I emerged from the tree line and started walking toward him. I had to walk about a hundred yards to get to him. As I walked, I watched the other Hueys to see if anybody was going to get out. Except for a pilot and copilot, they were empty.

Hope and Glory, what in the hell does that mean? Is it the Hope of these soldiers they can defeat the communists and the Glory if they do, or what? By now it didn't matter to me one way or another what it meant. I just wanted to get rid of this shit and get out of here. I could see Lucky with his M-16 trained on the man standing outside the Huey. I was about fifty yards from the man when he suddenly turned toward me. I instantly recognized him and stopped dead in my tracks.

"WHAT THE FUCK!"

Standing before me was Colonel Khuan, the Cambodian I had delivered packages to just a week ago on Operation Dragon Flower. For some reason, though, this didn't surprise me much. I don't think anything could surprise me at this point. He stood there wearing a Laotian uniform, flying here in a Laotian helicopters, and grinning like he thought he was king shit. I knew this Vietnam thing was pretty screwed up, but I didn't realize everything over here was totally fucked. It was real clear to me I was not being told the truth about these operations. There were no U.S. POWs being traded on Operation Dragon Flower. I was sure that Operation Hope and Glory was *not* to supply arms to guerrilla forces to battle communism. I didn't understand Khuan's role in this whole game, but I knew he wasn't an intelligence agent of any kind.

"Well, Khuan. I can't say I'm entirely surprised to see you," I said as he strutted up to me.

"We meet again, Sergeant. I asked your superiors for you to make this delivery. I trust your journey was a pleasant one?"

"I have your cargo. What do you want me to do with it?"

He stood there grinning at me. "Just show me where it is. My men will load it into the helicopters."

I walked over to the underground bunker and unlocked it. I didn't have time to open the door before one of the pilots moved me out of the way. He opened the door and went in the room. The three pilots started taking the duffel bags and bags of rice to the helicopters. As they loaded the cargo, I thought about the booby traps. I considered waiting until they were all in the room, then blowing it. For some reason I had an intense dislike for these men and wanted to treat them like the enemy they were. They weren't soldiers; they were something else, something evil. I couldn't put my finger on it, but I knew there was something.

As one of the men brought a rice bag from the room, it snagged on the side of the door and split open. Out poured rice, but something else fell to the ground. Before the man had time to put the bag down, Khuan hit the man in the face with his fist and started yelling at him. The man quickly picked up the contents of the bag and hurried to the chopper. I walked over to the doorway to see what was going on, but Khuan stopped me before I could get a glimpse of what had fallen from the bag. It was obvious that whatever was in the bags was something I wasn't supposed to see.

It took about an hour for them to load the three helicopters. I told Khuan I would help him load his cargo, but he insisted his men do it. I wanted to get closer to the bags to see if I could tell what was really in them, but Khuan made sure that wasn't going to happen. Once the bags were loaded, Khuan ordered the men back to the helicopters. Lucky had stayed watching us while Khuan was on the airstrip. It was too late to blow up the cargo, so all Lucky could do was try to avenge my death if Khuan decided to pull a double cross. The helos were loaded and ready to leave when Khuan came over to where I was standing.

"It looks like all of my supplies are loaded. Tell your superiors that this shipment will help my army a great deal. Make sure they know I will expect to hear from them in the future about more supplies," Khuan said before he turned and walked away.

I guess he knew from our last meeting I had no intention of shaking his hand. This time he didn't even offer it. I didn't respond to his comment. I just stood there and watched as he climbed into his Huey and flew away. Once Khuan was out of sight, Lucky came walking over, still holding his M-16.

"Ain't that the shits," he said as we stood there watching the helicopters disappear over the tree line.

"This is a real fucked up war. If we would have seen him a month ago, he would be dead right now."

"You know he's dirty, don't you?"

"Yeah, I know. I think I know what we've been hauling around for the last week, too. One of the bags of rice broke open, and I saw something fall out of it. I'd bet my balls it was opium, heroin, or both." I listened to Khuan's helicopters slowly fade away . . .

Debra

By the time Lucky and I stopped drinking and talking about Hope and Glory, it was almost 2000 hours. The booze had knocked the pain in my thigh to a dull ache. The bullet hole had stopped oozing, and I was getting to where I could almost walk without much of a limp. My concern now was getting everyone home.

I finished getting dressed and we went downstairs for dinner. In the lobby we found Debra with a friend of hers. Debra introduced us to Cindy and said she had made reservations at a seafood restaurant just down the street. We left the hotel and found the night perfect for walking. The hostess, who knew Debra by name, met us outside the restaurant and showed us inside to our table.

"I thought you might like a little change," Debra said as she smiled and winked at Cindy.

Cindy was a local businesswoman and quite lovely. She took to Lucky right off. It looked like they were going to have a real good evening.

Knowing the situation Lucky and I were in, Debra took care not to say anything that might compromise us. She told Cindy that Lucky and I were businessmen from Oklahoma checking out local hotel properties. The night was perfect for forgetting our troubles, and we were going to do our best to do just that.

Debra performed like a pro, keeping the conversation light and entertaining. We stayed at the restaurant until 2330, then headed back to our hotel. Lucky and I both walked with a bit of a limp, so Lucky told Cindy we were in a car crash a few days before back in the States. Of course that made Cindy feel sorry for Lucky and want to tend to his injuries. I smiled as I wondered how Lucky was going to explain to her how he got a bullet hole in the ass.

When we reached the hotel, Lucky and Cindy disappeared. Debra had arranged a separate room for Lucky for the night. I asked her if she wanted to come up to my room, and she said yes. As we reached the room, Debra took my room key and unlocked the door. She took me by the hand, and I followed her into the suite. Once inside she closed and double-locked the door, turned down the lights, and took a bottle of wine from the freshly restocked refrigerator.

"You don't have to worry. I know you've had a rough time, and I think it's time for you to relax a little," she said as she poured me a glass of wine.

"Thanks, Debra; you can't imagine how right you are," I told her as she handed me the glass.

She looked at me with her large, dark eyes, as if she were looking into my soul. Her long hair, tan skin, gorgeous face, everything, was perfect. I had much the same impression when I first met her in a hot tub in Washington, D.C.

I had been in D.C. for a week and a half getting some specialized training. I hadn't been at my Maryland hotel a week when I met Debra, the assistant manager. One night, about ten-thirty, I was in the hot tub relaxing. Debra came out and sat in a deck chair next to the hot tub we started talking. We must have talked for two hours before she said she had to go. I thought she had to leave because she was married, but she said it was because she needed some sleep. She had to work the next day.

As I sat there in the hot tub, I could hardly keep my eyes off of her perfect body. She was tall, about five foot eight, and looked like a model for Victoria's Secret. Full, round breasts, small waist, perfect hips, and long legs—high speed, low drag all the way. She clearly had the brains and a great personality to match her looks.

As she walked away, I imagined her naked in the hot tub with me. Being the man that I am, we weren't talking about the temperature of the hot tub or engaging in mindless small talk. We weren't even having sex. We were fucking. Fucking like animals.

Only in my dreams, I thought as she walked away. Debra was all class—not someone I wanted to show my animal side to. As she walked away, she said if I was there the next night, she might join me. With an invitation like that, there weren't too many things on this earth that would keep me away.

I only had three more days in D.C., and I was going to make the best of it. The next evening the hot tub was mine. I had talked the night manager into closing it early and letting me stay. Around ten o'clock, Debra walked in wearing a robe. As she opened her robe, her beauty almost took my breath away. It was almost embarrassing. I was acting like a teenager on his first date. She climbed into the hot tub and slid up next to me. We talked for more than an hour that night. I got to know her as a real person, not just a hard body. She was great.

Debra and I saw a lot of each other over the next three days. She spent every night with me and even acted as a tour guide around

Washington. When I left, she made it a point to tell me that her door was always open. We kept in touch, and every time I was in D.C. I looked her up. One thing that really blew me away about her was that she was just as much as an animal in bed as I was. . . .

I had finished most of a dozen Coronas before dinner, so I really didn't want to drink anything more. I wasn't much of a wine drinker, either, but this wine tasted especially good. As I looked into her eyes, I could sense she was here to take care of me. I put down my glass and gently took her in my arms. I stood there holding her for several minutes. The tenderness of the moment made me almost want to cry. This was the first time I could relax in weeks without worrying about somebody trying to kill me. Debra took my hand and led me to the couch in front of the sliding glass door that overlooked the ocean. She opened the door, and we sat down. She took my head and guided it to her lap as I stretched out. I lay there on the couch looking up at Debra's face as she stroked my forehead with a touch, like a soft breeze, quietly drawing the fear and anger from my soul.

I first thought we would make love like we had done in the past. My head rested against her soft breasts as I looked up at her. It was odd, I thought. But I didn't want to make love to her. I wanted her to hold me, protect me, and I knew she sensed that as she stroked my face.

I quickly became totally relaxed and at peace. All my fear and worry were gone. I felt no anger, no rage, and no need for revenge. I wasn't alone any longer. I was lost in Debra's world. I was safe. The sound of the ocean was soft in the background. I felt I should say something, so I started to speak. She pressed her fingers against my lips and told me to rest. I closed my eyes and was consumed by her warmth. The sound of the ocean and the gentle rhythm of Debra's heart were all I was aware of. I felt comfortable there, at peace.

Since my second divorce, in 1990, I hadn't trusted any women. But for some reason I knew I could trust Debra. We had no strings attached to our relationship, and I guess that made a difference. And I knew I didn't have to trust her with much of my life, just a few quiet moments.

I woke to the sound of Lucky charging into the room. I jumped to my feet, expecting an army to come crashing through the door behind him.

"Relax, I figured you were up by now," said Lucky with a huge grin on his face.

I stood there looking at him in complete confusion. The last thing I remembered was sitting with Debra on the couch. I must have fallen asleep during the night and Debra had left without waking me. I looked around, but she was gone. The sun shone brightly through the glass door. My watch said it was almost 1030 the next day. I must have slept for ten hours. Lucky had obviously enjoyed his night. He was bouncing around the room like a kid who just lost his virginity.

I saw that the wine Debra and I were drinking had been put away and the glasses cleaned. In their place, I saw a note on the coffee table.

The note read:

Chance,
I hope you slept well, my precious friend. I couldn't bear to wake you when I left. I had to leave for Rio this morning, so I won't be able to see you off.
Take care, my sweet; you know my prayers are with you. If you ever need me, you know I'm here for you.
Love, Debra

I was sad I couldn't see her before I left. She had done more for me than she would ever know.

But Lucky and I had to hurry to get to the airport and catch our plane at 12:00. I showered quickly and we left the hotel for the airport.

"I guess you had a nice evening," I said to Lucky as we got into the cab.

"I think I'm in love," Lucky replied.

"Yeah, that's what I figured by the look on your face. How did you explain the hole in your ass?" I asked.

"I told her somebody tried to carjack us and I was shot as we heroically fought off the attackers," replied Lucky.

"You're shittin' me," I said in amazement.

"No, she believed every word. She really wanted to make me feel better after that. She said I must be some kind of superman or something," he told me.

I looked at Lucky, then busted out laughing. *Some things just never change,* I thought. No matter how bad things got, I could always count on people like Lucky to come through and remind me what guys like us are really about. Animals.

We made it just in time to catch our flight to Miami by way of Montego Bay, Jamaica, and went right to the gate to board. We were able to get seats next to each other toward the back. The flight was only about half-full, so we had several rows of seats to ourselves. As the plane headed out over the gulf, Lucky started to talk about the mission again.

"I don't want to talk about that right now," I said. "Tell me about Cindy."

"Damn, what a woman! She took me to my room and jumped me like I've never been jumped before."

"So, is this the next ex–Mrs. Lucky?" I said jokingly.

"Hell, no. I didn't even get her last name. We never got that far in a conversation. I guess she was too impressed with a real man for a change. I did get her telephone number in case I was ever in the neighborhood, though."

Lucky and I managed to talk about everything but the ambush. We even bet to see if one of us could get a date with the flight attendant.

Lucky tried every line I had ever heard. I stayed with the quiet routine and was able to get a phone number from her: 1-800-STICK-IT.

"So, how was Debra last night?" asked Lucky.

"You wouldn't believe it if I told you. She was so great, I didn't even know when I fell asleep. She is one in a million, that woman."

I wasn't about to tell Lucky what really happened. After all, I had the team honor to uphold. I doubted he would believe me if I told him the truth anyway.

"You know we might run into some trouble in Jamaica," I told him.

"I was just thinking about that," said Lucky. "You know more people there than I do. Think you'll have any problems?"

"I doubt it. I haven't been there in some time, and I never flew into Montego Bay."

"I'll be getting off the plane first, so if you have a problem, I wouldn't be able to help," said Lucky.

"No problem. You just get yourself back to Colorado; I'll take care of any problems."

Colorado

As the captain announced we were landing at Montego Bay, the flight attendant handed Lucky a slip of paper with another phone number on it. I guess he won the bet. We had a twenty-minute layover, so I told Lucky it was best not to be seen together. We would sit in different sections of the plane, and I would talk to him again in Colorado. The plane pulled up to the gate, and we prepared to get off. Lucky moved to the front of the plane so he could get off before me.

When I reached the terminal, I headed to the rest room to shed some clothes. *God, I am scared shitless and I feel so feel alone,* I thought as I walked into the rest room. I guess Lucky was more of a security blanket than I had realized.

I needed a little time to think, so I found an empty stall, went in, and closed and locked the door. It's funny, the things you think about when you're sitting there. I looked at the three gray walls, reading the graffiti and thinking about Lucky, my most trusted friend. He'd always been there. Wherever I was, he was always there, going through the same shit with me. I suddenly realized that except for Lucky's girlfriend in Colorado, I didn't have a clue what Lucky did when we weren't working. The only time we were together was when we purposely met somewhere or when he came to my place. All I knew for sure was he disappeared from the face of the earth when we weren't on a mission.

I could not stop the fear from erupting as I started to comprehend what I was thinking. Was it possible that Lucky could be the mole? Could I have been so wrong about someone I trusted more than anyone on earth? The thought terrified me. I knew I had to suspect everybody, even Lucky.

I had to enter the States as quietly as possible, so I decided it would be safer to take another plane. Lucky would probably check on me when he got to Miami and would find that I wasn't on his flight. If I knew him as well as I thought, he'd know I'd taken another flight and would go on to Colorado by himself.

I waited until the rest room emptied before I left the stall. I took off the shirt I was wearing and stuffed it under some paper towels in the trash can. I had a T-shirt underneath with some stupid design on it. I figured it was good enough for the trip to the States, so I didn't worry about buying anything else.

I went back to the ticket counter and asked if I could exchange my ticket for a later flight. The ticket agent said the next flight wasn't leaving until that night, so I took it. I had time to kill, so I grabbed a cab and headed for lunch. The cab driver took me to a restaurant that was about five minutes from the airport and dropped me off. I paid him twenty bucks and went in.

I wasn't very hungry, so I ordered some iced tea and sat next to an open partition that looked out onto the street. I have a habit of sitting in restaurants facing the door so I can watch everything. As I sat there staring at my drink, I thought of Debra, Lucky, the team, and the mole. The world seemed to vanish as I became more focused. I was going to be in the States soon, and I had to find a way to determine who the traitor was, if there even was a traitor. As I looked up at the many tourists walking by, I didn't know if I should be envious of them or glad I wasn't one of them.

I had several hours to kill, so I decided to take a walk and think. As is typical with Jamaica, the streets were loaded with people trying to sell their goods. I didn't want to be bothered, so I decided to get off the main tourist routes. Before long, I realized I had walked to the very poor section of town and the people there didn't appreciate an intruder.

"Hey, man, what you think you doin'?" yelled a man from across the street.

"Nothin', man, just walkin'," I said.

Suddenly he came up to me with three of his friends and stopped me.

"What the fuck you mean, man? You don't belong here," he said.

I wasn't in the best of moods, and I didn't want to screw around with this guy. I figured I was in a part of town where if I did get into trouble, I would be on my own.

"Look, pal; I'm not looking for any trouble. Just leave me alone and I'll be out of here," I said.

"I'm not your pal, asshole. You ain't leaven' until you give me your money," the man replied, staring at me.

His three friends had gathered around me, not leaving me a way out. I knew this could go to shit, so if I had to I was going to make it short and sweet.

"Look; you're making a real mistake here," I said. "I'm not giving you my money or anything else. Just let it be before someone get hurt."

"No, man, you're not leaving and someone is going to get hurt."

Spooky

Then the man took a swing at me, barely missing my face. I grabbed the man's wrist as it passed by and pulled his arm out straight. Before I knew it, I had snapped. I attacked him like an animal, not caring about the consequences.

I smashed his extended elbow with my other fist. I could hear the bones as they broke. As he bent over, I kicked him in the throat as hard as I could. A gush of blood came from his mouth, and he fell to the ground. Another man lunged at me, but I blocked his arms and grabbed the back of his head, pulling it down as I tried to drive my knee through his face.

As the second man fell to the ground, I felt someone pulling at my shirt. A third man had tried to stab me with a knife but missed. His knife had gone through the loose fitting T-shirt and was caught as he tried to pull the knife back.

I grabbed his hand with one hand and hit his elbow with the other, forcing his arm to bend. As it bent, I drove the knife into his stomach. As he fell to the ground, I turned to see the other man running away.

I stood there for a moment, looking at the three men lying around me. Two looked dead, and one was crying like a baby. Suddenly I realized that people were yelling at me as they came from their houses. If I was going to get out of here, I had to go now. I started running as fast as I could, pushing my way through the growing crowd. As I glanced back, I saw several men had started chasing me.

I ran several blocks before I realized I was finally alone. For some reason the men had stopped chasing me. I was covered with sweat and blood from the fight, and I couldn't go to the airport looking like that. I started looking for a place to buy some clothes. I found a shop, bought a shirt that was too small and some cheap pants, and headed back to the airport. I made sure I didn't find myself walking down any more streets that were off the tourist routes. And I've made it a point since to stay out of Jamaica.

My plane was on time, so I boarded and settled back for the quick flight to Miami. It took less than two hours before we were preparing to land, not even enough time for a meal. That was just fine with me; I was ready to get back on U.S. soil. Once I reached Miami, customs would be my last hurdle. I was hoping customs here was still more of a dog and pony show than a means of monitoring the mass of people coming into the United States. If it wasn't for the drug dogs smelling everyone's crotch, customs wouldn't have any real function at all. The agent asked me for my passport, never really looked at me, stamped it, and didn't even question why I didn't have any luggage.

I tried to stay with crowds of people so I wouldn't be noticed, then headed for the domestic ticket counter. I had to try to look like everybody else so the many government types wouldn't pay close attention to me.

After I purchased my ticket to Colorado Springs, bought a new shirt, and had a quick lunch, I was broke. I figured Lucky had already gotten there, so I could call him at his girlfriend's house in Manitou Springs and tell him when I'd be in so he could pick me up at the airport.

The trip to Colorado Springs took over three hours. When I arrived, I called Lucky and told him I needed a ride. He said everyone had made it OK and was there waiting. It would take about forty-five minutes to get to me, and I was to wait outside the baggage area on the curb. It took closer to an hour before Lucky showed up. I didn't recognize him at first, as he was driving a taxi. He borrowed it from his girlfriend, who was a cabdriver in Colorado Springs. Lucky opened the door, and I climbed in the backseat, just like a fare.

"Any problems?" I asked.

"None. Everyone made it OK. I checked if anyone made any phone calls. Nobody did. Everybody stayed together."

"How's Sue? She OK with this?"

"Yeah, she's fine. I didn't even owe her money. How do you think we should handle this?" asked Lucky.

"Let's not tell the rest of the team what kind of insurance we have. I need to buy some time before we spill our guts. I'll make a phone call to let those fucks know we're back. I won't tell them what happened. I'll just tell them everything got all screwed up and we had to boogie. I'll drop a couple of hints so they'll know we think we might have been set up. They'll figure we still trust them and that we think somebody else might have set this up, like the drug cartel."

"That'll work. I've already called our buddy with AT&T. We'll route your call to D.C. so they won't be able to trace us."

"Great. That's going to make things that much better."

It was going to take about an hour to get back to Manitou Springs. Lucky said he had an errand to run for Sue, but it would take just a few minutes. I told him to take his time; I needed to make sure I had everything straight in my mind what I was going to do. I knew I had to get to Washington, D.C., as soon as possible. I had to meet face-to-face with some people and get answers. It was safer to go alone, but it sure would be nice to have some backup. I'd have given anything to be able to let the team know what I was going to do, but I couldn't tell anyone, not even Lucky. If there were a mole in the group, we'd all be dead the minute I gave up my plan.

I knew the team was anxious to know what to do next. The first order of business was to make sure the mole would want to wait until all the insurance was gathered before he made his next move.

Over the years, Mike worked behind the scenes to collect valuable government documents, memorandums, and private notes implicating the higher-up officials who had the powers to safeguard us. Mike cultivated a friend who was a maintenance supervisor and routinely worked on mechanical problems within top-secret government buildings. Any time something broke or didn't work properly, his crew was called in to fix it. If a fax jammed or copy machine ran out of toner, he fixed it. If a shredder quit shredding, he made it work. And, most important, his crew emptied the trash. Mike's prize document was a memo to then-president Reagan that I'm sure Congress and the press would have given anything for.

We also had things from the reign of Frank Carlucci, John McHahon, William Casey, George Bush, and our ace in the hole, Bill Colby, all while they worked with the CIA. Even William Crowell from the NSA wasn't immune to bits of information failing to reach the shredding room. We had copies of maps, directives to military leaders, shredded memos between CIA heads, code books, and tapes of radio intercepts. Lucky had a couple of friends in the NRO (National Reconnaissance Office) that didn't trust anybody, either, and kept us supplied with interesting tidbits for our collection of Cold War memorabilia. It took a few years before I really understood what the NRO was, and yes, the world is, in fact, wired.

The things I had personally collected pertained mostly to the black operations in Central and South America. A "hit list," as it were, of drug lords and political puppets that had fallen from grace with the United States. I managed, on a couple of occasions, to take pictures of good guys having meetings with bad guys. I even got a copy of a tape of a recorder that had been placed in a hotel room air vent and recorded one of the day's leading U.S. politicians having a little kinky sex with a Panamanian "professional."

Possessing such documentation was incredibly dangerous. I was careful about who on the team had information and worked my ass off to keep them quiet about it. Mike, Lucky, and I had the lion's share of dirt, but neither of them knew who on the team had what. I knew that Dave and Opey had nothing, and I had to decide with Lucky and Mike separately whether we should share anything with them.

Sue's house in Manitou Springs was outside of town, nestled in the hills at the end of a half-mile dirt road leading from the highway. The house backed up against huge boulders, the perfect place for cover and safety. Sue lived by herself in the fifty-year-old house she had bought from her grandfather. She had dated Lucky off and on for five years. Sometimes they wouldn't see each other for almost a year, but she was very laid back and didn't seem to mind. Small doses of Lucky were probably all one woman could handle anyway.

Sue's house had its own security system, three very big dogs that thought Sue was their mother or something. Sue was an ace with a handgun and did everything she could to be self-sufficient. She really had the temperament for covert ops. She worked for cash and didn't pay taxes, and I don't think she even had a Social Security number. She was just about perfect to baby-sit the team until we were ready to make our next move.

Lucky and I got to the house at around 1600 hours. Everything seemed quiet outside, a bit too quiet for me. Even the dogs weren't making noise. Lucky sensed it, too, and parked a little way from the house. As we got out of the car, Lucky left the keys in the ignition in case we had to make a quick exit. As he closed the door, I opened the back driver's side door; then I made my way around to the rear of the house, where I could see what might be going on. My heart was pounding again. Things were too fucking calm. Was everybody dead? I climbed some rocks overlooking the back of the house and waited for Lucky to show himself.

Too many things reminded me of an ambush. The absence of any activity was usually a dead giveaway. I expected Sue's dogs to be out in the yard, alerting her to any visitors, but they, too, were gone. It seemed that even the birds had quit singing. I had to smile thinking of how well Lucky and I worked together. We had not said a word about what we were doing, and yet we were both on the same page. At least, I hoped we were both on the same page. If Lucky was setting me up, then he was really the master. I truly believed he was on my side.

A few minutes later Lucky showed himself at the sliding glass door at the rear of the house. His shirt was pulled out, and his pants were unzipped. He had an immense grin on his face, and he looked like he had just gotten a blowjob. *You son of a bitch,* I said to myself. Sue appeared on her knees, sticking her head between his legs. She smiled at me and waved for me to come in. As soon as she was gone, I gave Lucky the finger.

Inside, Sue met me with a cold beer, hugged my neck, and said she was glad to see me again. I asked her if she had a surprise for me, too, but she just laughed and slapped me on the butt. She said Mike, Dave, and Opey were in the back room asleep. I walked to the back room, stuck my head in the door, and yelled, "GUN!" as loud as I could. All three of the sleeping beauties about shit trying to find a place to hide.

"Greetings, boys," I said and returned to the kitchen.

Sue had some leftover spaghetti, so I heated it up in the microwave and anticipated eating home-cooked food without having to check my back every second.

Mike was the first to pull himself together. "Shit, Chance. You scared the piss out of us," he said, his hands still shaking.

"Good. It's not time to kick back and take life easy."

"Have any problems on your trip?" asked Mike.

"Not really. Just thought all of you were dead when we got here is all. Where are the dogs? You guys eat them?"

Dave and Opey came into the kitchen and sat down. Both of them just sat there and watched me as I took my plate of spaghetti out of the microwave and sat down at the bar to eat.

"Don't even think about it. If you touch my plate I'm going to cut off your balls and cook them in the microwave," I said without looking up at them.

Everyone stopped what they were doing and stared at me. They didn't know if I was serious or not.

"Just kidding. If you're hungry, help yourself," I said. "Listen," I continued. "I know we have a lot to talk about, but let's eat and have a few beers before we get down to business. I think we all need to relax a little before we start. Is that all right with you?" I wanted everyone's tongue to be as loose as possible as I watched each of them drink his share.

Everyone said it was, so we ate at the dining room table and Sue broke out the Corona and Coors beer. We devoured everything she had in her kitchen, and the five of us finished off about a case of beer. Pretty soon we had relaxed, cleared off the table, and reached the point of talking about what we should do.

"I know everyone wants to get on with their lives," I told the group. "I informed you a couple of days ago that we have insurance that will help us with that. Some of us have been tucking away intelligence we could use as bargaining chips in case we found ourselves in a situation like Paco was in a few years back. Well, we are, and it's time to play hardball with whoever is trying to fuck us. From here on out the rules of engagement will be strictly ours."

"Chance, Mike and I have gathered enough information to make Big Brother shit little green apples clear into the next century," said Lucky. "If anything happens to me, the information I have will automatically be mailed to one of the surviving members of the team."

"That's how Mike and I have it set up also," I stated. "We will divide our information between all of us. You each have to make arrangements so that in the event of your death the information you have will be sent to a surviving member. If, for some reason, those who remain believe the death was the beginning of someone getting rid of the team, the information needs to be sent out. Is everybody with me so far?"

They all nodded.

"OK. When you get your information, do not tell any member of the team what you've done with it. The only way we can guarantee the security of the information is if each of you deals with it secretly. Only you need to know where it is and how you plan to get it out. You've all had to tuck something away for safekeeping before and know what to do.

"Here's the worst-case scenario. If we all get it at the same time, make sure the information will get sent to the *Washington Post*, the *New York Times*, CNN, and members of Congress and anyone else who might give a shit about the U.S. intelligence taking out its own men. It's already an automatic thing with me. I have given certain people instructions as to what to do in case something happens to me. For their sake, I don't give them a clue of what the information is they will be sending out."

"When will Opey and I be getting a portion of the insurance?" asked Dave.

"Soon. We have to get it all together; then we'll get back together and give it to you," I said. "We also need to let Washington know we are alive. My guess is they still are wondering what has happened to us. Plus it's essential that they don't know how many of us got out. Most important, it's crucial no one make any contact with Washington until we can get all of our information together and divided up. I'm going to tell them we need their help, but we need a little time to recover. They're going to expect us to lie low or even disappear like Paco did, but I think we should do just the opposite. We all need to go back home and show ourselves to people we know, not hide. If we hide out and they come gunning for us, our disappearance won't be noticed. Everybody understand so far?" I asked.

"Are you shittin' me!" Dave stood and looked at the other men.

"I agree," said Opey. "Chance, you've got to be kidding."

"No, he's not," Mike disagreed. "We've got enough classified shit stashed to make the next administration wish they never got into politics."

"Look," I said. "Don't take any assignments for God's sake. Don't go to any federal buildings. Don't even go to your regular post office; use a mail drop. We all need to have a piece of the insurance, and only then can we breathe easier.

"In the meantime, if they're that interested in us, they'll send people to check on us. If we're watching for it, we may get an idea of who is behind this.

"We will meet again soon with all the information and divide it up between us. Does everyone understand?"

Though I did not know who the mole might be, this meeting with all the insurance in one place would be his only chance to complete his mission, which was to finish the fob started in Colombia and dispose of the insurance.

"Everybody needs to go back home as if nothing has happened. Tell your friends, family, or neighbors that you went on a week long private rafting trip here in Colorado. Make sure everyone knows who you were with. Let them know if something happens to you, they need to try to get hold of one of us. Make sure you leave our pager numbers where anyone can find them in case something happens. Any questions?" I asked.

"Yeah, I have one," said Opey. "When will we get together again?"

"I'm not sure. Not for a few weeks anyway. Lucky, Mike, and I will coordinate between ourselves on that. We will decide on where and when at the proper time. Until then, it's not a good idea to be in contact with each other. If it's absolutely necessary, use pay phones, pagers, and your scramblers. Do not use a cordless or cellular phone for a tactical conference. If we are compromised, we are dead. This mission is not over. It's just beginning."

We spent the rest of the night getting loose. I had gone outside and disconnected the phone so no one could make any unexpected phone calls. I told Sue what I was doing, and she'd been around Lucky long enough to understand.

We didn't get drunk; we vented. Our anger had reached the point where we had to do something with it. If we didn't, someone would do something stupid, and before too long someone innocent or even not so innocent would end up dead. The pain of losing our fallen brothers began to emerge, and before too long the tears began falling. People that do covert ops don't confront and deal with loss very well. Most of the time they bury the sadness deep in their minds, never to bring it up and face it. But we couldn't help it this time. Razz and the rest were too important to be forgotten. For a short time we cried and remembered our dead friends, and this was something we never did, especially in front of someone like Sue, who, we didn't know very well, except for Lucky.

Sue displayed an incredible understanding of the male ego. As soon as the emotions began to emerge, she quietly went into another room and let us reveal a side of our personality that was kept private. None of us, including me, ever allowed anyone to see what we thought was a weakness. This night was the exception. We didn't break down and let it out as we probably should have, but we did express our grief. Though we'd all been told that we had to deal with loss, not bury it, I, for one, never had time for that. It was much easier to lock emotion away and worry about it later. But later never came. I guess that's why people like us live with such persistent demons and lose perspective about the value of human life. Strangely, it took three of my closest friends' dying for me to figure that out.

Around ten minutes to one in the morning, I woke Sue and asked her if I could use the aluminum case Lucky had given her. Because we had planned to use Sue's house as an alternate safe house, we had stocked it with a few mission-essential supplies. The aluminum case held a satellite telephone I had picked up a couple of years earlier.

As I entered the living room with the phone, everyone fell quiet. Lucky knew what the case was, but the others weren't sure.

"It's time. Lucky, is Dan standing by?" I asked.

"Yeah. He said he would be working until five A.M. I told him we would be calling him between midnight and four."

Dan Fraziar was a friend I had met a couple years before. He used to work for the NSA as an electronic intercept guru, but after several years he burned out and went to work for AT&T as a troubleshooter. He worked in Denver, Colorado, at their main office and had access to all the electronic switching we needed to make a call to Washington without being traced.

Before I had a chance to set up the phone, Dave had picked up the regular telephone.

"Shit!" he said excitedly. "The phone's dead!"

"Relax, Dave. I disconnected it so we wouldn't be bothered by anyone."

I set up the sat phone and dialed Dan's private number in Denver.

"Your dime," came Dan's voice over the phone.

"Dan, long time, how've you been?"

"Same old shit. Just fixin' other people's fuckups. How about you?"

"You know. Trying to make a living. You know where we're at, don't you?"

"Yeah. Your partner called me yesterday."

"Could you call that number in five minutes?"

"Sure. I know the game. Give me five minutes and I'll fix you guys right up."

Lucky had already explained to Dan what we needed. Dan missed fucking with people and liked getting back into the game every now and then. He had left the NSA with an attitude and liked to help people like us when he could. He could make it almost impossible for anyone to trace us, especially at 4:00 A.M. eastern time. With Dan's call to us, the originating call would be just a little more obscure. By routing the call through a dozen states, a couple of communication satellites, and a few more Earth stations he made sure by the time somebody back east got around to tracing us the call would be over.

I went outside and reconnected the house phone and waited for Dan to call. The team sat around the coffee table staring at me. We were all thinking that soon our former bosses would know we were alive and could try to finish the job they had started back in the jungle.

I woke Sue again so she could answer the phone just in case someone else called. It didn't take long for the phone to ring, but we still jumped.

"Hello," Sue said, having little trouble making it sound like she had just woken up. She hesitated for a moment, then handed me the phone.

"Dan?"

"Your communication wizard is here to help you."

"Here is the number I want you to place for me. Seven-o-three eight-two-four one-o-one-o. As soon as the operator picks up the phone, drop the line to the alternate phone."

Dan had found us a pay phone out in the middle of nowhere. As soon as the person on the other end of the line answered, Dan would make the computer think the call had originated from that pay phone. The whole trick depended on the alternate phone being one that no one would pick up. If Dan didn't find a phone that was totally private, we'd end up connecting to the pay phone and have to do the whole thing all over again.

As Dan made the link, my heart began to pound and my palms started to sweat. The call would reveal whether our plans had succeeded so far. I heard several clicks as the signal relayed through Dan's communication web. Then came a moment of dead silence, before the line began to ring.

"Good morning, CIA," said a voice on the other end of the line.

"David Chance calling for William Coltan. Priority call Zulu three-one Tango nine-one-seven. ID Whiskey four-five Bravo."

"Mr. Coltan has retired from the agency. Can I connect you with the night supervisor?"

"No, ma'am. This is a priority Zulu three-one call. Please connect me with Mr. Coltan. Now!"

"Yes, sir. I will connect you right away."

Bill Coltan was the one person in the government I knew monitored the pulse of all black operations, even though he was in retirement. I had only spoken directly with him a few times, but I was sure he would be able to get the message to the right people. When we first spoke, he told me to call him if I ever had a problem and needed serious help.

After a few moments the operator came back on the line. "Go ahead, sir. Mr. Coltan is on the line."

"Chance, this better be damn important, calling me at this hour."

"Yes, sir, it is. Have you heard anything about Spooky 8?"

"I understand they were on assignment down south. Other than that, nothing."

"That's correct, sir. We were south, but we ran into a serious problem and were able to make our own way out."

"Damn, Chance. Did you lose anyone? Where are you now? How did it happen?"

"I'm not sure about anything right now, sir. I think we might have been set up, but I can't be sure. We were able to get out before anybody could tell where we were. I'll tell you more about it when I see you."

"What can I do for you?" he asked. "Where are you now? I can send some people to take care of you."

"That won't be necessary, sir. We're safe. I just wanted to let someone know we were OK. I can't imagine who might be behind this, but I think there might be a security problem. I think the cartel might have gotten wind of our mission and waited for us."

"You might be right. We have been tracking down a few leads that deal with internal security. It's good you made it back safely. Get back here as soon as you can so we can debrief. Maybe together we can figure out what is going on."

"No, sir. I don't think that is a good idea right now. A few of us have been working on a little insurance policy for just this kind of thing. We need a little time to get things together before we come see you."

"Insurance? What do you mean?"

"I can't say right now, sir. Just know it's very strong insurance. As soon as things die down, I'll come to Washington and see you. It won't be for a few months, though. We've decided to go inactive for a while."

"Chance, listen very carefully. You can trust me. I'll take care of everything. I want to get to the bottom of this as bad as you do. Take your time. Go home and get some rest. I know you've been through a lot. When you're ready, come see me. I'll help you any way I can.

Don't talk to anybody about this until you talk to me first. Do you understand?"

"Yes, sir, I think so."

"No, damn it. You need to understand. Clear everything with me first. Take no action on your own. Everything is going to be fine. Whatever this insurance is, forget it. I'll take care of everything. Do you understand?"

"Yes, sir, I understand. Take no action on our own. Clear everything through you first."

"That's right, Chance. Don't worry about a thing. You call me when you're ready. Everything is going to be fine. Where are you? Can I help you get your men home?"

"No thanks, sir. That's all been taken care of. Everybody is already where they need to be."

We had been on the phone for almost five minutes. If I stayed on any longer, a trace would find us.

"I've got to go now, sir. I'll be in touch."

I hung up the phone before Coltan could respond. The guys stared at me, no one saying a word.

"OK," I said. "They know we are alive and well. When I told Coltan about a security breach inside the organization, he said he had already been checking it out. He wants us to do nothing without checking with him first. I told him we were inactive, and that was OK with him. He said get our insurance together and we'll go from there. Lucky, did you ask Sue about some money?"

"Yeah," he answered. "She's got a few thousand she can give us."

"Great. The thing to do now is all go home, get some rest, and get on with our lives while Mike, Lucky, and I get our shit together. I, for one, am going to take it easy until Coltan contacts me. Then I'll head to D.C. and find out what is going on. Anybody have any questions?"

"That's it? Just fuck it, go home, and pretend like nothing has happened?" Mike sounded as pissed as I was.

"No, Mike. You need to maintain. This will only work if we all can keep it together. You, Lucky, and I will need to get together and figure out how we are going to divide up our insurance. Then we all meet again. That's what we are going to do."

"Fuck it." Now Dave exploded. "This is just great. Our government tries to kill us while we're doing a fucking job for them. We make it out and you just blow it off."

"Listen, you guys; can it." I stood and leaned over Dave. "You know very fuckin' well I'm not going to blow it off. We need time. Pull your head out of your ass and think. Until we can get our shit together, our ass is still hanging out in the fuckin' wind."

I walked to the dining room window and took a few deep breaths. I needed to stay focused on the men. I had to support them, but I had to lie to them at the same time.

"We have to do this right. Nobody needs to die because we got stupid. You can bet your ass we are not going to sit by and let them hunt us down. Before we can do anything, they have to think we are playing their game. So we will go home for a few weeks and chill. Get a job, get laid, I don't give a fuck, but stay cool, and don't do anything stupid. Be visible. As long as they think we aren't going to do anything on our own, they aren't going to come after us right away. I told Coltan we were gathering our insurance. They'll watch us, but they won't attack. Not yet. Anybody have a problem with that?"

I didn't think anybody was going to challenge my decision now. They knew I was in control of the situation and I was going to do all I could to get everybody through this.

"Lucky, you have any problems?"

"No, not at all."

"Mike?"

"Whatever you say, boss."

"Opey?"

"You're the man. I'll do anything you want."

"Dave?"

"Shit, I'm sorry. I just lost my head for a second. You're right. That's the only way to play it right now."

"OK then," I said. "We are all in agreement. We go home and chill for a while. Lucky, Mike, and I will get our shit together. After we've done that, we'll all meet. Let's keep communications between us to a minimum. Figure our phones are tapped and we all have shadows. That's no problem; we've been there before. Right?" They all nodded yes.

As I looked at the survivors of Spooky 8, I still couldn't believe that one of them might have tried to kill the team a few days before. If that was true, nothing on this earth could stop me from dealing with him, no matter which man he was. This unbelievable act would mean unbelievable action, and I knew that I and only I would have to deal with it. The rest of the team might want to share in the act, but it ultimately fell to me.

The sun started to rise over the aeons-old rocks that surrounded Sue's house. It was the beginning of a new day and probably the start of the most challenging and dangerous part of our lives.

It was time for everyone to get back home. Lucky would stay here, but the rest of us needed to make arrangements to get where we felt the safest. I told everyone I was going to visit some friends in Oklahoma. Mike and Dave were going to catch a plane from Colorado Springs, and Opey said he was going to visit an old girlfriend in Denver. We decided we would all go to the bus station in town and then go our separate ways from there. We had nationwide pagers, so I could reach everyone when it was time to meet again.

I could sense the men felt apprehensive about going home, feeling like they were exposing themselves to someone waiting for them to finish the job. I tried to assure them that everything was going to be OK. I told everyone to call people at home they could trust and meet them away from home. At least they would see a friendly face as they got back to their homes and lives.

The next morning, I gave each man $500 from the money Debra

had given me. I called the local Hertz rent-a-car and told them I was traveling back to the Northwest. I asked if they had anybody delivering a car there that I might codrive. The lady said she didn't, but there was a special on one-way rentals, so I took it. I told Mike, Dave, and Opey good-bye, and Lucky and Sue took me in the cab to the Hertz agency across town.

Lucky said he was going to hang out in Manitou until he heard from me. Sue said she was going to take real good care of him and get him a job driving a cab, but Lucky told her to forget it. I knew he'd be OK, cab or no.

They dropped me off at the Hertz place, then sat across the street making sure I got a car. I had just enough money to rent the car, buy gas, and eat as I drove the 1,200 miles to my Washington home. I didn't tell Lucky about my real destination; I guess I couldn't bring myself to trust even him at this point.

I signed the papers, headed out the door, and waved at Lucky and Sue to let them know everything was all right. I found the car and drove it across the street to thank them and say good-bye.

"I want to thank you again, Sue. You've been a great help."

"You know it's always my pleasure. Are you going to be all right?" she asked.

"Yeah, I'll be just fine. We'll all be fine."

"I don't know how you do it," she said. "Every time I see you, you're always in control. Do you ever get afraid?" she asked.

"Oh, I guess so. I just don't have time to be afraid most of the time," I said with a smile as I drove away.

As I turned to wave one last time at Lucky, we gave each other the thumbs-up. The trip home was going to be a long and lonely one, so I settled in for some serious driving.

I'm a person who likes to get the job done. Being stuck in a car for fifteen hours wasn't my idea of a good time, but I figured the sooner it was over the better. I would stop only for gas, food, and to take a leak every now and then. I found a rock 'n' roll station on the radio, cranked it up, and headed north. The roads were good, very few cops and traffic lights. I headed north to Wyoming, then on to Montana. One thing about Montana: the roads are straight, there is nothing there, and if I slowed below seventy I got passed.

I managed to drive mindlessly, for the most part, and the time flew. But about three in the morning I started thinking about Lucky and Sue. She seemed to understand his ways. If she didn't, she was awfully tolerant of him. I envied them in a way. It must be nice to have a good woman to come home to. I had to laugh when I thought about what Sue had asked me. Was I afraid of anything? Sue, if you only knew.

D.C. Safe House

The Saudi security detail was over before I knew it. And after the "wheels-up" party, I said good-bye to the other men on the detail and headed to the airport. They thought I was headed back home, but I was going to rent a car and start my real mission in the Beltway.

I had a couple of friends in the D.C. area but decided not to tell them I was here for fear that their phones might be bugged. The more I thought about it, the more my gut knotted up. I couldn't trust anyone. I couldn't tell anyone. I was as alone as anyone could possibly be.

Hertz was out of cars, but Budget had a Ford Taurus available. They wouldn't let me pay cash for the car, so I had to use my credit card. When you're trying to travel unnoticed, you never use your credit cards. But the rental agency assured me that they wouldn't charge against it if I paid cash when I returned the car. I gave my card to the agent and she gave me the keys.

I needed to find a place to stay for a few days, and my first spot was going to be the Marriott in Manassas, Virginia, just outside of D.C. I had spent several weeks there training people for a security company based in Oakton, Virginia, and knew the staff. I was sure if they had a spare room, I could stay there without officially registering and they would keep my presence quiet. As I pulled into the front drive of the hotel, I couldn't help noticing that the hotel looked a little run-down. I went to the front desk and asked for Charleen. The desk clerk said she didn't work there anymore.

I used a pay phone in the lobby to call the number I had. She didn't answer her phone, but I had her address, so I decided to go over to her apartment and wait.

I met Charleen a couple of years earlier while in Washington, D.C., doing some training for one of the international security companies based in the D.C. area. She worked at the hotel we were using to conduct the classes. During my nine weeks there, I got to know Charleen real well. She is one of those people who act as if they have never met a stranger. She has such a nice personality and is so outgoing you can't help but like her. After the training cycles had ended, we parted close friends.

I had no idea if Charleen would return home with someone, so my adrenaline pushed my senses into the "hunter mode" as I waited. It was as if I were on another black operation. All my senses were peaked and ready. Nothing was missed. Every movement, every sound, every smell was noticed.

I'd been in the parking lot for a half an hour when a Ford sedan pulled slowly into the lot. I was parked at the back of the lot, so I wasn't noticed by the driver of the Ford. As I watched it, it slowly cruised the lot as if they were looking for something or someone. I lowered myself in the seat so my head wouldn't be seen and watched as it passed me. Two men were in the front seat, both scanning the parking lot. As they passed, I noticed the car didn't have a government or tax-exempt license plate. I saw a cellular antenna but no others.

My first thought was to wait for them to leave, then get away. As I watched, I waited for them to stop or other vehicles to race into the parking lot. If this happened, I knew I was discovered and I was going to get out any way I could. If I had to run over someone, I would.

Just as the sedan got a few cars past me, it stopped. My heart started to pound as I watched the car door swing open and the passenger get out. As I began to start my car, I heard a woman's voice yelling from the apartment.

"It's about time you got here! Couldn't you follow directions?" the woman said.

"Sure, baby. I just couldn't remember what apartment you lived in, that's all!" the man yelled back.

The man and woman ran to each other and hugged. The driver parked the car, got out, and went inside. I took my hand off the ignition key and wiped my sweaty hands on the seat.

I didn't know what kind of car Charleen drove and the parking lot bore no apartment numbers, so I decided to go to the door and take a chance that a man wouldn't answer. As I got to the door, I thought I heard a man's voice coming from her apartment. *Shit,* I said to myself. I went back to my car and drove out of the parking lot to look for a pay phone. I thought I had better call to make sure.

At a 7-Eleven down the street, I called Charleen from a pay phone. The phone didn't ring twice before Charleen picked up.

"Hello."

I smiled as I heard her enthusiastic voice again.

"Hi, Charleen; it's David Chance."

"Oh, my God, David. It's so great to hear from you. Where are you?"

"I'm here in Manassas on a little business. How are you?"

"I'm just great. Are you here long? Where are you? Can I come and see you?" she said.

That was what I wanted to hear. I was pretty sure she didn't have a husband, and the excitement in her voice told me she really was glad to see me.

"I'm just down the street. I came by your apartment, but I thought I heard a man's voice, so I didn't want to intrude. I decided to call you first before I came by."

"Oh, God, that was just my brother. He just left when you called. If you're that close, get your butt over here. I can't wait to see you."

"Charleen, I'm here on business, private business, and I need your help. It's one of those things where I can't let anybody know I'm here, not even your mother."

"Oh, David. Are you in trouble or something?"

"Not in trouble, but it is something. I need to stay with you for a few days if I can. But if I'm in the way at all, you need to let me know now and I'll get a hotel somewhere."

"No, no, you won't be in my way. Let's not talk about this over the phone; get over here."

"Thanks, Charleen. I'll be there in five minutes."

In the parking lot, Charleen recognized me and ran to the car. I didn't even get the door completely open before she had her arms around me.

"Oh, David, it's so nice to see you. How long are you going to be here? How long can you stay with me? You can stay here if you like. Are you by yourself?"

I never found Charleen to be at a loss for words. I couldn't fit a word in edgewise until we entered her apartment. As she opened the door, I couldn't help looking behind it and scanning the room. I noticed everything, looking for any sign that we weren't alone. My senses still stood at full stage, and they weren't going to come down for a while.

"Slow down, Charleen. Let's relax for a few minutes. We'll have plenty of time to talk. So, tell me, how've you been?"

"I've been great, just working as usual," she said as she stared at me.

Charleen is incredibly attractive, with a drop-dead gorgeous body. It was hard not to think about just telling her to shut up and get naked. It had been far too long. We continued the small talk for about an hour. She told me all about her new job, her family, and the boyfriend she no longer had. For a short time I was able to put the mission on hold, almost.

"Charleen, I'm really glad to see you. I wish it were under different circumstances, but I need to talk about why I'm here."

"This sounds serious. Are you in some kind of trouble?" she asked again.

"Trouble, no; need your help, yes. Please listen to me very carefully. You have to completely understand what is going on, and you have to make a choice about helping me."

My mind was a blank. What was I going to tell her? I was making this story up as I went, and I hoped it made some kind of sense.

"Do you remember the last time we were together—you know, the classes?"

"Yes, I remember."

"Do you remember when the men in the suits came to visit me in my room, just before the school was over?"

"Yeah, the ones I told you looked like FBI or something."

"That's right, those guys. Well, they weren't the FBI, but they were members of the government. They worked for the government intelligence; I sometimes work for people like that."

"Yeah, I know," she said. "I talked with your friend Lucky about you. He told me you and him did some work for the government like that."

"Well, a few weeks ago Lucky and I were working out of the country and we ran across some intelligence that was very important, very sensitive. It was so important that special people were sent to bring the information back here to D.C. Some of the information was left by mistake, and I'm here to make sure it gets where it's supposed to. Do you understand so far?"

"I think I do."

"Good. I have to find out who has that information now without anyone knowing I'm looking. That's why it's very important that no one knows I'm here snooping around."

I couldn't bring myself to tell her what was really going on. I didn't trust her enough for that. More important, I wanted to keep her as safe as I possibly could. If she didn't know the real story, she would be looked upon as an innocent civilian caught up in the game. If I told her the truth, she'd be an expendable liability.

"What do you want me to do?"

"Listen, Charleen. You need to understand you could get in trouble if certain people knew you were helping me. I'm not supposed to let civilians help me in any way. You aren't supposed to know anything about what I'm doing."

"I understand. I have friends who do work that they can't tell me about. You can trust me. I won't tell anyone, not even Mom."

Charleen was serious now. I don't think I had ever seen her this serious. I felt she knew the situation was important to me and she wouldn't let me down. She was a very smart woman and was quite savvy in the "Washington way." She was going to work out just fine.

I took her hands and, meaning every word of it, said, "I can't tell you how much this means to me. I don't think I would be able to go any further without your help."

We spent the rest of the afternoon catching up on times past. Charleen was a joy to be around. At about eight that night, I realized what time it was.

"Man, Charleen, I'm getting hungry. How about I take you to dinner?"

"Oh, shit, I was supposed to be at work at seven. I'm late," she said in a panic. "I turned my phone off so we wouldn't be disturbed, and I forgot to check the time."

"Are you going to get in trouble with your boss?" I asked.

"No, not really. He thinks he can't make it without me. I'll call him. It'll be OK."

Charleen called her boss at the restaurant she managed. It turned out that he hadn't shown up, either. It was a slow night, and the assistant manager hadn't called Charleen yet. Charleen told her that she was running a little late and would be in shortly, then hung up the phone.

"How about I take you to dinner? You can follow me to work in your car. I've always got people in there that come to see me, so you will fit right in. Don't worry. It's a slow night; nobody will pay any attention to you."

"I'll tell you what," I said. "You tell me how to get there, and I'll stop by after I take a shower and freshen up."

"Sounds like a deal. I'll shower and get out of here so you can have some time." And she headed for her bedroom and closed the door.

I sat in her living room listening to her take a quick shower. I couldn't help thinking about walking in there, stripping down, and getting in the shower with her. I think she would probably have liked that, but all that would have done was make this arrangement too personal, too close. I knew if I did that, I would be fucking up my safe house for good. This wasn't the time for that. Maybe later, when I had what I was looking for.

Charleen soon emerged looking like a million bucks. She gave me the directions to her restaurant and kissed me on the cheek. She worked about two miles from the apartment, and it was real easy to find. I went into the spare bedroom and lay down on the bed to relax. I hadn't closed my eyes when the phone rang, scaring the crap out of me. I wasn't going to answer it, but I listened for the answering machine to pick up.

"David, it's Charleen. If you're there, pick up the phone."

"Hello, Charleen."

"Are you coming? It's been almost two hours."

"Two hours, are you shittin' me?" I said as I looked down at my watch. It was 10:30.

"I'm sorry, Charleen; I must have fallen asleep. Is it too late to come down?"

"No, your timing is perfect. There isn't anybody here except a friend I want you to meet. Get cleaned up and get over here. I have a thick steak waiting for you."

"Great. I'll be there in fifteen minutes." And I hung up the phone.

I rushed and took a quick shower, threw on some clothes, and headed out the door. I was in my car leaving the parking lot before I realized I was a lot calmer than I had been earlier. It took about ten minutes to get to the restaurant, park the car, and go in. Charleen was standing at the front door talking to a customer when I walked in.

"Good evening, sir; your party is waiting for you," she said as if she had never seen me before.

"Ah, yes, thank you," I replied, a little confused.

"Right this way, sir."

I followed Charleen as if I had a clue as to what she was doing. As expected, my senses were back at a full stage of alert. I didn't know what was going on except Charleen was acting as if she didn't know who I was. I followed her to a table in the back where a black-haired woman sat alone at a table set for three.

"Here you go, sir," Charleen said as she winked at me, then made eye contact with the woman.

"It's OK David. I'm Linda, Charleen's friend. I'm the one she told you about over the phone that she wanted you to meet."

I wasn't exactly thrilled about Charleen's calling Linda, but after a while, I realized she was who she said she was. For the next two hours we sat, talked, and laughed at the stories that Charleen and Linda told about each other. By the time we left, I felt pretty comfortable with Linda, and I was secure in knowing she wasn't going to tell anybody about me. Charleen locked up the restaurant, and I followed her back to her apartment.

When we got inside, Charleen wanted to stay up and talk some more, but I said I was pretty tired. She showed me where the extra linen was and emptied a drawer in the dresser of the spare bedroom. We stood in the hallway for a few more minutes, then said good night and went to bed. My mind was still in a cloud as to what to do, but at least I had a place to stay and somebody I could trust—partly, anyway.

I went right to sleep—well, as asleep as I could get. As usual, my senses were still on alert, so I heard everything that went on. I heard Charleen get up to get a drink of water from the kitchen. I listened to the next-door neighbor's radio playing quietly all night. I could even hear a cat prowling around outside looking for a field mouse or possibly another cat. At one point I lay wide awake, thinking about the woman sleeping just down the hall. She had made a point of telling me that she slept nude, and if she was trying to turn me on, it worked. For more than an hour, that's all I thought about.

About 0530 the next morning the sun was shining brightly in my bedroom window. Everything was quiet outside, so I decided to get up and sit on Charleen's back patio. I made some hot spiced tea and watched the morning come to life. I must have been lost in the morning, thinking about home and getting free of the contract still out on Spooky 8, because I didn't hear Charleen get up and come into the kitchen. Before I knew it, she had come up behind me and put her arms around my chest, kissing me on the neck. She scared the shit out of me, and I almost reacted in a bad, very bad, way.

I jumped up, spilling my tea, turned, and faced Charleen ready for whatever.

"Oh, God, I'm sorry, David; I didn't mean to startle you. I thought you heard me coming."

"My fault; I wasn't paying attention. Are you OK? Did I scare you?"

"No, no. I'm OK. I think you scared me about as much as I scared you."

"Man, that's one way to get your juices flowing in the morning," I said, trying to get my heart back down to an acceptable rate.

We both had a laugh, then went back inside. Charleen showed me where her breakfast cereal was and said she had to go into work early today to do payroll. She would be back around 3:00 P.M. I told her I didn't know if I would be here, but if I wasn't, I'd see her later that evening.

"Is there anything I can get you while I'm gone?" she asked.

"Yes, there is. I'll need a cellular phone. Can you lease one for me, and I'll pay you cash for it?"

"Sure. Where do you want the number to be from, Virginia, Maryland, or D.C.?" she asked.

"A number out of Maryland would be just perfect."

"No problem. Anything else?" she asked intently.

"Maybe one thing. Do you have any binoculars?"

"Sure, in the hall closet. My mom got them for me. She thinks I watch birds with them; I don't. I sometimes watch my neighbors, though," she laughed. "Anything else?"

"I don't think I'll need anything else for now. Thanks, Charleen."

"OK then," she said. "I'll see you later today. If you need anything, call me at work or here."

She closed the door, leaving me to the job at hand. I found the binoculars in the closet. I also noticed an 8mm camcorder in a bag on the shelf next to the binos. I didn't need it now, but it was good to know there was one available.

My first order of business was to watch the areas where I knew people like me got a lot of their orders, the place where many black operations are routinely born. I had to make my way to an area about four blocks from the Arlington Visitors Center, a place called the Becker Research Institute on South Hays Street just three blocks off of Highway 1 (Jefferson Davis Highway).

The building isn't much to look at, a modest three-story structure that looks like an old office building. But looks are deceiving. The people that made the decisions several floors underground are what I was interested in. Those people who work for the CIA, NSA, and Department of Defense and make the decisions that send people like me on missions nobody will take responsibility for.

The Pentagon was only a few miles away, and the Becker building was said to be one of many linked by an intricate and clandestine underground tunnel system. Over the years, I had only traveled in a few tunnels myself, having passed through underground stations with secured branches leading off in a myriad of different directions. I was never told where I was or what I was seeing, but it didn't take a genius to figure out where all roads led.

This part of Arlington was always busy with traffic, so I didn't think my nondescript rental car would give me away. Surveillance cameras monitored almost every government building I'd ever been in. Some I could see. Many I couldn't. Needless to say, I had to be careful and plan my every move. I didn't know a single person in Arlington, but my plan was to try to recognize someone who either we had worked for in the past or perhaps had given us a briefing or intelligence at some time. If by chance I did see someone that looked familiar, I was going to follow him and find out where the went and, if at all possible, force a contact with him. I needed to start somewhere, and I figured grabbing somebody was as good a beginning as any. The advantage I knew I would have was that the bureaucrats who worked in these underground facilities would be scared shitless to face someone like me. I was counting on the presumption that it wouldn't be all that hard to make one of them talk. There was a small sandwich shop across the street, so I decided to go there, casually have lunch, and watch.

For almost an hour I picked at my meal and watched as people came and went from the building, mostly college-age people and mostly women. I figured they must be a part of the legitimate work that went on there. I'd sat too long and was about to leave when I noticed a small door into the building that was only accessed from a side street and across a lawn. I hadn't caught it before, so I ordered coffee and hung on a while longer. As I sat and took stock, I realized this was the hot spot I'd been looking for. Middle-aged men entered, and I never saw them leave. It was a nice day with plenty of human cover, so I moved out to a small park and sat under a tree reading a book like the rest of the people were doing. I had no idea if there was a school in the area, but I didn't care; I was acting like most everybody else. I stayed until about five o'clock and catalogued everything I could think of in my mind. I didn't want Charleen to start to worry this early in the game, so I called it a day. I found my way back to Interstate 495, got off on 66, then took 28 back to Manassas.

When I got back to Charleen's home, she was waiting for me.

"I thought you might have left or something." She was obviously a bit concerned.

"It took me longer to get back than I had expected. I forgot how bad the traffic can be here," I said, trying to make her feel better. "I hope you don't think I would leave like that. Do you?"

"No, not really. I was just a little worried," she replied. "I have a cellular phone for you. It's one of those flip phones with a Maryland number. I got a couple of extra batteries with it. I hope it's OK."

"This is just perfect. Thanks. How much do I owe you?"

"It's sixty dollars a week plus airtime. If that's too much, I'll try to find you another one tomorrow."

"No, this is just right. Thanks again for helping me," I said as positively as I could. "How was your day?"

"Payroll got all screwed up, but I got it figured out by two o'clock. After that, Linda and I went shopping. How about you?"

"Didn't do much today, just drove around looking at the sights. Thought about going into D.C. and looking around. Maybe you can go with me the next time and show me around."

I knew if I made it a point to go to the same place every day, somebody was going to start to notice my car. I figured that after a while I could get Charleen to take me around to the different places I needed to watch. Then I could mix it up with my rental again when I found who I was looking for.

"I don't have to be at work until eight tomorrow night. How about you and I doing a little sightseeing tomorrow?"

"That would be just great," I said. "I would like to go to the Capitol and drive around there and possibly drive by the Pentagon if we have time."

"We'll have plenty of time for that. I'll be your tour guide; you just tell me where you want to go."

"Charleen, do you know where the Turkey Run Recreation Area is? It's past 123 on the George Washington Memorial Parkway."

"I've never been there, but I sort of know where it is. It's supposed to be a nice, quiet place."

"Yeah, that's what I hear. Maybe we can have a picnic there one afternoon."

The Turkey Run Recreation Area is an area open to the public that happens to be just north of CIA Headquarters. CIA Headquarters is located in a rather remote area west of the George Washington Memorial Parkway in Langley, Virginia. The last time I'd been there, the only signpost I saw that indicated the road leading to CIA Headquarters read: FAIRBANKS HIGHWAY RESEARCH STATION.

I was hoping to find a couple of military buddies that had been "sheep-dipped" and were working for the CIA. *Sheep-dipped* meant they had been discharged from the military, then hired by the CIA or NSA to do intelligence work. The last I heard, one of them had screwed up and was working at the front gate at CIA Headquarters. I hoped I could contact him there, then meet him later.

Unless Charleen knew where the CIA was located, I wasn't going to bring it to her attention. I figured the less she knew, the better. It wouldn't take long before those responsible for Spooky 8's ambush would realize that I hadn't gone home after making it back to the United States. They would know I was probably in the D.C. area, and it wouldn't be long now before people would be getting together to decide how to handle me. My plan was to take her 8mm camcorder and set it up pointing at the CIA parking lot. I'd let it run until the batteries ran down, then check it to see if I could spot a familiar face. I knew it was a long shot, but I didn't have anything to lose.

"I'll take the day off and we can go into D.C. in the morning, take stuff for a picnic that afternoon, and enjoy a little nightlife later."

Charleen had cooked dinner and it was almost done. We spent the rest of the evening enjoying each other's company. I was getting tired, so I headed off to my room.

"By the way, do you mind if I use your camcorder? I saw it in the closet when I was getting your binoculars. I would like to take a few videos to take home with me."

"No, not at all. It's brand-new. I put it in that bag, but I haven't figured out how to use it yet."

"Great. I'll just get it and charge the batteries tonight." I took the camcorder from the closet, gave Charleen a hug, and said good night.

She had a real nice Sony 8mm camcorder with three long-life batteries. All three were dead, so I hooked up the charger and got them charging. She had a couple of new tapes in the bag; one was 90 minutes, and the other was a 120 minute tape. I had never seen a 120-minute tape before, but two hours would be great if I could only get the batteries to last that long.

One battery would last around an hour and a half, but I needed at least three. She had several different kinds of patch cables in the bag, so I decided to use them to wire the batteries in a parallel circuit to get the longest possible run time. With a little luck, I could get the camcorder to record at least three hours and possibly four. My plan was to leave the camcorder in a bush by the CIA Headquarters and then pick it up later.

Daytime Nightmares

At seven o'clock the next day, Charleen greeted me with a big glass of cold orange juice. She woke me from across the room—obviously she'd learned a lesson from my freak-out the day before. Breakfast waited on the kitchen table—eggs over-easy, bacon, and toast. *I could get used to this,* I thought as I sat down at the table. She was wearing an incredibly sexy robe that was split up the side. It was *very* hard to keep my mind on breakfast. Well, the bacon and eggs anyway.

We sat and talked about what we were going to do on our tour around D.C. She had all kinds of suggestions as to where to go, so I let her make the itinerary. I didn't want to spoil her fun by making all of the arrangements. I had specific places I needed to check, but as long as we got to them sometime that day, the rest of the adventure would be hers.

We left the apartment around eight. It was a little cloudy, and it looked as if it might rain before the day was through. Charleen had packed a picnic lunch and put a large blanket in the trunk. I had borrowed a gym bag from her to hold the camcorder, binoculars, and a throwaway camera I had bought at a 7-Eleven. Our first stop was going to be the Vietnam Memorial. I hadn't been there in some time, and I wasn't real thrilled about going there now. There's something about that big black wall that really gets to me. The first time I saw it was with my high school sweetheart, Susan. We had gotten back together after our twenty-year high school reunion. I had been working in D.C. at the time, so she met me for a weekend. Thank God I had someone with me when I lost it and started crying thinking about all of my buddies who had died.

Charleen and I left Manassas heading north on 28, connected with 66, and headed east toward D.C. As we approached 123, I asked Charleen if she minded if we took a little detour to a town called Salona Village. It's a small place between Langley and McLean and just off of Highway 123. It's one of those obscure little places that most Americans don't know exists but where highly classified activities and people could be found. She said it was perfectly all right, so we headed that way.

As we got close to Salona, I tried to remember the location of a building where I had received an intelligence briefing from a member of the remote viewer project. The first time I met a remote viewer, I thought he was whacked-out and had obviously done too many drugs in the sixties. He claimed he could "go" to faraway places and tell me what they looked like, find certain buildings and smaller items like rooms or documents, or examine equipment, just by using his mind. I thought he was a Twilight Zone reject until he started proving he could do these things, regularly.

The small, weathered sign out front read: SRI EXTENSION OFFICE. *SRI* stood for Stanford Research Institute, which for years managed the remote viewer program from California before the government took it over and screwed it up. I didn't say anything to Charleen, but this was a place that I most definitely wanted to watch.

This was one of two buildings that I personally knew black ops were being managed from. I was sure that officially the remote viewer project was dead, but unofficially it was alive and well. This building still had a variety of communication antennae on its roof and at least three floors underground that I knew of. If there was a mole and he did come back to D.C., I was betting this would be a place he might visit. Information is information, and the remote viewer angle was just as good as anything else. Hell, they may have been looking at Charleen and me as we made our way there.

Charleen asked me if I wanted to stop anywhere in Salona. I said I couldn't remember where anything was and apologized for the detour. It was still early, so we had plenty of time to tour D.C. We passed a sign that said we weren't too far from the Turkey Run Recreation Area. It was almost eleven, so Charleen suggested we stop there and have an early lunch.

Charleen had packed a picnic basket in grand style: barbecued ribs, potato salad, and wine. We took our time and ate on paper plates and drank from Dixie cups. After a casual lunch, we decided to go for a walk. As we walked, I thought about Salona and the Becker building. These were the two places I had to concentrate on.

"Are you OK?" she asked, obviously concerned.

"Oh, yeah. I'm just thinking. I need to be getting on with why I'm here. I guess I feel a little guilty about not getting it done. That's OK, though. You and I will enjoy today, and I can get back to my business tomorrow."

The most of the park was closed off, so my plan to get close to CIA Headquarters through the park would have to wait. It was probably a long shot anyway. We drove back into D.C. just about the time the sky opened up and dumped an inch of rain on us. We sat in the car near the Vietnam Memorial for over an hour talking and waiting for the rain to stop. But it didn't look like there was going to be any end to it, so Charleen came up with the idea of going to visit a friend of hers that worked at a hotel close by.

The Hyatt Hotel was across the Key Bridge from Georgetown. It was also across from the Rosslyn Metro Station, which led to downtown D.C. Charleen's friend Beth was the public relations manager for the hotel. Charleen said she had met Beth a couple years ago at a hotel managers' convention. They had become good friends and would every now and then go out together on the town. Charleen said she liked being around Beth because she worked in the heart of D.C. and always had great stories to tell.

The rain poured down as we pulled into the Hyatt. We had the valet park the car and went in and found a seat in Hugo's Sports Run Sports Bar inside the Hotel. I was still a little hungry, so I ordered pasta salad while Charleen went off looking for Beth. We had a place next to the window, so I sat and watched the people running by in the pouring rain. It wasn't long before Charleen returned. And as I stood to greet her friend, I was met with a "flash from the past" that took my breath away.

"David, this is my friend Beth. Beth, this is another good friend, David," Charleen said proudly.

I couldn't believe my eyes. *I know her,* I thought to myself. Beth looked like a woman I had met while staying at a hotel close to the Pentagon the year before. I was in the bar one night when this beautiful woman approached me and asked me to buy her a drink. I did, and we sat for a while and talked. She told me her name was Beth and that she was a manager at one of the hotels in D.C. She was very comfortable to be with, too comfortable. We talked about D.C. and why I was there. I had told her that I was attending a meeting sponsored by the National Red Cross on international disaster relief. Of course the story was total bullshit, but she had no business knowing why I was really there anyway. My story was well rehearsed, and she wasn't able to get any information from me. A few days later I accidentally bumped into her outside the same government building where I was attending my briefings. We met later for dinner, and after I got to know her she told me what she was really doing. I learned she was a test. Her job was to meet and talk to guys like me and try to get them to tell her why they were in D.C. It was one of the many games the government played to make sure people doing business with them weren't talking when they shouldn't be. I knew she wasn't supposed to tell me that, but by the way she was talking, she was tired of the game and was making a career change anyway. I doubted that Charleen knew anything about Beth's other life, so I wasn't going to mention it unless she did.

"It is very nice to meet you, Beth. Please, can you join us?" I asked.

"I'd love to. David, you look like someone I know. Have we ever met before?"

"That's funny. I was just thinking the same thing. You look like a woman I met last year," I said, hoping she would remember.

"Of course. You bought me a drink, and we had a lovely talk. You were doing something with the Red Cross, as I recall."

Damn, what a memory, I thought. I was pretty sure she wasn't in the business anymore, but I still wasn't about to trust her.

"Wow, I'm impressed you remembered. You're right. I was considering getting involved with the Red Cross. I thought I wanted to be part of their disaster relief efforts. It turned out to be more time than I could spare. How about you? What have you been doing?"

"Well, I've just been working here, and I love it. I'm responsible for the public relations for the hotel. I get to meet all the important people who come in, and I also get to travel a lot. I can always find a convention or trade show to go to. That's how I met Charleen."

"Beth and I met at a trade show in Bethesda. We were interested in the same booth and were asking questions of the vendor. After a few minutes, we were talking to each other and forgot all about the poor guy. We decided to hang out together, went to the bar to tease men, then went out on the town and had a really great time. We've been good friends ever since."

"Oh, I get it. You were out teasing men when I met you. Well, it worked," I said, realizing that Charleen didn't know Beth's past career.

"Wow, this is so weird, you two knowing each other. I guess it really is a small world, especially here in Washington," Charleen commented.

Yes, it was weird, me running into Beth. And Charleen and Beth being friends made it too weird. I couldn't help being suspicious. I knew that our intelligence agencies have groomed people from birth to accomplish just one task. And the bullshit chitchat didn't dispel my trepidation.

We talked for more than two hours. Beth would get paged and have to run to a phone, leaving Charleen and me to talk about her. Every time we were alone, I questioned Charleen about Beth. For every question I asked Charleen had a completely believable answer. The best I could tell, they were just friends by chance, not design.

Around three in the afternoon the rain finally stopped. We had taken up far too much of Beth's time, and Charleen was anxious to continue our tour of D.C.

We spent the rest of the day walking around D.C. I surprised myself by not crying at the Vietnam Memorial this time. In fact, as I looked at the memorial I thought about how many of those names were of men who died not in battle but doing our government's dirty deeds, delivering packages to the enemy or assassinating officials of a bordering country. Instead of feeling guilty for being alive, I felt sorry for those that weren't. I wondered who else was out there in the same fix as I was, trying desperately to stay alive because of something they had done in the name of freedom and the American way.

On the way back to Charleen's apartment, I asked her to stop by a Budget car rental place. I told her I had to check on something about my car and it would only take a minute. The Budget place was about ten minutes from her apartment. We pulled in, and I had her wait in the car while I checked inside.

What I wanted to do was rent a car just like the one I already had. I was going to use the car as a plant car to put the camcorder in and leave in a parking lot. Each day I could go and switch cars without Charleen noticing the difference. I didn't think she would pay any attention to the license plate. The young man behind the counter didn't look old enough to drive, let alone rent me a car. I asked him if he had a 1991 blue four-door Ford Taurus available. He checked and said he didn't, but he had a white one.

I told him that I was going to leave the car at my office and I needed it to be a blue Taurus because my business partner, who was getting the car there, was expecting a blue one. I told the guy that I couldn't get ahold of my partner, so I couldn't tell him the car was going to be white. He said the closest one was in Falls Church. I said that would be perfect and to have them hold it for me. I had to put the car on my credit card, but I made sure they wouldn't charge against it until I returned the car. I said I would only need it for a week, signed the papers, got directions to the Falls Church address, and left.

When I got back to Charleen, I said everything was fine and we headed back to her place. Neither one of us was hungry, so we sat outside on her back porch until about ten; then I turned in. Charleen had to work the late shift, so she stayed up and watched TV. I told her I would probably be gone by the time she got up and that I would see her when she got home. I told her to wake me up if I was asleep.

My plan was to have the camcorder set up in the gym bag I borrowed from Charleen. I would set the bag on the rear deck of the Taurus and record the activities at the SRI building in Salona for as long as possible. I was going to buy another 8mm camcorder and set it up just like Charleen's so that all I would have to do would be drive up, park the car, and leave. When I returned, I would get into the other car and take it home to view the tape. If everything went as planned, nobody, including Charleen, would be the wiser.

I was up by six the next morning. I made a couple of test recordings to make sure the camera was working properly and would record through the small hole I had made in Charleen's bag. Everything worked perfectly. I wanted to be parked on the street next to the SRI building no later than seven. I wanted to tape the people going in and out in hopes of spotting someone I knew. If that happened, I would come back, wait, follow him, and try to get him alone. Once I had him, I was committed, and I was going to do whatever necessary to get answers.

I got to Salona Village about ten after seven. I got lucky and parked my car about twenty yards from the front door. I made sure the camera was working and pointed at the building, got out, locked the door, and walked off in a different direction as if I were going to work. Actually, I went looking for a taxi to take me to Falls Church to pick up the other car. As luck and planning would have it, there were plenty of taxis around at that time in the morning bringing people to work. I waved one down and had him take me to the address I had for the Budget car rental place. As we were going, I asked him if he knew a place where I could buy an 8mm camcorder, cheap. He said he knew of a pawnshop not too far from here and would go by and see if they were open. The pawnshop was still closed and wouldn't open until 9 o'clock. I wrote down the address so I would remember how to get back; then we headed for Falls Church.

The blue '91 Ford Taurus was waiting just as promised. One problem: it was a two-door. It was the only one they had, so I had no choice but to take it. By the time I got back to the pawnshop, it had opened. I told the owner what I wanted, but he didn't have one in stock. I asked him if he knew anyplace that did, and he said he would check a few of his friends' places for me. He found one in Vienna.

The Vienna pawnshop had everything from TVs and VCRs to camo fatigues and MREs. It was kind of a military surplus/pawnshop kind of a place. The storekeep had a Sony 8mm camcorder that looked to be in good condition, so I bought it. He also had spare batteries and tapes, so I bought what I needed and headed to a sporting goods store to find a bag like the one I had borrowed from Charleen. One thing about this area: if you drive around long enough, you'll find about anything you need. And I did. The bag was an exact match, and I was on my way. I had to stop at a Radio Shack to get some wire and things to modify the batteries to get the record time I needed; then I was headed to Arlington, to the Becker Research Institute to watch its activities.

I found a place where I could see the door I had spotted earlier. As I sat there, I tried to modify my camcorder batteries and watch the building at the same time. I didn't want anybody to see me working on the batteries. It would be real easy for someone to mistake what I was doing for making a bomb. That's all I need, a bunch of local SWAT guys surrounding my car and getting me out at gunpoint. That would be real good for my cover. I put a newspaper against the steering wheel, rolled down the windows so I could hear anybody walking nearby, and went about my business.

It didn't take long to wire the batteries together. I had to charge the batteries before I could use them, so I decided to put my project in the trunk and head over to the little café for lunch. As I closed the trunk, I notice a man entering the back of the Becker building.

For an instant I thought I knew him. I only caught a glance, but I was sure it was Bates. It was exactly the man I wanted to see, the son of a bitch that sent us on the mission.

God, could this be true? Was that who I thought it was? Could I be that lucky?

I had to go sit in my car and try to regroup. My first instinct was to crash through the door, chase him down, put a gun in his mouth, and find out what the hell was going on. But I knew that was a real bad idea. I had to collect myself and get back to basics. If it was Bates, I could be in some real bad shit before I could get out of D.C. If he saw me, I knew it would be only a matter of hours before they tracked me down and killed me. I had to get away from plain sight immediately.

I drove off and found a spot concealed from the building a couple of blocks away, in a parking lot of an apartment complex. *With my luck he lives here and will walk right past me,* I thought. My vantage point was just about perfect. I could see the side of the building where, if he came out the same door he went in, I would be able to see him come to the street.

There was a neighborhood store across from the apartment building with a pay phone outside. I put my baseball cap on and ran across the street to look in the yellow pages. I was looking for a costume shop or possibly a beauty salon that had men's wigs and stuff. As I looked through the phone book, though, I became more and more paranoid about being seen. I quickly got tired of fumbling with the damn phone book on a chain, so I ripped it off the wall and took it back to the car. I kept watching the store to see if anybody saw me. The girl behind the counter looked like she was talking on the phone and didn't see a thing.

I found a costume shop and called it. I asked them if they had a makeup kit for men. The girl said I should try a theatrical supply store and gave me the number. I called and talked to a young woman who told me she had just what I was looking for. It was a kit for men that had stick-on mustaches and beards, eyebrows, and even different dyes for hair. She was about ten minutes away, so I told her I would be right over.

The lady at the store was real nice. I was hoping she wouldn't notice how wired I was. My senses were on the highest alert now, and I knew I must have looked like someone stoned on speed. She showed me the kit and even helped me with a mustache. There were several different sizes, shapes, and colors in the kit. She found one that was close to my hair color, then showed me how to glue it on and take it off.

I had used them before, but I didn't want to draw any special attention, so I let her show me. I told her I was going to use it for a fantasy with my girlfriend. She thought that was very cool and asked if I would come back and tell her how it went. I said of course I would, paid in cash, and left with the mustache in place.

With a thick mustache, cheap wig, dark glasses, baseball cap, and long-sleeve sweatshirt, I was pretty sure nobody would recognize me too quickly. I wasn't planning to get that close to anyone. Not yet, anyway. Looking like Groucho Marx crossed with a sick Fabio, I couldn't help smile. Whatever works, though. I returned to the Becker building and waited.

I sat in the parking lot of the apartment building until after seven, but there was no sign of Bates. My eyes were starting to have a hard time focusing, and the rain had started again. Maybe I'd imagined the whole thing. I set up the cameras there in the apartment parking lot and left.

Charleen was already at work by the time I got back. The house was dark, but I could smell her perfume, and I wished she were there to talk to. I wasn't hungry, so I went into my bedroom and lay down. She had left me a note on my pillow.

David,
Beth called and wanted to talk to you. She asked if you could call her when you got in. Her number is 703-525-1234. Hope you had a great day; talk to you when I get in.
Charleen

As I looked at the note, I felt like a condemned man about to have his last meal. *What on earth could Beth want to talk to me about?* I thought. *Is she calling to tell me I'm through, the bad guys are outside my door, and I might as well just give up now or what?*

I sat on the bed and stared at the note. I didn't know what would be the best road to take. I could pack up now and head for home. I could change my identity and disappear. I thought for a minute, then took a deep breath. Fuck it, I'm here, and I'm not leaving until I get some answers or die trying. I walked to the kitchen and dialed Beth's number.

"Good evening, Hyatt Arlington. How may I help you?" came the cheerful voice over the phone.

"Good evening. This is Dr. Mitchell Brooks. We are having a meeting there next month, and I was trying to reach Beth Williams. I had a couple of questions I needed to ask her; is she still in?" I asked, sounding as professional as I could.

"Yes, sir. Let me ring her office. Please hold."

My heart pounded as I waited for Beth. This was either a legitimate call or a way to make sure I was here before the final curtain fell on my last mission. I noticed the sweat glistening on the back of my hand as I gripped the phone.

"Good evening; this is Beth Williams. May I help you?"

"Hi, Beth, David Chance. I had a note to call."

"Hi, David. Are you at our friend's house?" she asked.

"No, I'm not. What's up?"

"I need to call you back. Give me a couple of minutes, and I'll call you right back. Can I get your number?"

"Give me ten minutes and I'll be at Charleen's," I said.

"Thanks, Chance. I'll call you back there in ten minutes."

Chance! Shit, this was it, I realized. Charleen never knew I went by "Chance"; how would Beth? I ran to the front window to see who was coming, then remembered Charleen kept a .380 pistol in her nightstand by her bed. I ran to her bedroom and took out the Beretta. It was a great little gun and in almost new condition. I pulled the magazine and checked it. It had eleven hollow point rounds and one in the chamber. I wanted to make sure the pistol worked, so I ran back to my bedroom, took out a folded pair of socks from my drawer, and held them over the muzzle. I lifted the sheets from the end of the bed and buried the muzzle as deep into the mattress as I could. *Blam,* it went off as I pulled the trigger. The sock absorbed the muzzle blast, so all Charleen could see would be a small hole in her mattress. It was small enough that I doubted she would even notice. I figured I was going to make a last stand in Charleen's apartment. Whoever came through the door was going to take a bullet. I took one bullet from the magazine and put it in my pocket. I wasn't going to be taken alive.

I went to the kitchen and sat on the floor with my back against the wall so I had a clear shot of the front of the apartment. There was an occupied apartment behind me, so I figured whoever it was wouldn't get too crazy with a shoot-out. As I sat there, I tried to listen for the phone in the apartment behind me. If the phone started to ring and nobody answered, that would tell whoever was calling there was no one there to get hit by a stray bullet. This could get real bad, real fast. I kept the room as normal-looking as possible, only moving one chair so it wouldn't be in my way when I moved after my first volley of fire.

I waited, sweat running down my forehead, weapon trained at the front door. *Rrriiinnnggg,* went the kitchen phone.

Shit! I said to myself. The phone scared the crap out of me. I had to take a moment before I could answer.

"Hello."

"Hi, David; this is Beth. Sorry it took so long to get back to you," she said in a very pleasant voice. "I had to move to my private phone. The one I answered was part of the house phones, and they're sometimes recorded. So, how was your day?" she asked.

I had to sit for a moment and calm down. My paranoia had almost gotten to the point of a terrible disaster. My shirt was soaked in sweat, and my killer instinct was ready to explode.

"Ah, fine. Drove around doing a little sightseeing. How about you?"

"Work as usual. David, the reason I called is, well, I want to talk with you, you know, about when we first met. I think I have some things I need to explain."

"I don't think I know what you're talking about, Beth. We met in a bar and had a few drinks. You explained what you were trying to do over dinner, and that was that."

"Not really, David. I need to tell you a few things more. Can I come over?"

Beth sounded quite serious. At this point, I didn't have anything to lose. If she was working for them, she was going to see what I was up to or try to find out what I knew. If she was the one going to kill me, this would be the time.

"Sure, Beth. Charleen won't be home until around two."

"Great. Charleen doesn't need to know what is going on, OK?"

"No problem. If she calls, should I tell her you're coming over?"

"No. It'll be like I just stopped by. Thanks; I really appreciate you listening to me. I'll be over about nine."

I didn't know what was going on, but I steadied myself and worked as if I were in control. No matter what Beth's plan was, I felt sure I could deal with it.

Charleen called shortly after I got off with Beth and said she might be a little late and wasn't going to be home until after 2:30 A.M. I said that was fine and I was probably going to go to bed early anyway. She said she would let me sleep and talk to me in the morning. I put the room back in order and made sure Charleen's nightstand drawer was like it had been, except for Charleen's pistol, which I kept under a couch cushion, just in case.

About nine-thirty, Beth showed up. I could tell she had gone home and changed her clothes after work. She wore shorts, a T-shirt, and a zip-up sweatshirt. She carried a small handbag, and by the way her clothes fit, I was pretty sure she wasn't wired or packing. I still didn't trust her, so I turned on the radio in the kitchen and in both bedrooms.

I wanted to fill the air with as much background noise as possible. I found a radio talk show and tuned all three radios to it. The more conversation, the harder it would be to filter it out.

She wasn't smiling as she entered the living room. Once inside, she suddenly turned and started to open her handbag.

Unexpected Angel

Pulling out a glass case, she put her glasses back in her handbag and said, "Hi, David. Thanks again for letting me come over."

"Hi, Beth. You sounded like this is important. Let's go over to the couch, and you can tell me what this is all about."

I made sure she sat at the end opposite the gun cushion.

"David, I've got something that has been bothering me since I saw you the other day. I have to level with you. When we met last year, it wasn't by accident. I was supposed to meet you in that bar. I told you my job was to talk to anybody that looked important and get them to tell me all about themselves and their work. That was only part of the truth. I was there for you specifically that night. My job was to seduce you and get you to tell me about the briefings you were attending."

I almost lost it. It all became clear. I'd been look at as a potential problem long before Easy Breather in Columbia. I had been told years ago that security was critical to black operations and that our loyalties would be tested. Tested at any time in any way. I had kept up my end, but in the end it meant nothing. I held it together and just stared at Beth, waiting for her to continue.

"Please, David, try not to be mad at me. It was my job. I didn't know anything about you other than your name was David Chance and you often went by 'Chance', you worked on classified government projects, and you had a security clearance. My job was to make sure you were qualified to keep your security clearance; that's all."

Sounded believable, but I couldn't help feeling there was something more to her story.

"OK, you lied to me about your job. I understand that completely. But since you're being so honest, why in the hell are you really here? I don't believe that is all you wanted to tell me."

"You're right. There is something else. I later found out other things about you, things you should know. When Charleen told me about you, I didn't put it together, not until I saw you. David, you are going to be set up. I was told your team was going to be killed."

"What the fuck do you mean, my team was supposed to be dead?"

I grabbed the gun from under the cushion and put it to her throat. Beth was so shocked she couldn't say anything.

"Time's up, Beth. You'd better start talking or I'm going to end it, right now."

"Please, David. I'm on your side. I don't work for the government anymore. You've got to believe me."

I didn't have much choice at this point. If she had set me up, I would be dead now, so maybe she was on the up and up. I lowered the gun and sat back on the couch.

"I'm sorry, Beth. You're right; my team *should* be dead. You need to tell how you knew."

Beth relaxed some and took a deep breath. "A few months after I met you, I was doing the same thing to another guy, a sailor, no, a navy SEAL; I found him at the bar getting drunk and loud. I sat down and got him to buy me a few drinks, and we talked. He started telling me about his experiences in Vietnam and the things he had done since then. He was really pissed off by the way he was treated by the government. He was in D.C. trying to get someone to listen to him about what the government had been doing secretly over the last twenty years. So, I helped him back to his room and told him he could tell me about it; I would listen. He told me about going into Cambodia and Laos and doing all kinds of crazy things." Beth sounded almost in tears.

"It's OK, Beth. I understand you're upset. Please, try to remember all the things he told you."

"It was the things he did after the war that got to me. He said he and his team did a lot of tying up of loose ends. He said they went after people that could hurt our country and got rid of them: drug dealers, traitors, spies, and things. But he couldn't stand it anymore when he found out that Americans were being killed. Not bad men, but just because they were loose ends to some intelligence agency. He told me that some members of his unit had disappeared and he wasn't going to disappear like them. He said he talked to some friends of his in the government that gave him all kinds of stuff, pictures, names, and information about people, Americans that our own government had killed.

"Your team came up, David. He said Spooky 8. He said since the early eighties he had known about your team and of what you did after Vietnam."

My mind was trying to stay clear, but a fog of rage was starting to roll in. I had to fight it and the panic that threatened to overtake me and make me say or do something rash. I still didn't know what she was after or if this song and dance was a setup in some way.

"Tell me what he said about Spooky 8."

"He said he thought you guys were probably dead by now. He said he was told you had turned into a traitor and that you were training terrorists. He was supposed to track you down and get rid of you, but he refused. He knew you were just like him, a team doing the government's dirty work. He wasn't going to kill any more Americans that were caught up in the government's bullshit. He said he hid out for a while until he found some people that would help him."

The questions came pouring out: "Have you seen him since? Can you get in touch with him?" This was a man I had to meet, or at least I had to find out what he knew. I had to trust my instincts now, and in my gut I felt Beth was telling me the truth.

"I see him every now and then. He comes to the bar at my hotel every few weeks," she said.

"Do you know his name?"

Beth dug through her bag, pulling out a small address book. "Yes, here it is. Stacey, Kevin Stacey. All I have is a phone number."

"Do you think he would meet if you called him?"

"I guess so, but I've never called him before."

"That's OK. Would you give it a try?"

"I can try. He has become real weird lately, very paranoid, but I think he would meet me."

We had talked for hours, and Charleen was going to be home soon. I told Beth I would be home tomorrow, after nine. I wanted to retrieve the car I had left in Salona and set it up to watch the Becker building. Beth said she would call me between nine and ten in the morning to let me know if she had gotten ahold of Kevin.

As soon as Beth left, I took the Beretta, put the one bullet back into the magazine, and put it back in Charleen's drawer. A hot shower and a cold Corona would be the perfect end to a not-so-perfect day. It actually took a couple of beers to calm me down to the point where I could sleep. I glanced at the alarm clock on the nightstand as I turned out the light; it read 2:27 A.M.

As I lay there, I thought about Charleen and hoped she would get home soon. I was in a mood to see how far our nightly talking could go, but before I knew it, I was asleep.

I awoke the next day to the sound of Charleen taking a shower. That was odd, I thought. She wasn't in her bedroom shower; she was in the one next to mine. I lay there with my eyes closed just listening to her. She turned the water off, and I could hear her drying off. I was wide awake now, fantasizing about her coming into my room, still wet from her shower, and climbing into bed with me.

I hadn't completed my fantasy when I was startled by the sound of Charleen's robe dropping to the floor and the sheet being slid back as she climbed in bed next to my naked body. She was still warm from her shower and not completely dried off. She didn't say anything, just snuggled up real close and lay there.

I didn't say anything to her, just wrapped my arms around her and enjoyed her body next to mine. I could feel the water from her shower still on her body as my fingers slowly traced her spine to the small of her back. She slowly opened her eyes and smiled as she said good morning. I smiled back, then gave her a long, tender kiss.

I'm sure she knew my intentions weren't all that honorable, since I was as hard as a rock. She grinned as she pressed her hips against me and asked if I was having a private party or was glad to see her. I told her I was real glad to see her and kissed her again, slowly, this time, and deeply.

The feel of a woman's body next to mine was something I hadn't experienced in a long time. I closed my eyes, not really thinking about who it was, just savoring the moment. The slow kissing and caressing quickly turned to serious foreplay as I let Charleen take me to another place, another reality. Holding me, touching me, kissing me, devouring me.

Slowly the lovemaking turned to play. We found ourselves laughing uncontrollably as we fell to the floor. Feet and butts in the air, we laughed until we cried. We played on the floor like a couple of kids until we were both covered in sweat. I sat there looking at her body shining with the perspiration of our playing. I stroked her skin as she sat motionless, watching my hand circle her breasts.

The play soon turned to passionate, hard sex. We released all our anxiety, and it wasn't gentle or slow; it was truly primal.

We finally fell apart, exhausted. When our breathing slowed, we held each other in a long and comforting embrace. Before long we started to feel cold, so we took a hot shower together.

Charleen finished showering before me. She dried off, put her robe back on, and went into the kitchen while I shaved. I could smell breakfast being cooked as I got dressed. The clock read 8:45, which startled me at first. I knew Beth was going to be calling, and I wasn't sure how I was going to handle it if Charleen was still here.

Sure enough, Beth called just as I was sitting down to eat. Charleen answered the phone as I tried to pretend I didn't know who it was.

"Well, good morning, Beth. What's going on?" Charleen asked as she winked at me and smiled. "Yeah, he's right here; hang on," she added, handing me the phone.

"Good morning, Beth," I said, trying to swallow my food.

"Did you tell Charleen I came by last night?" Beth asked.

"No, I just got up," I replied, hoping she could follow what I was really saying.

"Good. I talked to Kevin, and he said he would meet me for lunch."

"Great. What time tonight are we having dinner?" I replied.

"He'll be in the restaurant's sports bar at my Hyatt at eleven-thirty this morning. I told him to wait for me and I'll meet him before noon."

"Hang on; I'll ask Charleen."

I was glad to see that my ability to carry on a bullshit conversation with someone standing there watching me was still up to par. Beth was smart. She read between the lines as I made up this crap.

"Beth wants to know if seven will be all right for dinner tonight."

"Yeah, that's perfect. I have to be at work in half an hour, but I'll be through by five," Charleen said as she noticed the time and ran to get ready.

"That's just fine, Beth; we'll be there right on time. Thanks for calling, and I guess we'll see you later," I told her.

"I'll be in my office. When you get to the hotel, call me and I'll point him out. Be careful, David; this guy's no fool."

"Great. See you tonight." I hung up the phone.

Charleen was headed out the door, so I had just enough time to get to Salona Village, switch cars, and get over to the Hyatt. Everything was coming together just as I hoped.

The trip to Salona was quicker than the day before. I wanted to get the car to the Becker building, but I didn't have time to do it right then. I parked my car with fresh batteries in the camcorder, set it up, and locked the door. I walked the half-block to the other Taurus and checked it for tickets or other police markings. Apparently, nobody had paid any attention to it being parked overnight. I got in and sat for a minute before I started the car. *What if somebody knew I left the car there?* I thought. Was the car going to explode when I turned the key?

"Screw it," I said, and turned the ignition. The Ford snapped to life. I was in such a hurry, I didn't even take the gym bag from the rear deck as I pulled out onto the main road back to the highway. I headed for the Hyatt as fast as traffic would allow. I didn't want to be late for the meeting with Mr. Stacey, or whatever his name was. I knew it was going to be close, but if I did it right, I would have time before the meeting to check out the café and make sure it wasn't a setup.

I had taken Charleen's Beretta from her nightstand just in case thing didn't go as planned. For all I knew, Stacey could still be on his ops and I was just another assignment. If that was the case, I was going to bring a world of shit into Beth's hotel as I put a bullet in Mr. Stacey.

All the way there, all I could think about was getting answers. For some reason, I didn't have a bad feeling about this meeting. I was cautious but anxious. I was hoping I wasn't letting the desire of getting answers cloud my judgment.

By the time I reached the Hyatt, Beth was almost in a panic.

"I'm sorry, Beth; I had to park and walk here. Is he still here?" I said to her over the house phone.

"Yeah, he's here. He's sitting in the back next to the planter in the corner by the kitchen. He's had a few drinks and seems a little nervous. I told him I had to go to my office for a minute, but that was over twenty minutes ago."

"Good. At least he's still here. What's he wearing?"

"He's wearing blue jeans and a dark green windbreaker. He has a briefcase on the floor next to his left leg."

"Thanks, Beth; you did great. Is there an exit through the kitchen?"

"Yes. Go through the kitchen, turn left, and down the hall. You'll see the sign. It's funny; Kevin asked me the same thing."

"Anything else you can tell me about him?"

"He's got a gun. I saw it under his jacket when he sat down. Be careful," she said nervously.

"Everything's going to be fine. I'll talk to you shortly."

I had the fake mustache in my pocket, so I put it and my sunglasses and baseball cap on before I left.

The little warning alarms were going off in my head. Not loud, but loud enough. I decided to make a little diversion before I got to him. The table next to him was empty, so I called Beth and had her get him to the house phone for a moment. It worked. The hostess went around asking for Kevin Stacey. He didn't respond at first but then gave in and signaled to her. She told him that Beth needed to talk to him on the phone, and he got up with his briefcase. As he did, I walked past him, bumping him slightly, and sat at the table next to him. If he was watching at all, he would become very concerned if when he returned he saw someone new sitting at the table next to him. But I knew if he noticed me as we passed it would help things look normal.

I sat down and was reading the menu when he returned. He seemed anxious and started looking at his watch. I gave him about five minutes before I got up and went over to him.

"Excuse me, but are you Kevin Stacey?" I asked.

"Who wants to know?" he replied with an obvious distrust. "No. You're mistaken."

"No, Stacey," I said. "I'm not mistaken."

"Who are you? What the fuck's going on?" he asked as he started to tense up.

I pulled the Beretta from my waist and shoved it in his side.

"Look, Stacey, or whatever your name is; I know you're packin'. If you even think about it, you're a dead man. I don't have anything to lose right now. I'm one of those men the government's trying to dispose of, one of those loose ends. You are about the only thing I got going right now, so let's don't make this any harder than it already is. Agreed?"

He sat there a minute, frozen, not even breathing. He knew I meant every word I was saying. Like me, I could tell he had a talent for looking into a person's soul. And I could tell he could see a man pushed to the limit. A man that didn't have anything to lose and was willing to go the distance to get answers. Even if that meant putting a bullet through his chest.

"I don't know what the fuck you're talking about," he said as he stared.

"Here's the deal," I told him. "I think we need each other. I'm going to put my gun away. The next move is yours. You can accept that, put a bullet in me, or walk away. It's your call."

I watched his eyes and his constricted pupils starting to open. I knew he was controlling his adrenaline rush, backing down. I slowly withdrew the gun and put it back in my waistband. I made sure he saw me put it away and that it wasn't a trick. I then slowly pulled the mustache from my face and laid it on the table. It took a few moments, but the expression on his face changed completely.

"You're supposed to be dead."

"Don't believe everything you hear," was all I said.

Shark in SEAL's Clothing

I watched as the tension in Stacey's face drained and his breathing slowed. He stared at the glass of water in front of him. When he reached for it, I saw that his hand was shaking a little.

I waited a few moments before speaking.

"Look; I think we're in the same boat. You're right. I should be dead. I got lucky. They tried to get rid of Spooky 8 a few weeks ago, but we made it back. Kevin, I need your help. I'm not going to disappear without a trace. The lives of the men of Spooky 8 depend on what I do here in D.C. I think you might have information I need to keep us alive. Beth told me a little about your story. You know what's going on. You've been there. You're one of us."

He didn't say anything. His hand had stopped shaking, but an intensity that I hadn't seen before entered his eyes.

"Yeah, I'm one," he said. I could hear the anger in his words. And I could feel his rage building.

"It was in the eighties. I'd hurt my ankle on a training jump so I took a couple weeks off. They got a guy that used to be with SEAL Team 6 to fill in. While I was away, the team was sent on a mission to Central America; one of those 'easy breathers,' they said. They didn't come back, none of them. They got 'em. They got 'em all. When I reported back, they about shit. They didn't know I had taken some time off. My team was all former SEALs, mostly snipers. We were assigned to do black ops, just like you. Those civilian bastards. Those fucking civilian bastards."

I knew what he was going through. Losing your friends, your brothers, and a part of your soul. It's like losing your core being. Even after several years, his pain was still intense.

He took his briefcase from the floor and placed it on the table. He looked at me for a moment before he unlocked and opened it.

"What do you want from me?" he asked.

"I don't know what I can do for you, but I think you can help me. Beth said you had information about me, about Spooky 8."

"Yeah, I do. It goes back a long way, back to Vietnam. You and others."

"Tell me about it," I said a little too eagerly.

"Do you remember Operation Dragon Flower?" he asked.

Dragon Flower. Shit, I thought. *I knew that mission was the start of this bullshit.* Having Stacey mention that mission made me sick to my stomach. That was a secret mission that was never declassified. If he had information about it, that meant there had been some old skeletons dug up by someone.

"Yeah, I remember. That's when I first started doing this fuckin' shit."

"Well, a member of your team started long before that. A guy that went by the nickname Lucky. He was doing black ops in the sixties."

Stacey looked to be about Lucky's age, and I knew Lucky had done two tours in Vietnam before I met him. Lucky had told me he was involved in secret operations in Vietnam.

"Talk to me. Tell me about Lucky. Tell me about Spooky 8," I said, trying to let Stacey know he was with a friend, someone that cared.

"Lucky started in the early sixties. He was part of a Special Forces unit that was involved in covert operations in Laos and Cambodia. After his second tour, he got out of the game and was attached to a regular team. Then you came along. You guys were groomed for black ops. From the beginning, even in jump school at Fort Benning. You were groomed, and I don't think you even knew it. Lucky was put on your team to see if you guys were going to work out."

"How do you know all this?"

"In 1975, I volunteered for a mission. I was to track down and kill a member of the Cambodian military who was a key player in the drug trade coming out of the Golden Triangle. His name was Colonel Laung Khuan. I tried to take him out in '71, but all I was able to do was shoot off part of his ear. I really wanted this mission. I wanted to finish what I started four years before."

"The ear!" The memory of that first meeting with Khuan bloomed in my mind. I had wondered how his ear had been mangled.

Stacey continued. "I didn't know anything about you until I started reading his file. His code name was Dragon Flower. In the file was a short history lesson on your team. I read about your mission, Hope and Glory. Shit, they were setting you up even then. Hope and Glory was all part of Operation Dragon Flower. What did they tell you about Hope and Glory?" he asked.

"They said we were delivering humanitarian supplies. But I knew we were supplying guerrilla troops in the area."

"Bullshit, that was all bullshit. Remember those packages you delivered to Khuan just before that, you know, on operation Dragon Flower?" Stacey asked angrily.

"Yeah, they said it was money for information about POWs," I answered.

"Drugs, man, that was drugs. You delivered a sample of the drugs our government stole from the communists in the Golden Triangle and were trying to sell back. Shit, you delivered two hundred pounds of pure heroin to that son of a bitch."

Suddenly it became perfectly clear. Back then I knew something wasn't right, but I was a soldier. I wasn't paid to think. I knew it wasn't money. I had my suspicions, but I didn't want to believe I was doing something wrong.

"All that shit you and Lucky were watching, that was drugs. Nothing but drugs. Our fuckin' Special Ops guys were selling drugs to finance their little war. Shit, man, they were getting rich while Americans were dying."

The whole picture, my career, everything, was beginning to make more sense. We had been part of a huge drug deal in which members of the U.S. intelligence community were the dealers. The very thing I despised I had become, a drug dealer, a mule. It didn't matter that we didn't know what was going on. It didn't matter that we were just following orders. It didn't matter to them. It did to me.

"Can you prove this?" I asked. "What you're saying could turn our government upside down. It could make the Iran-Contra thing look like a sideshow," I said.

"Sideshow. Iran-Contra was a major player," Kevin said. "They used the Iran-Contra thing as an excuse for a lot of their drug smuggling operations."

Kevin turned his briefcase so I could see inside. A file about an inch thick lay on top. Across the top, a label read: DRAGON FLOWER. Stamped on the side in big letters was the word SECRET over a Department of Defense emblem. The file was on top of several more files, all with different names: Black Water, Thunderhead, Urgent Fury, Pokeweed, even files as current as that of Operation Just Cause. I thought how this old, brown, beat-up briefcase held the lives and political careers of hundreds.

"Jesus Christ. You're carrying that around with you?" I said in total amazement.

"Yeah. I can't trust anybody with it. Don't worry; if somebody tries to open it, it blows," he said, almost sounding like he wished someone would try.

"Can I read the file on Dragon Flower?"

"Not here, not now. Too public."

"Are you staying nearby?" I asked.

I was hoping he might entertain the idea of staying at the Hyatt. I wanted to have some control over his movements just in case he wanted to play hardball with his information. I had already checked with Beth about a pair of connecting rooms. She had them on hold until she heard from me.

"No. I live a few hours from here," Kevin replied.

"If I can get you a room, would you stay here for a couple of days? I'll pay for it," I said with a purposeful sense of anxiety.

"No, that's OK. I'll find a place. By the way, where is Beth? Is she in on this?"

"It was all my idea," I said. "She doesn't know anything about this. She mentioned you because she thought we used to do the same kind of work and we might know each other."

"How do you know Beth?" Kevin asked.

"I don't really. She's a friend of a friend of mine. I met her at dinner last night. Look; I've got to go. When you find a place, call me. I'll meet you here or anywhere you like."

I gave him my cellular phone number. I didn't want him calling Charleen and finding out where she lived.

"No problem," he said. "I'll get a place and call you tomorrow."

I got up from the table and walked to the lobby to call Beth. I stopped for a moment and watched Kevin through the window as he sat and read the menu. I wanted to see if he was going to split or possibly make a phone call. He didn't do either, just sat and waited.

Beth was in her office when I called. She had a few minutes between appointments, so she asked me to come to her office to talk. I hadn't asked her if she would do any big favors for me, but by the way she had been talking the day before, I was betting she would. I told her I would be there in a few minutes, then hung up the house phone.

Beth was just getting off the phone when I entered. I could see she was anxious to hear how our meeting went.

"So, how did it go?" she asked.

"Fine. I think he'll be able to help me. He has quite a story to tell, and he's got a bunch of stuff to back it up. I asked him if I could get him a room here, but he said no. He looks like he's going to have lunch. Beth, would you do something for me?" I asked.

"Sure, David. Name it."

"Go have lunch with him. I told him you didn't know anything about this, other than what you told me about him and me having possibly worked together. Convince him to stay here tonight. If he won't, take him somewhere, get him a room, and then call me and let me know where he is. Do you still have the rooms?"

"Yeah, just like you asked. Two connecting rooms, third floor, in the back by the stairs. Numbers 305 and 307. Number 307 is closest to the stairs. I have the rooms in my name, but I'll change them to yours if you want."

"If you don't mind, keep them as they are. Tell Kevin you will put a room in your name so he can't be traced. He'll like that," I said. "Would you do one more thing for me?"

"Sure," Beth replied.

"Get him to take you out to dinner tonight."

"No problem. He kind of likes me anyway. Nothing to get serious about, but he does have some stories to tell."

"Thanks, I owe you, big-time."

"No, you really don't. This is the least I can do for you," she said.

As I was leaving, I watched as Beth went in and sat down with Stacey. I was sure Beth could convince Kevin to stay at the Hyatt. If she couldn't, I knew she would call.

It was almost two in the afternoon, and I needed to get my rental car and camera over to the Becker Research Institute. I still had to find out who went into that building. When I returned to my car, I saw I'd gotten a parking ticket. *Great,* I thought. *That's all I need is to let the police know I'm here.*

I grabbed the gym bag, which had fallen on the floor, and put it in the front seat with me. I didn't want to forget it and have Charleen find it. I left the Hyatt and headed back to Charleen's. She wasn't home, but the note she had left told me she had talked to Beth and would see me when she returned around four-thirty.

My funds were running low, and I knew this mission could only last a few more days. I wanted to move the car from Salona to Arlington to watch the Becker building. I hadn't started the camera yet, so all I needed to do was get the car in place. I was hoping Charleen would be home so she could take me to Salona, but a taxi would have to do.

The taxi was going to take about ten minutes to get to the apartment, so I took the gym bag out of my car and shoved it under the bed. I figured I would check the tape and charge the batteries later.

I had the taxi drop me a few blocks from the Taurus in front of an office complex in downtown Salona. As I walked to the car, I started thinking about Bates going into the Becker Institute. I was hoping I would get lucky and see him again. If I didn't, I hoped the information that Kevin had would tell me if there was a mole in Spooky 8. That's all I could think about as I drove back to Arlington.

Finding a place to park to watch the Becker building was going to be more difficult than I planned. This was a busy place, and parking spaces were at a premium. I drove around for over half an hour before finding a place close to the café I went to on the first day. It wasn't as good as I had hoped, but at least I could see the front of the building. With camera in place and recording, I locked the car and found another taxi to take me back to Charleen's.

Time was getting short, and I still hadn't been able to watch any of the tapes. Stacey was my most solid lead, so I knew I would have to put off watching them. I also wanted to contact some people I knew who were actively engaged in politics.

Through a party with friends that lived here, I had met a couple of clerks who worked in the Hart Senate Building. It had been a couple of years, and I was hoping they would remember me enough to go and have lunch. They were desperately trying to be players in Washington, and I wanted to see if they had reached a position to hear anything of substance.

If Washington, D.C., were a ship, it would have sunk years ago from all the leaks from its lower-level employees. At the party where I met these clerks, all they could do was talk about the people they worked for and the unpublished affairs they were involved in.

I was also acquainted with Congressman Jared Tucker, who had been a member of a government oversight committee in the eighties. His committee had questioned a few of us civilian types about operations in South America a few years before. Of course I played dumb, saying I had no knowledge of what he was talking about. I didn't have to spend much time before their committee. Later we had gotten together with some of his committee members for a little informal gathering. For an elected official he seemed like a guy that knew an awful lot about covert operations. Information about most black operations was not something most elected officials were privy to. He knew too much specific information for me to believe it was coincidence. I thought now would be a good time to talk to him about what was going on.

But all of those plans would have to wait. Tonight my attention was going to be on Mr. Stacey. I figured I was going to have one shot at him, and it had better be center mass. The more I thought about it, the more I believed he was going to get as much insurance information from me to back up what he already had and then vanish. My little voice was screaming at me now to do whatever was necessary to get inside that briefcase, and I was going to listen.

It was after five by the time I got back to Charleen's. She was taking a shower when I came in and had laid clothes out for tonight's dinner. I yelled through the door, hoping not to scare her. She gave out a yell, and I knew the plan didn't work. I went in the bathroom to apologize and ended up conserving a little water by taking a shower with her. Now that was a good idea.

After our shower, I was in my room getting dressed when Beth called.

"David, it's all set. Kevin is staying at the hotel in Room Number 305. He doesn't know I already had the room. He's also taking me out to dinner tonight at eight. He said he'd make reservations at Jeffrey's. That's about a forty-minute drive from the hotel."

"Great," I said. "Try to get him to relax and open up to you. I need to know what his story is. He might slip up and tell you something. I'm sure it will take a couple of hours to get him to relax. Call me here if you find out anything."

"Do you need the room next to his?" she asked.

"Probably tomorrow," I said. "If you could, leave the key at the front desk in Charleen's name."

"You got it. I'll do that now. Anything else?"

"No, I don't think so. I really appreciate it, Beth."

"My pleasure, David. You and Charleen go and enjoy yourselves tonight. I'll call you if I learn anything."

Charleen asked what the plans with Beth were, and I told her that she had just had to cancel. I needed Charleen's help, but I didn't want to put her in any danger. I wanted to be honest with her without scaring her. I decided not to tell her exactly what was going on, just enough so she wouldn't ask too many questions. If for some reason she met up with Stacey, she could tell him what she knew as the truth.

"Charleen, I'm going to need your help tonight. I met with a guy today that somehow has gotten a bunch of information that pertains to me and some of guys I used to work with."

"You mean Lucky?" she asked.

"That's right, Lucky and others. This guy isn't supposed to have this stuff, and if this gets out, well, we could be in real danger. He said he was going to show it to me, but I think he's going to try to screw me over with it and then disappear. I need your help in getting a look at it to make sure it can't hurt me."

Some of the color left Charleen's face. She was realizing this wasn't a game and people could get hurt, primarily me.

"Let's get this asshole," she said. When she saw my jaw drop, she added, "I've always had a feeling about what you did. I'm not stupid, you know."

"I need you to help me tonight get a look at the information he has. Are you up for this?" I asked.

"Are you kidding?" she asked. "This reminds me of some of the things Beth and I did a while back. It was great; let's do it."

She surprised me again. She had been around, especially if she was spending time with Beth.

We waited until fifteen minutes after eight before we pulled into the Hyatt. I could see that Charleen was a little nervous as we pulled in and parked in the guest parking lot. I told Charleen there was a key at the front desk in her name and to go and get it. Without hesitation, she went in, got the key, and returned to the car.

"The coast is clear," she said. "I didn't see anybody I knew in the lobby."

"OK then. Show time," I replied.

As we walked through the hotel's front door and to the elevator, I made sure we were holding each other real close, so anyone who saw us would assume we were going to our room for the night. The door-man tipped his hat, as did the bellman. The woman behind the front desk never gave us a look. The elevator was open and waiting, so we entered. I pushed the button for the fifth floor.

"I thought we were going to the third floor," Charleen said with a curious look.

"We are. I didn't want anybody to know we got off on the third floor. We'll take the stairs down."

As the elevator door opened, I took Charleen in my arms and turned my back to the door. If anybody was there, I didn't want him to see me. She was startled at first but soon caught on to what I was doing. The hallway was empty, so we found the stairs and proceeded to the third floor. The door to the stairs would only allow us to enter the stairway and not return. I told Charleen to go down to the lobby and take the elevator to the third floor, then open the door for me. If there was anybody in the hallway, she was to go to Room Number 307 and wait until it was clear. I would be waiting on the stairs for her.

The halls were clear, so Charleen opened the door and we went directly to the room next to Kevin's. I told Charleen I didn't want her to be here if anything happened. I wanted her to go downstairs and wait for me in the bar but keep an eye on the lobby. Once she was there, she should call me to let me know everything was clear. Charleen hugged and kissed me and told me to be careful, then left. I unlocked the door between the rooms and listened to make sure there wasn't anybody staying in Kevin's room. It was quiet, so I phoned his room and let it ring several times, still listening at the door.

I knew it was now or never. I didn't know how long Beth could keep Kevin away, so I had to move quickly. His connecting door was locked, so I had to take the molding off the door and force the latch to Kevin's door open. I waited in my room to hear from Charleen.

I gave Charleen a couple of minutes to get to the lobby to make sure everything was clear; then she called and let me know everything was set.

As I went back into Kevin's room, I noticed my hand was shaking.

I wasn't used to burglarizing somebody's room in this country, especially Washington, D.C. I kind of smiled as I thought to myself that this was like the Watergate thing.

I stood just inside the room and took a mental picture of how everything was. If it were me, I wouldn't leave a room without some way of telling whether somebody had been here.

Everything looked normal. A small bag was on the bed next to one of the hotel towels. The TV remote was on the nightstand, and I could tell he had been watching television in bed because the pillows were bunched up. As I walked over to the bed, I paid special attention to the phone. A paper card was still leaning against the phone base giving long-distance dialing instructions.

I scanned the room looking for his briefcase. I didn't expect to see it in the open, and I wasn't disappointed. I didn't have much time, so I couldn't be as careful as I wanted in searching his room. A quick look under the bed, in the bathtub, and behind the closed window curtain revealed nothing. I slid my hand carefully between the mattress and box spring. Nothing. I checked the dresser for anything to tell him somebody had opened the drawers, then pulled each drawer open very slowly. Nothing. Behind the certain, nothing. The closet, nothing. I checked everywhere I thought he could put a briefcase. Nothing.

I was starting to get a little panicked. *Shit,* I thought. *Could he have put it back in his car?* I stood there for a moment and thought of what I would do if I were him; where would I put a briefcase? He might have put it in the hotel safe, but I doubted it. He couldn't get to it fast enough.

I had already quickly checked the closet, but I forgot to look up. I again slowly opened the sliding door and looked up to the wall above the door. There it was. He had taken a boot knife and stabbed it into the wall in the space above the door opening. He then hung the briefcase by the handle on the knife. You couldn't see it by looking on the shelf; you had to look back toward the door. *Just what I would have done!* I thought.

I examined the briefcase before I removed it from the knife. No wires, strings, or tape. Safe, I hoped. As I took it from the closet, I remembered what Kevin had said. If anybody opened it, it would blow. Was he saying that for my benefit? The sweat began to form on my forehead as I gently took it into Room Number 307 and put it on the table. I closed the doors between the rooms but didn't lock them.

I examined the outside of the briefcase as completely as I could but couldn't see anything that didn't look right. If this was an issue brief-case, I wouldn't see anything unusual, but it just didn't look like one. I saw that the combinations to the thumbwheel locks were both set to 000.

"Well, isn't that special," I said quietly to myself.

It didn't look like a courier's briefcase, just a run-of-the-mill Samsonite. I decided to take a chance.

I was betting the case was dead—there wasn't anything that was going to blow if I opened it. This guy had been drinking too much. He'd have blown himself up by now if it were rigged, I thought. All I had to do was figure out the combination and open it up. Piece of cake. I had opened several briefcases like this over the years, and I hoped this one was going to be as easy. After all, I had learned from the best. The government had sent me to lock manipulation school.

I had been in the room about fifteen minutes, and I was starting to get a little anxious. I needed to get the case open fast. As I put slight pressure on the latch button and started to turn the combination wheels, I couldn't help thinking, *What if it is rigged?* It was too late to worry about that now. *Just get it open,* I kept telling myself. One by one I turned the wheels until I felt a slight give to the latch. Seven, the first number, came. Then the second, six. Then the third, two. *Click,* the latch snapped open.

"You little shit. That's the caliber of your sniper rifle," I said quietly. "I bet I can figure out what the other number is."

I stared at the second lock. Was I as smart as I thought I was? My first guess would be to use the same number, 762, but I knew that would be too easy. My second guess would be to use the civilian number for the same caliber, 308. This was where things started getting interesting. I was betting he thought 308 would be the logical number somebody would use, but I wasn't just somebody. If the briefcase was wired to blow, it would go one of two ways: one, by just opening it up or, two, with the wrong combination. I was betting it would be with the wrong combination.

I remembered Kevin's story about his team. They were a bunch of SEAL snipers. Being they were navy, they probably had gone to the Marine Corps sniper school at Quantico, Virginia. Most sniper schools teach basically the same thing anyway. He did black ops like me, so I knew he was on his own most of the time. When I was on a sniper mission, it was usually long-range. He'd already used 762, which is the most common caliber used in sniping. I had to decide what would be the next caliber he most favored.

I narrowed it down to two: .243 and .300 Magnum. Both calibers were perfect for sniping. Both had great crosswind characteristics and hit hard. The difference was energy. The .300 Magnum was a bigger bullet and carried more force. With an ego like his, I was betting 300.

I dialed 300 on the second lock. My thumb shook as I held it close to the button that was going to either open the briefcase or blow me to pieces. I stared at it for a moment, took a deep breath, and pushed the lock. *Click!*

Answers

The latch released.

"I'm still here," I said quietly. I stared at the briefcase almost amused that I had unlocked it so easily. *Could it be this easy?* I thought. Sweat ran down my forehead as I looked at the unlocked briefcase. All I had to do was lift the lid and start reading files.

The possibility of it being rigged was all I could think about. I had come too far to screw up, so I wasn't going to get in a hurry. I knelt and examined the briefcase, paying special attention to the seam between the lid and the rest of the case. I was a bomb technician for the sheriff's office back home, and I'd give anything for some of my special technician's tools. I would at least be able to look inside without opening the lid.

Everything looked clean, nothing to tell me it was booby-trapped. It was now or never. I had to open the lid. I slowly stood and looked at my reflection and that of the briefcase in the mirror behind the table. My face shone with sweat, and I could see the arteries pounding in my neck.

"OK, let's see how lucky you really are," I said quietly.

I knelt back to the briefcase and placed my hands gently on each side of the lid. I wanted to open it just a crack and try to see any booby traps. I took the sharpened pencil that was lying on the table and put it in my mouth. I pushed the point against the crack between the lid and the bottom of the briefcase and held it there. Ever so slowly I opened the lid, just enough to slid the tip of the pencil inside.

OK, it was cracked. The pencil was holding the lid open a fraction of an inch. I then took the shade off the table lamp and held the bare bulb close to the side of the briefcase to try to look for any wires that might be hooked on the inside. I was looking for a wire or anything connecting the lid.

I didn't see anything, so I put the lamp back on the table, then pushed the pencil farther inside the briefcase. Now the lid was open about a quarter of an inch. I could see the papers and edges of files, but no wires or switches. It was time to see if this thing was really wired to blow. I had to stop for a moment and breathe. I hadn't realized it, but I'd been holding my breath from the start.

I wiped the sweat from my forehead and face with the sleeve of my shirt, took a couple of deep breaths, and got ready to open the lid.

Gently I started to lift the lid off of the pencil. As the pencil loosened, it dropped to the floor. Slowly, ever so gradually, I lifted the lid. One inch, two inches, three inches, the lid raised. Just as I was about to believe I had it made . . .

Rrrriiiinnnnnnggggg! The phone next to the bed rang and scared the shit out of me. I dropped the lid and jumped to my feet, staring at the phone. My heart raced as the phone rang a second time. It was Charleen's signal that Kevin or Beth was in the lobby. I had run out of time.

I turned and looked at the briefcase.

"Shit," I said. I had about two seconds to make a decision. I could take the briefcase and hope Kevin didn't use Beth or Charleen to get to me. I could just put it back and hope he showed the files to me, then get, or should I say take, the information from either him, the briefcase, or both.

"Fuck it," I said. I flipped the lid open, not caring what was going to happen. Nothing happened. It was all bullshit. There was no bomb, no booby trap.

A file folder marked: GIANT lay on top. I hadn't a clue what operation that was, and it wasn't of my concern. I dug through the files until I found what I was looking for. I thought if I only took the Hope and Glory file, Kevin might not notice it right away and I would have time to either put it back or get out of town.

I had put the folder on the table, closed the lid, and spun the lock when . . .

Click. I heard the sound of a hammer being cocked on a handgun.

"Find what you were looking for?" asked Stacey.

He had come back to his room and was standing in the doorway between the two rooms, pointing his gun at my head.

"Do more than breathe, and I'll end your story right here, right now," he continued. "Open the briefcase and put the file back. Do it slowly, or you're a dead man."

I watched him in the mirror as he eased up behind me. As I dialed the combinations on the locks, I watched him look to see if anybody else was in the room. Just as he looked to the bathroom, I back-kicked as hard as I could, knocking him back through the door into his room. I was on him before he had a chance to recover. The fight was on.

He swung at my face with his gun hand and missed. I grabbed his wrist and snatched the pistol from his hand. Just then he hit me with his other hand, knocking me back against the wall. He lunged at me, but I rolled to the side, spinning around and getting him in a sleeper hold. I choked him until he went limp.

My first thought was to break his neck and make it look like he had been robbed. But if I did that, I knew, Beth and Charleen would get involved, so I tied him up with the electrical cord from the coffeepot and the phone cord.

As I finished tying his feet, he came around: "What the fuck. You'd better kill me, you son of a bitch," he said. "Those files are the only things keeping me alive. You take them and I'm as good as dead."

"Shut the fuck up. All I'm taking are the files about me. I don't give a shit about the rest of this. Look; I could have killed you, but I didn't. I've got nothing against you. You're just like me, trying to stay alive. I need answers and you've got some."

We stared at each other for several moments.

"Take the fucking files," he said. "I don't give a shit anymore. I'll end up dead anyway. So will you."

"Bullshit! You'll end up dead if you want to, but not me, asshole. Somebody's gonna have to work for that honor. Look; I don't want any trouble from you. When I'm gone, you'll never see or hear from me again. Nobody will know where I got this stuff."

I finished making sure he wasn't going to get loose, then went back to the briefcase. I took the Dragon Flower and Dark Eagle folders out and closed the lid.

"You missed one," Stacey said.

"What?"

"You missed one. A folder, you missed one," he said.

I looked at him, confused.

"The folder marked: *Clean Slate*," he added. "It's about all the Spooky teams. If you're gonna take them, take the right ones. There's a guy in there called the Bagman. He's the one who is the plant. I don't know who he is, but he's in there."

I thumbed through the file until I found a folder marked: *Clean Slate*. I took it out and set it on top of the other three.

"Thanks, Kevin," I said. "I'm not going to fuck you over. I'm just trying to stay alive."

"Yeah, right," he replied. "The next time I see you, we'll see who fucks who."

I closed the case and threw it back on his bed. He started to say something else, but before he could, I knelt down next to him and punched him in the side of the head, knocking him out.

"You talk too fucking much," I said as I left the room and shut the door. As I went into the hall, I hung the DO NOT DISTURB signs on both hallway doors.

Charleen was talking to Chris, the bartender, when I entered the lobby. As soon as she saw me, she got up and came over.

"Everything go OK?" she asked. "I saw Beth getting off the elevator. She was by herself and got into a cab. I didn't know if you had talked to her or not."

Charleen didn't know about Beth's dinner with Stacey.

"No, I didn't see Beth. Anything else going on?" I asked.

"No, everything was quiet. Are you OK? You look like somebody hit you in the face."

"I ran into the door when the phone rang. I'm OK. I don't know about you, but I'm beat," I said. "Let's go back to your place."

"Do you want to stop and get something to eat?" she asked.

"No, not really. Do you have anything at home?"

"I've got a couple of steaks," she said. "I'll put them on the grill."

"That sounds great," I agreed, and we left the hotel.

We got back to Charleen's car and drove back to her apartment. Neither one of us said much as we headed west on 644 to Manassas.

When we got back to the apartment, Charleen started preparing the steaks. I sat at the kitchen table and started to read the file marked: DARK EAGLE—W45B7S8.

It was a complete history of the Spooky 8 operations in Central and South America. As I started reading the file, I was amazed at the amount of information Kevin was able to attain. He had memos, copies of after-action reports, photographs of the team, copies of maps and several intelligence reports, and a five-page document about Lucky and his past operations in Vietnam.

As I read it, I learned that Lucky had been around the block more than once. He was deep in covert ops in '68 and '69, in operations I had never heard of. I read where he had a problem with a CIA operative in Vietnam and it was decided that he should take a new career path. He was out of the business for a couple of years, until '72. That's when I came into the picture.

Operation Dragon Flower started in 1970 and lasted over eighteen months. I worked during the last few months of that operation. I was led to believe I had been trained to gather intelligence on missing POWs. It turned out I was gathering intelligence on drugs coming from the Golden Triangle in Southeast Asia. High-level intelligence officers planned to locate and steal the drugs, destroy the processing plants, then jack up the price and sell the drugs back to the drug lords for a huge profit. They were going to use the money to keep a covert war going in Southeast Asia and also give themselves a very lucrative retirement fund. It appeared that certain individuals in high places were laundering money and hiding some of it away in secret foreign and offshore bank accounts.

These weren't just a few civilian and military intelligence people working in Southeast Asia, however. I read the names of several politicians, some of them now in Washington, D.C. The file indicated that this operation was only one of many of this country's hidden agendas.

As I read, I was overwhelmed by what I saw. I knew that Kevin had to have a considerable amount of help to get this kind of information. I could only guess what Stacey's other files contained.

I had been reading the files for almost an hour when Charleen sat down next to me.

"You OK?" she asked. "You look like you've seen a ghost."

"Yeah, I'm fine," I said. "This stuff brought up old memories; that's all."

"Can you take a break? Our steaks are ready."

"Sure. Let's eat," I said.

I didn't want Charleen to know how important the files truly were. I turned the file over and went out to the patio, where Charleen had the steaks waiting. We ate, drank wine, and talked for over an hour. After we ate, Charleen cleaned up and I went back to reading.

How did I get to this place? I thought. *I'm just a guy who grew up in the Pacific Northwest. Just like every other kid I knew. I wasn't any different from anybody else.* Now I sat reading secret files that told me that certain parts of the government I'd worked for were among the biggest drug dealers in the world.

My hands shook as I looked at the pile of papers in front of me. I felt sick to my stomach and disgusted. I was enraged that I had become a part of this agenda without having a clue what I was really involved in. The idea of being a pawn in a game that technically didn't even exist to the rest of the world was too much to handle.

I got up to get a drink of water from the sink to try to calm down. As I looked at my reflection in the window, I took the glass of water and threw it across the room, breaking it against the refrigerator.

Charleen came running into the kitchen. "Are you OK?" she asked.

I couldn't say anything for a moment. The anger had reached an all-time high.

"This game is going to end, now," I said.

Now it was my game and my rules. I knew there was no use trying to hide or run. It was too big to ignore but too powerful to fight. So I decided not to play. Not by their rules, anyway. I turned and looked at Charleen.

"Yeah, I'm just fine," I said coldly. "Sorry about the glass. I got a little angry."

"That's OK," she told me. "Why don't you get some air? I'll clean this up."

I went our on the back porch and stared at the starry sky. Those files were mine now. If Stacey hadn't made a copy of it, that was his problem. Whoever had supplied him with this information was going to have to deal with me if he wanted it back. I didn't care anymore. And if I went, so would everybody whose name appeared in the files. I went back inside and back to my reading.

I opened the file marked: CLEAN SLATE. This was about as close to a "smoking gun" as I was going to find. Stacey had gotten his hands on memos, letters, and other documents that outlined the systematic purging of all Spooky teams involved in Operation Dark Eagle. There was a memo in code talking about a plan written by former CIA director Tracy in 1987. This plan gave instructions on how to get rid of all "Special Project" (Spooky) teams used in Central America. There were letters written in code from the Department of Labor to the State Department giving orders to officials in South America to terminate Spooky teams.

One letter explained that all information about Dark Eagle was being purged from personnel files and military and civilian archives and that the remaining members were in the process of being debriefed. *Debriefed* obviously served as their way of saying "eliminated." One official letter was even signed: "William Edward Bates."

"Bates! That son of a bitch," I said.

The man who assigned our missions had signed the order to debrief my team. With a stroke of a pen, we no longer existed. I doubted if Kevin could have had any information on my last operation, Easy Breather. If he had, I would have known he was one of them. The date on the Clean Slate documents was shortly before I went to rescue Paco. He to had been debriefed by Clean Slate.

These letters explained the letter I had received in 1989. It was a coded letter from someone I didn't know in the CIA. It warned me to be careful and that something was going on with the Spooky teams.

I wasn't sure at the time what it meant, but because it used the same code I had been using, I knew it had to be legit.

I finished scanning the documents, looking for any more references to Spooky 8. I didn't have time to study these files completely. My time in D.C. was over, and I needed to get out. As I turned over the last page in the Clean Slate file, there was a hand-written note addressed to me:

Chance,
You have what you came for. I knew I couldn't just give it to you. You're like me—you had to get it your way. I hope this will protect you as it has me. Only you and I know what you have. Use it wisely. Trust no one!

Watch your ass, Kevin

The note was written in pencil on the back of paper from the hotel. I realized he was an ally after all. He could trust no one, not me, not even himself. He knew he couldn't just give me what I needed. If he was ever questioned, he could tell the truth: he hadn't given me anything. I was wrong about him. He hadn't lost his honor. I also knew I would never see him again.

I closed the files and took them to my bedroom. As I was putting them into my bag, Charleen came in.

"You gonna be all right?" she asked.

"Yes. I'm just a little overwhelmed by all this."

"I can tell," she said. "Anything I can help you with?"

"You've already done so much. I can't tell you how much I appreciate it."

Charleen didn't say another word. She walked over to me, put her arms around me, and gave me a slow, passionate kiss; then we made love the rest of the night. When I woke, I found Charleen had already gone to work.

It was time to wrap things up. I needed to get the other rental car

Spooky

back, so I called for a taxi. The Ford was right where I had left it. I grabbed the gym bag from the rear deck and drove to the Falls Church Budget place to return the car. I had enough money to pay cash for the rental, so I didn't have to use my credit card. I started to feel panicked. Reading the files on Spooky 8 made me realize how dead I was supposed to be, and D.C. was the worst place for me to be seen. I had to get out. I grabbed another taxi and headed back to Charleen's apartment as fast as possible.

The Final Message

With Charleen at work, I could make my arrangements without having to explain why I had to leave in such a hurry. When I got back to the apartment, I almost started to call the airlines to find a flight. But before the first one had a chance to answer, I hung up the phone. I was back on maximum alert, and my paranoia told me to just go to the airport and catch a flight. If Charleen's phone was bugged, I didn't want to let anybody know my plans until after I was in the air.

I grabbed the gym bag and stuffed it in my travel bag. I took the tape from Charleen's camcorder, "un-wired" her batteries, and put it all back in the closet. I didn't have time to replace her videotapes, but I didn't think she would mind. I made a quick search of her apartment for anything I might have forgotten, then wrote her a note:

Charleen,

I'm sorry I had to leave in such a hurry, but something came up and I had to catch the first flight out. I wasn't able to replace your videotapes, but I'll send you some as soon as I get home. I won't be home for a couple of weeks, but I'll call you as soon as I am.

Thanks for all you've done. You have helped me more than you'll ever realize. I hope the next time we are together we can just have fun.

Thanks again, David

I knew she was going to be upset, but I couldn't help that now. I wanted to contact Beth before I left, but that, too, would have to wait. I had to get back to the team, figure out what to do with the files from Stacey, and decide how to deal with Bates. I didn't get any answers about a mole, and maybe there wasn't one. Maybe it was just Bates all along.

When I got back to the Hertz parking lot, I realized I didn't have enough money to pay for the car and buy a plane ticket, too. I didn't want to use my credit card until I was safely away from D.C., so I decided to leave the car in their parking lot. I would call them when I got back to my side of the country and let them know I had had an emergency and had a friend drop off the car. I grabbed my bag, then caught the shuttle to the terminal.

At first I was planning to go home, but as I rode to the terminal I decided to try to reach Lucky instead. I figured he was still at Sue's and I needed to act on Stacey's information. Before I bought a ticket, I called Sue's, hoping Lucky was still there.

"Hello," came Lucky's voice over the pay phone.

"Lucky, Chance. How are things going?"

"Damn, Chance, I thought you'd died or something. Mike and Dave are here. Mike's got his insurance and Dave pulled in here last night.

I've been trying to call you for over a week. Where in the hell have you been?"

"I had to take a trip. I've got answers that you're not going to believe. I'm going to fly into the Springs tonight. Are you going to be around to get me?"

"Yeah, I'll be here all night. Call me as soon as you get in."

"Great. Lucky, I want you to come and get me alone. Don't tell the rest of the guys I'm coming. I've got something that we need to go over. Try and get ahold of Opey. We need to get everybody together."

"Yeah, no problem," Lucky said. "I'll call him now and have him fly in as soon as he can."

"I still haven't gotten a flight, so I'd better go and find one," I told him. "I'll be in either tonight or tomorrow. Don't go anywhere until you hear from me."

The sound of Lucky's voice was very calming. I knew I could always depend on him. Knowing that Mike and Dave were with him made things a lot easier. Once I had everybody together, I would reveal Bates. I needed everyone on my team. I needed their strength.

United had a flight that was leaving in fifteen minutes to Denver, Colorado. I had only carry-on baggage, so if I hurried, I could make the flight.

I hadn't gotten my seat belt fastened when we started to taxi to the runway. The plane wasn't half-full, so I had the entire row of seats to myself. As the plane climbed to its cruising altitude, a huge weight seemed to lift from my body. As I left D.C. I felt like I had when a helicopter came and got us at an extraction point after a mission. I knew I wasn't completely safe, but I was a lot safer than where I just had been. I wished I had been able to spend more time with Charleen, but I was glad to be leaving. The past couple days had overloaded my senses with information. It was time to put it all in perspective.

As I sat and looked out of the window of the 737, I realized that I had been running on adrenaline almost the entire time I had been in

D.C. I was suddenly physically and mentally tired. I wasn't sleepy, just worn out. I couldn't think straight, so I decided to sit back and enjoy the flight.

I had no intention of sleeping, but the next thing I heard was the intercom telling me to put my seat back up because we were landing in Denver. I had slept the entire flight.

Denver's Stapleton Airport was a madhouse as usual. I wasn't sure what flight I could take to Colorado Springs, so I asked the first person that looked like she might know what was going on. The woman at the United counter said I could catch one of their United Express commuter flights. It left in thirty minutes, so I bought a ticket and headed for the gate. I had just enough time to stop and call Lucky. I told him I would be in Colorado Springs in about an hour. Lucky told me Dave and Mike were out at the local bar getting ripped, so they would never know he was gone.

As expected, Lucky met me by the curb, but in Sue's old International pickup. I laid my bag on the seat between us and climbed in.

"How was your flight?" Lucky asked as we left the airport.

"Fine. I could use a cold drink and some sleep and I'd feel a lot better. Let's not go back to Sue's yet. Find a cheap hotel; I've got some things to show you."

"No problem. I know one about thirty minutes from Sue's place."

"Perfect," I replied, staring out the window. "I've been in D.C. You're not going to believe what I found. Did you get ahold of Opey?"

"Yeah, he'll be in tomorrow night. D.C.! Are you crazy?" Lucky said. "You took a hell of a chance going there. You should have called me. I'd have gone with you to watch your six."

"I had to go alone. If anything happened to me, you had to take care of the team. I was OK; I stayed with Charleen."

"Charleen! How is that choice hunk of prime anyway?" Lucky asked with a little chuckle.

"She's just great. I think she just keeps getting better-looking."

"Did you get any of that, Chance?"

"You know me. I was all business."

Lucky and I looked at each other, then burst out laughing. He knew there was no way I could keep my hands off her. When Lucky first met Charleen, he tried for a week to get in her shorts. She would tell Lucky that she was "all business." That became a joke between Lucky and me.

We didn't say anything more until Lucky pulled into a small roadside motel a short way from Sue's house.

"Is anybody going to notice your car here?" I asked.

"Probably. This is where I come when Sue gets pissed off at me and I need to get out for a while. I have a running account with the manager. Besides, I get him laid on occasion, so he lets me have a room for nothing."

Leave it to Lucky to find a way to beat the system. We didn't even have to check with the front desk. Lucky pulled a room key from the glove box, and in we went. The key was to Room Number 8. That seemed appropriate for the occasion. It was away from the front, and we parked where the truck wouldn't be seen from the road.

The room was typical of a "joint" I would expect to find Lucky spending a few days in. Clean but well used, it did have a shower, a TV, and a bed. There weren't any visible signs of roaches, so it was just fine for me, too. I took the folders I had taken from Kevin and laid them on the bed. I then took the gym bag from my travel bag and took out the camcorder. I dug around until I found the tapes I had taken and tossed them to Lucky.

"Hook up this camera to the TV. I took video of some of our old stomping grounds in Washington, D.C. I think you'll be amused. The patch cords are in the gym bag. I think there's still a tape in the camera of the old SRI building where we briefed with those remote viewer dudes. I haven't looked at any of them yet, so we need to go over them anyway. Start checking them out while I take a shower."

I went in to take a shower while Lucky hooked up the camcorder to the TV. I was beat from my trip, so I turned on the shower as hot as I could stand it and just stood there, letting the hot water beat away my tension. I could hear Lucky laugh when he started watching the tapes. I figured he would get a kick out of seeing his old alma mater.

I was in the shower over half an hour before I came out to see how Lucky was getting along.

"You asshole, why didn't you take me to D.C.?" Lucky asked sarcastically.

"I told you. I needed to go alone."

"Well, you weren't alone on this tape."

"What in the hell are you talking about? I was all alone. The only people that knew I was there were Charleen, her girlfriend, and a navy SEAL I met."

"Have you looked at this tape?" Lucky asked.

"No. I told you, I didn't have time to look at any of them. I figured my plan to videotape a couple of buildings looking for clues was a wash. Why?"

"Did you see anybody there that wasn't supposed to be there?"

"Yeah. I ran into that fuckin' Bates. Wait until you read those files," I said, pointing to Stacey's files.

"I think you'd better sit down and watch this." He was dead serious. He wasn't joking around. I could tell by the look on his face something was wrong, very wrong.

"What was the last thing you said when we were all together at Sue's?" Lucky asked.

"Nobody do anything. Take no assignments, and do not go to D.C."

"Exactly. I think somebody had other plans," Lucky said as he rewound the tape on the camcorder.

Lucky started playing the tape of the SRI building in Salona Village. He let it run for a few minutes, then fast-forwarded it. He stopped it when a pretty woman passed the camera and walked into the building.

"The woman? I don't know her," I said.

"No, not the woman. Just keep watching."

My eyes were glued to the TV screen. A couple more people had passed the camera when suddenly my mouth dropped open. A man carrying a black bag passed in front of the camera, stopped, and looked directly at it. He stood there looking around, then turned and walked through the front door of the SRI building.

"That son of a bitch, the fucking Bagman. Stacey said the guy was called the Bagman. Opey always carries that fucking bag," I said with obvious anger in my voice.

"I don't know about you, but that looks a hell of a lot like our Opey to me," Lucky said as he froze the picture on the TV screen.

"Yeah, it does," I agreed, shaking my head.

Lucky started the tape again, and just as Opey passed, Bates appeared and followed him through the door.

"When I was at the Becker Institute in Arlington, I was setting up the camera and I saw Bates. It was just for an instant before he went inside. That motherfucker Bates set us up, and Opey is our mole. I was starting to believe we didn't have one."

I had all the evidence I needed. I had him on video. Him and Bates together.

"You know what has to be done," Lucky said, still staring at the TV.

"Yeah, I know. We need to have all the team together. We can't tell anyone until we're all there. Shit, who knows? He might have a friend on the team," I remarked sadly.

"You don't believe that, and neither do I."

"Enough of this; we've got other things to deal with," I continued. "While I was in D.C. I met a guy that used to be a navy SEAL. He did black ops like us and got screwed over like us. But he got pissed off and did something about it. He's got all kinds of files on secret operations our government has been doing since the sixties. He had a complete file on Dragon Flower, Hope and Glory, Dark Eagle, and a very special one: Clean Slate. I have the files, and we need to go over them one page at time and decide what to do," I said as I threw the files from the bed.

The rest of the night Lucky and I were bent over the files. Some of the information we already had, some was worthless to us, but most was worth its weight in souls. The file that Kevin had on our days in Vietnam confirmed many of the things Lucky and I had believed were going on behind the lies. Kevin had enough evidence to hopefully start a major investigation into several secret operations of this government's many intelligence agencies. Several of the names were people involved in operations including Easy Breather. Between what we already had and this new intelligence, I was sure we could negotiate a deal that would keep everyone safe from being "debriefed."

The sun had come up before we were through going over the files. Neither of us realized how late, or how early, it had become.

"You said you got ahold of Opey?" I asked Lucky.

"Yeah. Called him on his SkyPager. He called me right back."

"We need a little time to prepare for him. You have his number?"

"Yes, right here," said Lucky.

He gave me Opey's SkyPager number, and I called him on Lucky's cell phone. Within a few minutes, Opey returned my call.

"Opey, Chance. How you doing?"

"Great. Working part-time for a vet. How are things with you?"

"Everything is going as planned," I said. "When are you leaving for the Springs?"

"Tomorrow morning at nine. I don't get into Manitou Springs until four-thirty. I have a three-hour layover in Tucson at noon," he said.

"Great. Then we'll see you tomorrow." I hung up.

"OK, let's get out of here. We need to get to the team. We are going to intercept him in Tucson tomorrow," I said.

We packed up the files and tapes and headed for Sue's.

Sue's house was like another country. There were no neighbors, no city, no cars, and no people. It really was a great place to have a private meeting. The fridge was full of beer and frozen pizzas, and we were set. Mike and Dave wanted to have a little fun, but they could tell by the way Lucky and I were acting that this wasn't going to be much of a party. As soon as we got to Sue's, I got down to business.

"Lucky, you and Mike get your information. We need to get to this," I said.

"Shouldn't we wait for Opey?" asked David.

"No," I said. "He's not in the loop any longer. We'll get to him later; first we need to go over our plan."

I explained my meeting with Kevin Stacey and the files I had taken from him. The Dragon Flower and Hope and Glory files mostly pertained to Lucky and me, but Dark Eagle and Clean Slate were about the entire team. We spent the next four hours going over the files one page at a time.

It gave them a good idea of how we all had been played as pawns in this game over the past twenty or so years and how we had become a liability to a certain group of people in the government. It was now easier to get rid of us than to monitor us.

They understood that the information we had was something that any good investigative reporter would have a field day with. We weren't important, just a bunch of mercenaries that couldn't fit in with society, but the documents we had were something else.

My plan was to divide all the information we had between the four of us, each having a piece of everybody else's pie. No single person would have all the information on one specific mission or person. If one of us was compromised, the others would have enough information to barter for his safety. They would have to get to all four of us to have all the pieces of the puzzle.

I then instructed each member of the team to take his information and make three copies of it. They were not to keep a copy with them but have the original in a place where they could get to it, then take the other three copies and give them to three different people they could trust. These people shouldn't knew each other or know anything about what the packet was. These people would have instructions on what to do if something happened to the team member who gave them the packet. I told the team members they needed to make arrangements so if they were to disappear or get killed by mysterious circumstances, the people who had the packets were to try to reach another member of the team. If they couldn't reach anybody on the team, they were to get their packet of information to major newspapers somewhere in the country. I suggested the *Washington Post, New York Times, Chicago Tribune*, or *LA Times*. They should never tell anybody where all the copies were—that was their insurance.

We had all been trained to make it next to impossible for anyone to find all the information. When it was time to deliver our message, there would be no question of how serious we were and what we wanted. Collectively, we decided that all we wanted was to be left alone. We didn't want money or any other material thing, just to be left alone and not hassled in other ways. I knew that if the government wanted, they could make our lives miserable by using the IRS or the ATF or even making it impossible to get a good credit rating or job. They had the power to ruin our lives without ever having to touch us. They could do it to any member of our family or friends. I knew how rotten they could be, and I was going to do my best not to let that happen.

The information was divided and gone over again, and I had each man explain in detail what he needed to do. I wanted no misunderstanding between the team. After all the questions were answered, I put everything away except the videotapes and the Clean Slate documents and prepared to talk about Opey.

"OK, guys, I've got something to say that isn't going to be easy," I said as everybody quieted down and directed their attention at me. "I think we all have had some feelings about our last mission. We've all had questions about who set us up and why. As far as why, I think we have a pretty good idea. As far as who, we know it was members of our own government.

"There were some things that happened in the jungle that we haven't been able to answer. One: who shot T J in the back, and two: who put the two bullets in Santana's radio? At first I thought we had a sniper stalking us. But now I know that wasn't the case. When we were last here, I told everybody to go back home and try to take up your normal lives. I gave specific orders not to take any assignments and, under no circumstances, go to Washington, D.C. Was that clear?" I asked.

"Yes," said Mike. "You told all of us not to take any jobs and, above all, don't go to D.C. for any reason."

"Mike and I got together and thought about this. We agreed that was the best thing to do," Dave added.

"You know about the information from the SEAL, but there's something I haven't told you. First, you need to read this document again," I said as I laid "Clean Slate" on the table. "This is the memo written by Ed Bates informing the government of our scheduled 'debriefing.' On page three, it talks about a man he calls the 'Bagman.' The Bagman was assigned to make sure the debriefing was carried out."

"Debriefing, hell. You mean killing us," Mike said.

"That's right, Mike. At first I didn't know who this Bagman could be, not until I saw this. I want you to watch the videotape I took while I was in D.C. It's of a building that has been used as a black ops headquarters by the government for over twenty years. It's where Lucky and I went for mission briefings. Lucky, would you start the tape please."

Lucky started the tape and let it run for a few moments. Then he fast-forwarded it to the same place where he had stopped it for me. Dave looked up at me, and I could tell he knew he wasn't going to like what he was about to see. Lucky let the part of Opey walking into the building pass without stopping. I was sure he wanted to see what the reaction was going to be.

"What the hell?" Dave said loudly. "That was Opey going into that building. What the fuck was he doing there?"

"Opey's the Bagman. He's a mole," I told him. "He works directly for Bates. He was put on the team to make sure we didn't compromise his boss. His job on the last mission was to make sure we didn't get out alive."

Everyone fell deathly silent while Lucky rewound the tape and stopped it at the point where Opey turned and looked in the direction of the camera. I could feel the tension in the air. I knew the disbelief that Dave and Mike were feeling. The thought of a mole festered emotions that none of us had ever felt, a hatred and rage so strong, so intense, that even Sue's biggest shepherd felt it. He stood and looked at all of us, gave a little whine, and left the room.

"That rotten bastard," Mike said.

"We have to deal with him," I said. "He'll be here tomorrow afternoon. He's flying into Tucson before he gets to Denver. He knows this place, so we can't bring him here. I want to intercept him in Tucson and take him somewhere; anybody have any suggestions?"

"Yeah, I do," Mike said. "I've got a hunting cabin in Mexico. It's about five miles from Santa Ana, a hundred twenty miles south of Tucson. It takes me about three hours to drive from there."

"How remote is it?" Lucky asked.

"It's been my secret getaway for ten years. My closest neighbor is over a mile away. I take a road across the border that's not watched by the Border Patrol. It's on private land, and the owner gave me a key to his property. Hell, my ex-wife never even knew I had it. There's a small cabin on it, but it doesn't have any power or phone. I have a generator to run the house and the pump for the water well. It will hold all of us OK."

"What's the terrain like?" I asked.

"Hilly. It sits in the middle of three hundred sixty acres. There's trees and a creek on it."

"That will work just fine. We'll need to rent a van to get from here to Tucson. Then we'll all drive to your place, Mike. Lucky, we'll need the sat phone for this. I need the bubble machine [voice scrambler] so the NSA will have trouble figuring us out."

"What in the hell are we going to do with him?" Dave asked.

"I think we all know what has to be done," Lucky answered.

We all looked at each other. Nobody wanted to come out and say it, but we all knew. To us, there weren't any options open to someone that had betrayed the team like Opey.

I sent Dave and Mike into town to rent a full-size van. Lucky got the satellite phone and plugged it in to get the battery charged up. I asked Lucky to dig out the sterile weapons I knew he had stashed.

He had two old Soviet Tokarev TT-33 pistols. They both looked like they had spent time at the bottom of a lake somewhere, but each functioned perfectly. He also had a Smith & Wesson Model 39 9mm that had been modified to take a suppressor that Lucky happened to also have. Finally, he showed me an old Colt 1911 .45, and all were completely clean and untraceable. I knew these were probably weapons that Lucky had used in his early days of special operations. Each of us had traveled to Colorado with our own weapons, but we wouldn't bring them on this trip. About two, Mike and Dave showed up with a nine-passenger GMC van with tinted windows all the way around. We spent the rest of the day making sure we each knew what to do with our insurance. We would use Opey to get our message across to his boss, Bates. I suggested that everybody try to get a couple hours rest because tomorrow was going to be a long day and we still had a fourteen-hour drive ahead of us.

I grabbed a pillow and a blanket and went out onto the back porch to one of the lawn chairs Sue had. A perfectly clear sky displayed an incredible sunset. I lay on the lawn chair and stared at the sky, thinking about all the things that suddenly were happening.

In just a few weeks, my life had completely gone down the toilet. A few months ago, I was a normal guy trying to scratch out a living in the civilian world sub-driving a school bus. Now I was getting ready to give members of our "secret government" an ultimatum.

I felt numb as I looked into the heavens. I had no fear left, only anger. I knew that we all felt the same way. We didn't have anything to lose now, only our lives to gain.

Dave came out to the back porch and sat down next to me. "I'm scared, Chance," he said almost in tears. "I can handle almost anything, but this has got me really bugged out."

"I'm scared, too, Dave. I'd give anything if this was different, but it's not. I don't think it was our fault. I don't think there was anything we could have done about it. We all made a choice to do what we did. We all knew the future was going to be an unknown, and we did the best we could."

"I just want it to end. I'm out of this for good. I don't ever want to get involved with anything again," Dave said, visibly trying to relax.

"Yeah, I know what you mean. All we have is each other, and you can count on that. Always remember that, Dave. You will never be alone. We will always have each other."

Dave and I sat and looked up at the sunset. We didn't say anything for several minutes. Finally I spoke again. "This is going to work. Don't you worry; this is going to work. We're gonna be just fine," I said as I covered myself with the blanket and closed my eyes.

"Thanks, Chance," Dave said and went back inside.

I was awake as Sue's dog came out to see what I was doing. Dave had fallen asleep on the couch, and Mike was asleep on the floor. The TV was still on, and the other dogs had gone back inside. I could tell the team knew the importance of the day because there wasn't a single beer bottle to be seen. They did like to drink, but not when they had to be at their best.

Nobody said much as we got ready for the drive to Tucson. We checked our weapons, the satellite phone, the scrambler, and any other equipment we had that was going on the trip. We all knew we might be gone for a few days, so everybody brought enough money for the trip.

We left for Tucson before nine that evening. It would take a little over fourteen hours, but I wanted to be there in plenty of time to set up. I didn't know what Opey's agenda was going to be or if he really was going to be alone.

The trip was expectedly quiet. Each of us took turns driving while everyone else tried to grab some sleep. We all knew what had to be done, and there was no need for discussion.

As we got close to Tucson, I went over everyone's assignment.

"Opey doesn't know we are going to meet him. He has a layover for a couple of hours, and we need to make sure he is alone. Dave, you and Mike set up a stakeout and locate him as he deplanes, but don't let him see you. Once you've spotted him, watch him for fifteen minutes or so. I'll be sitting out front waiting to hear from you. If he looks like he isn't alone or if he looks hinky in any way, the mission is terminated. We leave. If everything looks good, come and get me out front. I'll go in and make contact with him. Lucky will be out front in the van. Lucky, as soon as you see me go inside, you'll know that I've gone in to get him. Pull the van to the curb and wait. Mike and Dave, cover me as I make connect. You two follow me out to the van and get in after I have him inside. Contain your anger and don't let him know what's going on. Let's not spook him. Once he's inside, we'll head for Mexico."

Everyone understood the plan and was ready. We had a couple of hours before we needed to set up, so we decided to stop and eat before going to the airport. After breakfast, Lucky dropped us off away from the terminal entrance, and we split up and walked into the terminal separately. Mike and Dave each went to the gate that Opey would be coming through. I went out front and pretended to wait for a ride, reading the paper. I had put on my fake mustache, sunglasses, and cap to look as different as I could. I had a couple of newspaper to keep me occupied.

Dave spotted Opey first. Mike soon saw him as well and came out to tell me that they had him in sight and were waiting it out. Fifteen minutes later, Mike came out again and told me that everything looked cool. Opey was sitting by himself reading a magazine. I got up, gave Lucky the thumbs-up, and went in to get Opey.

He didn't recognize me when I first sat down beside him. It wasn't until I turned and talked to him that he realized who it was.

"Opey, good to see you."

"Shit, Chance, I didn't recognize you. You scared the shit out of me. What the hell are you doing in Tucson?" he asked.

"All the guys are here. We decided to party a little, so here we are. How was your flight?"

"It was fine. A little far to party, isn't it?"

"No. Mike and Dave had to come through here, too, so Lucky and I decided it was just as easy to meet here. Got any baggage?"

"Nope. Just this."

All he had was the same black knapsack-type bag he always carried. As I looked at it, I realized how stupid I had been. Everywhere he went he held on to it like a security blanket. That's why he's called the Bagman. *Dead man,* I thought to myself.

"Good. Let's get out of here."

We got up, and Opey followed me out to the van. I spotted Mike, who was keeping his distance, watching to see if anybody was with Opey. I opened the sliding side door to the van, and Opey got in. Dave and Mike had gotten to the van and climbed in immediately behind Opey. Mike sat next to Opey while Dave climbed into the seat behind them.

"Mike, Dave, good to see you guys. Hey, Lucky, you're lookin' as old as ever," Opey said, trying to be cheerful.

"Hi, Opey," Lucky replied without looking back at him.

"Hi, Opey. How's it hangin'?" said Dave.

"Great, just surprised to see everyone."

"We decided to get to my place and relax; you'll love it," Mike said.

"Your place. We're not going to Sue's?"

"No, we're not going to Sue's," I said. "I decided we needed to go to a different place. We have a lot to do, and we can't be bothering Sue for the rest of her life."

"Cool, sounds good to me," Opey agreed.

Lucky, Mike, and Dave all acted like nothing was wrong. I knew the anger each felt and was amazed at how they acted out the plan. Opey didn't have a clue we knew who he was. The trip to Mexico seemed more like a road trip for a bunch of guys than a trip to decide the fate of our lives.

It didn't take long before Opey realized we were headed for Mexico. "What's going on? I know you guys, and something is bugging you."

Opey was beginning to get nervous. His voice was starting to crack, and he was getting a panicked look on his face. I had told everybody that if everything went smoothly, we weren't going to hurt him, but if he started getting hinky, we were going to tag and bag him.

Opey made a grab for his bag, which was on the floor between his legs. Dave immediately grabbed both Opey's arms and pulled him back against the seat. He starting yelling as Mike took a roll of duct tape and put a piece of tape over his mouth. Mike taped his ankles and hands together. Dave frisked the bound Opey, and Mike grabbed his bag and opened it. Inside he found clothes, a cellular phone, and what looked like a pager. I had seen the pagers before and knew this was a locator transmitter used by government agents. When activated, it was picked up by satellite. Since Opey had grabbed for it, it probably wasn't on, but I wasn't going to take a chance. I took it from Dave and had Lucky pull into the first convenience store he came to.

We passed through a little town about twenty miles from the Mexican border. A Quick Stop was just a block away, and Lucky pulled in.

I shoved the S & W 9mm in Opey's chest and said, "If you so much as breathe loudly, I'll put a bullet in you right here."

Sweat poured off his forehead. He was trembling almost uncontrollably. Mike and Dave looked pumped to the max.

I tossed the transmitter in the back of a Coors beer truck that was unloading at the store, went in and bought a Pepsi, then casually walked back to the van. Opey hadn't moved. Mike and Dave were looking at the traffic to see if we were being followed. I climbed back in and told Lucky to go. He calmly left the parking lot and proceeded to drive around town to shake anybody that might be following.

After I pulled myself together, I turned to Opey and said, "Listen to me very carefully, Opey. You have only one chance to come out of this easy. I know who you are and why you are on the team. I knew you were in Washington. I saw you with Bates. I met the man that was assigned to debrief you. He gave me your complete file. We know what you did in the jungle. We know what you did to T J and Santana. Do you understand me?"

Trembling with fear, Opey nodded yes.

"You need to realize that you, too, were going to be 'debriefed.' You are going to help us. You have nothing to loose and everything to gain. You are going to call Bates and tell him we know all about you, him, and Operation Clean Slate. You are going to tell him we have information that will put him and his group out of business permanently. You will call him directly, at his private number. Do you understand?"

I pulled the tape from his face. He gasped so hard I wondered if he'd pass out.

"I can't do that. They'll kill me," he said.

"Then fine. I'll kill you right now."

I cocked the 9mm and put it to his heart. I looked him dead in the eye.

"Good-bye, Opey," I said so coldly that it even shocked me.

"*OK, OK,* I'll do it. I'll call!"

"Good. Now sit back and relax. If I think we are being followed or I think you have another transmitter on you, I'm going to carve you up looking for it, and I'll take my time doing it. Do you understand?"

"Oh, God, please. I don't have anything. There is nobody following me. Please, Chance, I was following orders. You would have done the same thing," he pleaded.

For the next hour not a word was said. I left the tape off of Opey's mouth. Mike and Dave continued to watch for a tail. Mike told Lucky how to get to the property that would get us over the border and to

Mike's place. I sat calmly and watched the scenery passing quietly by the van. I realized how much of a coldhearted animal I had become, and it wasn't bothering me at all. It wasn't bothering any of us. We all knew it was something we had to do. We knew somebody else had forced us into this. It wasn't our choice this had happened, but it was our choice to finish it.

When we started getting close, Mike started telling us about his place. I made sure the radio was loud so if Opey was wired, they'd have a hell of a time hearing us. Opey understood the situation he was in. He knew his only chance was to do exactly as I said.

Mike's cabin was rough, to say the least. It looked as if it had been there since the turn of the century. The windows were boarded up, and the place was overgrown with weeds. Mike explained that as long as he kept the outside looking like shit, nobody bothered the place. He said it'd been this way for years and he had never had a problem. There were two outbuildings a short distance from the house. One looked like a single-car garage, and the other looked like a small tool-shed.

Mike unlocked the door to the smaller building and started the generator. Dave and Lucky helped Opey from the van into the house. Inside, the house was a different story. It looked as clean as anyplace I had ever seen. Everything looked new. If I didn't know I was in Mike's house in the sticks, I would have thought I was in a downtown apartment.

They brought Opey in and sat him on the couch. Lucky and Dave went back out to the van and brought in our gear. I could see that Opey's arms were numb from being taped behind him, so I cut the tape from his wrists and then taped one hand to his leg. I figured I would give him one hand at a time. He said he had to take a leak, so I had Mike take him to the bathroom. I told him if he tried to escape, he would be tracked down and shot where he was found. I knew he didn't have any idea where he was, so it would be pointless to run.

By the time we got settled in, it was after six in the evening, and I didn't want to wait any longer to make our phone call. I saw that Opey was about at his stress limit, silent and motionless. I told Mike to take off all the tape and let him stretch.

"Opey!" I yelled, trying to bring him around.

As he broke from his trance, the fear started to come back to his face.

"Opey!" I said again. "Get it together. It's time you made your call. Before you do, there are some things I want to show you. Everybody, get your insurance out. I want Opey to see what we have so he can tell Bates."

Lucky hooked up the camera to the TV and started the tape.

"I want you to take a look at yourself on the big screen. I don't want any doubt in your mind about how I know what I know."

Mike and Dave dug out the files they had for insurance. Lucky started playing the tape of Opey walking into the SRI building. As his profile came up on the screen, Lucky froze the frame so Opey could stare at his picture. He tried to turn away, but I forced him to watch. Then the rest of the team laid out what information they had in front of him on the table.

"Pick it up, Opey; look it over. I want you to be completely familiar with what we have. I want you to be able to tell Bates that we have what we say we do. You can do that, can't you?"

"Yes, sir, I can do that. I'm sure they will believe me."

"Good. They need to believe every word you say."

Opey spent over an hour looking over the files. He knew he was fucked. He knew what we had was more than enough to cause real problems. He knew I was deadly serious and the only way he was going to make it was to do everything he was told. After he had finished, Mike taped him back up and tied him to a chair. We were going to wait until the next morning before we made our call. I wanted Bates to be at work when he got his wake-up call.

It was exactly 6:00 the next morning when I got out the briefcase that contained the satellite phone. I told everybody to gather up their stuff and put it back in the van, they took Mike outside and asked him if there was a place where we could go to make the phone call. I wanted a place away from the house where we couldn't be seen from above or from the road. He said he knew of a place not a twenty-minute walk from the cabin. We walked back into the house and got ready to leave.

"OK, it's show time. Let's go, Opey; it's time to make your phone call."

Opey sat there for a moment and stared at me. I didn't even blink as I stared back, waiting for him to get up.

"I told you, the only way you are going to make it easy is to do everything I say. You've never known me to lie to you. Now get up and let's go."

That seemed to reassure him that he was going to make it. I hadn't ever lied to my team before. He knew I was a man of my word, and he knew I meant what I said. Mike and Dave looked at me a little puzzled as I told him that. They had thought they knew what I was going to do, but now they weren't so sure. Lucky never said a word.

"Mike's got a place where I can set this satellite up. It's a short walk from here, so let's get going. Mike, you lead the way. Dave, bring up the rear."

We left the house and started walking toward a distant hill in the crisp morning air. There was a game trail that led us to a small out-cropping of rock that overlooked a valley. It was quite beautiful, no civilization in sight. You couldn't see any roads, power poles, or houses. It was as if we were totally alone in the world.

Lucky set up the sat phone as I talked with Opey.

"Why, Opey? Why did you do it to us?"

"I didn't know what was going to happen. I never knew they were going to try and kill you. They told me they wanted me to make sure you guys weren't setting up your own nest egg."

I listened as Opey tried desperately to come up with a story he thought I would believe. I had underestimated him for years. I never would have thought he had it in him. He was the one who always hung back and took care of everyone. He wasn't like the rest of us. He wasn't a gun nut or combat lover. He was just one of the best medics I had ever seen and had saved my ass more than once. In fact, there wasn't a man on the team that didn't owe his life to Opey. How could he do this to us?

"OK, Chance, the phone is set up, strong signal. The bubble machine is set to A twenty-six."

"Sit down, Opey. Next to the phone," I said.

Opey looked again at me, looking for any assurance from me that he was going to be OK. I gave him a half-grin and nodded my head yes. I wanted him to know that I was going to take care of him.

"Pick up the phone and dial. If you don't dial the direct number to Bates, I'm going to kill you, Opey. Do you understand?" I spoke just as calmly as if I were asking him for the time.

"Yes, sir, I understand," he replied.

Opey took the handset from the briefcase. His hands were shaking almost uncontrollably.

"Relax, Opey. I told you I was going to take care of you if you did what you were told. Dial the number."

"I can't. I can't do it!" he yelled and threw down the phone.

Mike ran over to him and grabbed him by the shirt and was going to hit him in the face. I grabbed Mike's arm and held it back.

"Back off, Mike. I gave my word. Now back off!"

Mike looked at me in anger. I knew he wanted to kill Opey right there, right then. Dave looked on in disbelief.

"This is the last time I'm going to tell you. Pick up the phone and make the call. If you don't, I will shoot you in the face."

This time Opey picked up the phone. He stared at me and then at Lucky as he started to dial. I couldn't see the numbers he was dialing, and I didn't care. I knew as soon as the call was over the number would be changed.

"Yes, sir. This is Opey. I'm sorry to call you on this number, but I have a situation here that requires your attention. Please set your phone to A twenty-six. Yes, sir, A twenty-six."

He looked at me as if to give me the phone.

"Tell him you are with Spooky 8. Tell him in your own words what has happened and what we have. Tell him all we want is to be left alone."

Opey nodded as if he knew exactly what to say, then switched to the scrambled mode.

"Sir, I need you to listen to me very carefully. I am with the members of Spooky 8. . . . Yes, sir, Spooky 8. Sir, they know everything. They've gotten a hold of a whole stack of files on your operations. They know all about Dragon Flower, Dark Eagle, Clean Slate, me, you, the senator, everybody."

"Tell him I have the files that Kevin Stacey had," I instructed Opey.

"Sir, Chance said he has the files that Kevin Stacey had."

There were a few moments while Opey listened to the voice on the phone. He didn't say anything at first, then told me, "He wants to talk to you, Chance."

I stood for a moment before I took the phone. I knew they were trying desperately to trace the call. The sat phone and scrambler would slow things down, but I knew they would pinpoint us soon.

"This is Chance; you've got one minute."

"Chance, what is it you want?"

"We have in our possession enough evidence to bury you and whoever you work for. I stole files from Kevin Stacey that go back to Vietnam. All we want is to be left alone. No money, nothing. Just our lives back. You know you won't be able to find all the information. I have instructed my men to make twenty copies and distribute them if anything happens to any member of the team or their families. *Anything!* Do you understand?"

By the time I was through, the rage had started to consume me.

Razz's and T J's faces flashed in my mind. I saw Santana's headless body and could smell his blood dripping from my back. I was talking to the man who had signed the death warrants of my team.

"You say that is all you want, but why should I trust you? How do I know you won't go to the press with what you have?" he asked, almost challenging me.

It was time to give my final message. I looked at Lucky and nodded at him slightly. Lucky knew what to do next.

"Listen, Bates, you spineless piece of shit. I know you sent Opey to finish your job. I know you want Spooky 8 eliminated. You will leave us alone or, I promise you, someday you will be on your knees as Opey is now, and you, too, will be debriefed."

Lucky had stepped around in front of Opey and had his .45 pointed at Opey's head. I dropped the phone from my ear and reached over and took the .45 from Lucky's hand. I turned and looked directly into Opey's eyes. He stared back, the color gone from his face. He knew what was about to happen.

"Please!" he cried. "You said you wouldn't kill me if I told him the truth. God, no, you gave me your word. I was just following orders. Please, Chance, you promised."

Then, abruptly, Opey stopped begging. He looked at me calmly and spoke without the slightest trace of fear. The pleading had all been just an act. It had always been just an act.

"Fuck you, you son of a bitch," he said calmly.

I suddenly saw the blond-haired American in the jungle who had said the exact same thing. I could see Opey putting two bullets into Santana's radio, then shooting T J in the back of the head.

BBLLLAAAMMMM! "That's for Santana."

BBLLLAAAMMMM! "That's for T J."

BBLLLAAAMMMM! "And that's for Razz."

"No, Opey, fuck you," I said as his body fell back against the rock.

I put the receiver back to my ear. All I could hear was heaving breathing as the now-silent man realized what had just happened.

Then came a click as the connection went dead. It was probably the first time in his life that Bates had been witness to the result of his work.

Mike and Dave stood expressionless, staring at Opey's body and what was left of his brains oozing out onto the rocks. The smell of gunpowder and blood again filled my nostrils.

"I think they got our message," I said and started putting away the satellite phone.

"I know what to do with the body," Mike said as he walked back toward the house. "Don't fuck up the rocks. Drag him off into the dirt!" he yelled back. "We'll cover him with the lime I use for dead animals, then bury that son of a bitch. In a few weeks, we won't even be able to find his teeth."

Lucky looked at me as if to say, "I know you had to do it." I was the team leader of Spooky 8. I was the one that had to terminate the mole.

At that instant we all changed forever. We all felt totally and completely alone yet desperately dependent on each other. We had come together in the ultimate act, the taking of one of our own.

We all had been through many terrible things in our lives, things that most people couldn't even imagine, but none as traumatic as this. A man who had been one of us, saved our lives as we saved his, experienced hell at our sides, in reality had turned out to be the worst kind of enemy. No, we would never be the same.

We put the mole's body in a deep grave and covered him with lime. We covered him with dirt, then with rocks and sage. We took special care to leave no trace of the incident. Lucky found the .45 casings and said he was going to make a necklace from them. We calmly, coldly sterilized the area and returned to the cabin. The mission was over.

As we drove away, we all looked at the place where Opey would spend eternity alone. Lucky slowed down, then drove us out the long dirt road, back to the world.

"We had no choice. I think we all knew that from the beginning," Mike finally said.

"Yeah, I know. It still doesn't make it any easier," I answered.

"Fuck him. He knew the risk when he started this game," Lucky said angrily. "He would have done it to us if he ever got another chance."

I knew he was trying to make everyone feel better, and he was right. Opey or somebody like him would always be out there, somewhere, waiting for that moment to finish the mission we called Easy Breather. It had to end.

"We need time now," I said. "We got our message across, but only time will tell if they took it seriously. Everybody needs to take care of business as soon as you get settled. I'm going home. I'm the only one they know is still alive for sure, and I'm not going to hide. If they want me, they'll have to come and get me. The rest of you need to make your own decisions as to what you're going to do. Take care of your insurance first. It's the only thing that will keep you alive. If something happens to me, you'll know they didn't take us seriously. Do what you have to do."

I had Lucky drop me off at the Tucson airport. I looked at my team one last time before I closed the van door. I didn't know if I would ever see any of them again, and a part of me felt as if it were dying. I felt an incredible emptiness in my soul, the same emptiness I could see in each of their faces. I had done all that I could do for them, and they knew that.

It would have been easy to let the moment completely destroy my spirit, but I also knew that, like so many times before, I would heal. The pain would lessen and the sadness would be buried. As I started to close the door, I turned and looked at Lucky, Mike, and Dave.

"We'll always be Spooky 8. Don't you guys ever forget that. I love you guys," I said before I closed the van door and walked away smiling.

Lucky honked the horn as I heard the side door of the van slide open.

"Hey, Chance!" Mike yelled. "Was it really all business with you and Charleen?" he asked.

All three of them started laughing.

"Chance!" yelled Lucky. "Say hi to the bogeyman for me."

"I will. We've become good friends over the years," I said as I turned and walked into the terminal.

Epilogue

I don't think I've ever felt so alone as I did on the flight back home. Never in my wildest dreams did I expect to be in the situation I was living in. My mind was exhausted and my spirit weak. I didn't care anymore what happened to me. If somebody was waiting for me when I got off the airplane, so be it. If I was being followed, it didn't matter anymore. I had done what I could to save myself and my team. If it didn't work, at least the truth would someday come out about Spooky 8 and the dark side of U.S. intelligence.

In a world inundated with deception, media disinformation, cover stories, and lies, it's impossible to know exactly what the truth really means. To this day I still don't know who Ed Bates really works for or if, in fact, that was his real name. Was it the CIA, the NSA, the DIA or a combination of them all? I don't know. I have my beliefs, but they're just my beliefs, and that, too, doesn't matter now. All I know for sure is a that very dark side of our government is in control.

When I got home, I didn't want to be around anyone. I didn't call my friends or listen to the few messages I had on my answering machine. I hid in my basement, wishing the world would just go away. I needed sleep more than anything else. I knew I would have to do battle with my mental demons, but I wasn't prepared for the war that was raging in my mind. For the first time in my life, I actually feared closing my eyes because of what I might see. The memories of years of life that, to most, didn't exist rose in my dreams as if I were there all over again. I relived the horror of feeling my friends die in my arms. I looked again into the eyes of the first man I ever killed. I saw again the men I had targeted in the scope of my sniper rifle. I saw the fear in the eyes of the three soldiers Paco and I had killed on Lago de Nicaragua.

Epilogue

I watched the defiance in Opey's face, not understanding why Opey had to do what he did. He felt no honor or loyalty. It was his job.

I had always told my men that they would have demons. Demons were a part of tragedy, a part of death that the living must deal with. I warned them never to give in, never surrender their will.

In time, my demons did retreat to the dark places of my mind. The sleep finally came, and peace now sometimes returns. I fought bravely against my fears and demons, and I wished my team courage in battling theirs.

It's now 1998, and we've gone through another national election. I can't help but wonder who was this time left in the jungles of deception as we brace ourselves for the final chapters of Bill Clinton's presidency.

Except for me, what's left of Spooky 8 is living out of the country. I saw them a few months ago for the last time. They have chosen not to be part of my world. I, on the other hand, decided to try this civilian world. I still find myself looking over my shoulder or missing my team almost every day.

Appendix

Term	Code	Term	Code
BANK	GO.	COAST GUARD	MY
▄▄▄▄▄	ZG	COCAIN	KZ
BARBADOS/O.N.I	NS	CODE/DYNOMITE	AN
BASE	DI	-CODE NOW-	PT
BATTERY	KR	COLD	MZ
BE	DA	COLONEL	BZ
BEFORE	HB	COME	PQ
BEHIND	US	COMMA	QI
BELIEVE	TM	COMMAND	XH
▄▄▄▄▄	ER	COMMO	UO
BEST	LY	COMPANY	LT
BETWEEN	UD	COMPASS	HQ
BEYOND	FV	COMPLETE	IZ
BIG	RN	COMPROMISE	LH
BIG COW	VN	CONCEAL	EN
BLACK	VS	CONCERN	HT
▄▄▄▄▄	FZ	CONFIRM	YR
BLOCK	MT	CONGRESS	AW
▄▄▄▄▄	RR	CONTACT	GE
BOAT	OM	CONTRACT	WR
BOB	OP	COOPERATE	SW
BORDER	GT	COORDINATE	JJ
BOTTOM	XZ	CORRECT	TP
BREAK	HW	COST	NX
BRIDGE	WO	COLUMBIAN	FG
BRING	JV	COVE	JQ
BUDGET/G. LNCHR	AE	CRITICAL	MQ
BUILDING	RC	▄▄▄▄▄	LC
BURST TRANSMIT	RX	CUBAN	LR
BUS	DU	CURACAO/▄▄▄▄▄	HN
BY	TD	CUSTODY	YS
		CUSTOMS	EZ
C.A.(CNTRL. AM.)	ZQ	CUT OUT	CL
C-119	BM	CURRENCY, U.S.	VH
C-123	DN		
C-130	BU	DHL	SB
CANADA	UB	DASH	DF
▄▄▄▄▄	KS	DATA	QC
CALIFORNIA	VV	DAY	FH
CAMP	RW	D.E.A.	IB
CAN	TT	DEAD	YE
CANCEL	PK	DEAD DROP	XU
▄▄▄▄▄	LL	DECEPTION/F.D.N.	AJ
CAPTIAN	QL	DECIMAL/M-26	AV
CAPTURE	RZ	DECISION	GL
CAR RENTAL	SQ	DEFENCE	QS
CARE OF	QO	DEGREE	DE
CAVE	ZC	DELAY/NON E.CAPS	AS
C.B.R.	PP	DELICATE	SH
CELL	JB	DELIVE	UI
CHANGE/VHF	AH	DEMAND	EV
CHECK	UT	DEMOLITION	SG
CHIEF	FU	DEPART	RH
C.I.A.	MU	DESTROY	GY
CIVILIAN	EJ	D.I.A.	PX
CLARIFY	WY	DIRECT	YP
CLEAR	MM	DISPATCH/E.CAPS	AR
CLOSE	VJ	DISTANCE	MS
COSTA RICA	NB	DIVERSION	JF
COAST	SD	DO	LJ

Term	Code	Term	Code
J.C.S.	QG	▄▄▄▄▄	HF
▄▄▄▄▄	VE	MERCEDES	GC
▄▄▄▄▄	SL	MESSAGE	UA
JAMIACA	XO	METER(S)	IT
JOIN	ZJ	MEXICO	NN
JUMP	OC	MIAMI FLORIDA	SS
JUNE	ZN	MILES	IF
		MILIMETER	CX
K.I.A.	MP	MINE/BOOBY TRAP	LF
KILL	HU	MINIMUM	EA
KILO	WZ	MINUTE	ZH
KILOMETER(S)	MO	MISS	PF
KNOWN	EX	MISSION	DI
		MISSILE	OJ
L.A.	JS	MINOR	QU
LAST	GB	MONEY/M-16	CC
LATITUDE	DS	MONTH	TI
LAUNCH	GA	MORE	NL
LEAVE	PU	MONTAIN	NC
LEFT	IJ	MOVE	ML
LENS	YJ	M.S.R.	VD
LESS	GU	MUST	SZ
LET	MJ	MY	QH
▄▄▄▄▄	OX		
LIBERATE	JC	NAME	JW
LIE	VQ	NEED	SY
LIEUTENANT	FR	NEGATIVE	HX
LIGHT	HK	NEGOTIATE/9MM	CH
LINE	ID	NEXT	LE
LIONS PAW	WF	NEXT OF KIN	VI
LITTLE	ZA	NICARAGUA	YG
LITTLE SANDY	VG	NIGHT	YL
LOCAL	DL	NIGHT VISION	FM
LOCATION	XT	N.O.E/105RR	BJ
LOGISTICAL	BS	NO	DR
LONGITUDE	NG	NORTH	RO
LOST	RL	NOT	RI
L.Z.	DW	NOT LATER THAN	TK
L.Z. SPIDER	CQ	NOTHING	PM
		NOTIFY	OE
M-203	CE	NOW	PG
MACHINE GUN	AC	NVG'S	XJ
MADE	MI	NUCLEAR	EO
MAGAZINE	NM	NUMBER	KC
MAIL	IY		
MAIN	BL	OBSERVE	FC
MAINTAIN	KX	OBSTACLE	EM
MAJOR/RIFLE	AB	OF	EY
MAKE	KU	OFF	NY
MAPS	FF	OK	OW
MARINE	GX	OKLAHOMA CITY	RU
MARTINIQUE	YV	OLD	BO
MANY	SO	ON	SF
MARIJUANA	KQ	ONLY	WA
MAXIMUM	OY	▄▄▄▄▄	LD
MAY	ZW	OP. FUND	IP
MEDIA	NR	OPEN	JX
MEDIC	LW	OPERATE	FT
MEDICAL SUPPLIES	EQ	OR/C-4	AM
MEET	IV	ORDER	HD

CENTRAL INTELLIGENCE AGENCY

PERSONNEL REPRESENTATIVE
Post Office Box 50397
Dallas, Texas 75250
(214) 767-8550

17 August 1989

Robert C. King

Dear Robert:

As of this date, your personnel records have been
transferred to ═══════════════════. You will no
longer be reporting to ════════ here in Dallas.

At the request of ═══════════════ you are
directed to communicate directly with your contact in
═══════════. It is my understanding that you already have
═══════════ name and contact number.

I have not been informed as to the reason why your
authority has been transferred, but I have been assured you
will be informed at the appropriate time. To my knowledge,
your classification will remain unchanged.

I have enjoyed talking with you and wish you only the
best in the future.

Sincerely,

CC: ═══════

This is a letter addressed to me dated the 17th of August, 1989. It contains a coded message (the thin line in the lower left corner) that warns of a possible CIA trap, and was the first real warning we received from somebody on the inside of "Black Intelligence."

February 12, 1992

Environmental Protection Agency
Office of Research and Development
Washington, DC 20036

Dear Samuel,

  This letter is in reference to project #W45B7. As indicated in a report dated March 3, 1987 by ▓▓▓ ▓▓▓, assets in this project were expected to be short term and produce marginal results at best. After considerable evaluation, it has been determined that #W45B7 areas S5, S8, S9, and S11, have become contaminated with toxic waste and are therefore no longer usable.

  You are authorized by the director to proceed with cleanup as soon as possible. You will be allowed 180 days to contain and dispose of any toxic waste. All other project assets are to be disposed of at your discretion.

Sincerely,

This letter, from a Department of Energy official to a figure at the Environmental Protection Agency, appears to be a request to end a series of projects. In reality, it was a government intelligence directive ordering the termination of the remaining teams operating under project #W45B7. The "S8" in the letter refers to Spooky 8.

OPERATIONAL AIRSTRIPS - TEXAS

BIG SANDY ~~███~~

Location:	~~███~~
Elev.:	390'
TPA:	1200' MSL, 800' AGL
Length:	L5100'
CTAF:	U-122.8
FSS:	Shreveport
VOR:	GGG 112.4D - Radial ~~███~~
	UIM 114.0D - Radial ~~███~~

~~███~~

Location:	~~███~~
Elev.:	1070'
TPA:	1900' MSL, 800' AGL
Length:	L3200'
CTAF:	122.9
FSS:	Wichita Falls
VOR:	SPS 112.7D - Radial ~~███~~
	BPR 116.5D - Radial ~~███~~

~~███~~

Location:	~~███~~
Elev.:	1230'
TPA:	2000' MSL, 800' AGL
Length:	L3800'
CATF:	122.9
FSS:	Austin
VOR:	AUS 114.6D - Radial ~~███~~
	STV 113.1D - Radial ~~███~~

~~███~~

Location:	~~███~~
Elev.:	410'
TPA:	1000' MSL 600' AGL
Length:	L3000'
CATF:	122.9
FSS:	Ft. Worth
VOR:	TPL 110.4 - Radial ~~███~~
	STV 113.1D - Radial ~~███~~

These are locations of commercial and private airports used for cover operations in Texas. Big Sandy and LZ Spider are two that I've used. It was believed that the Salvadorian Air Force used some of them to smuggle drugs into the United States for the CIA. There were also other locations in Oklahoma, Arkansas, New Mexico, Nevada, and Arizona. Outside the U.S. they used locations in Mexico, Argentina, Brazil, Chile, Cuba, Honduras, and even the Falkland Islands were rumored to have suspicious activity.

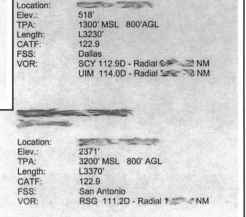

~~███~~

Location:	~~███~~
Elev.:	518'
TPA:	1300' MSL 800'AGL
Length:	L3230'
CATF:	122.9
FSS:	Dallas
VOR:	SCY 112.9D - Radial ~~██~~ NM
	UIM 114.0D - Radial ~~██~~ NM

~~███~~

~~███~~

Location:	~~███~~
Elev.:	2371'
TPA:	3200' MSL 800' AGL
Length:	L3370'
CATF:	122.9
FSS:	San Antonio
VOR:	RSG 111.2D - Radial ~~██~~ NM

~~███~~ **LZ SPIDER**

~~███~~

Location:	~~███~~
Elev.:	2595'
TPA:	3600' MSL 1000'AGL
Length:	L8801' (35R-17L), L2800' (7-25)
CATF:	U-122.8
APC/DEP:	Ft. Worth Cntr. 133.7
VOR:	BGS 114.3D - Radial ~~██~~ NM

EPA
United States
Environmental Protection
Agency

Office of Research and Development
Washington, DC 20036

06 April 1992

c/o Columbian Consulate
280 Aragon Avenue
Coral Gables, Florida 33134

Dear Eduardo,

I am writing to inform you that as of April 20, all funding
for project W202/CRP

will be terminated. It has been desided that this project
has not produced the results we had anticipated and is therefor
no longer considered for additional funding.

You will have six months from the end of April to dispose of
all research assets. Please transfer all pertinent documents to
our office as soon as possible. All physical property will be
disposed of at your discretion. This office will not require the
return any equipment used in your research project.

Because of the nature of the project, it is requested you take
action on this issue ASAP.

Best Regards,

This is the letter from a supposed Environmental Protection Agency official to our contact in the Colombian Government. The letter talks about project W202/CRP being terminated, but written in micro print in the thin black line under the heading was the sequence W 4 5 B 7 S 8. The way they knew the letter was authentic was by the split of the sentence and the misspellings of the word "desided" in the second paragraph. Often, sentence structure intentionally would be wrong, words misspelled, or dead people's names would be used to authenticate correspondence.